American
Military
Commitments
Abroad

American Military Commitments Abroad

Roland A. Paul

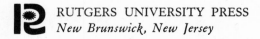

RUTGERS UNIVERSITY PRESS
New Brunswick, New Jersey

Library of Congress Cataloging in Publication Data

Paul, Roland A.   1937–
   American military commitments abroad.

   Bibliography: p. 215
   1. United States—Military policy.   2. United States—Foreign relations.   I. Title.
UA23.P37   327.73   72–4203
ISBN 0–8135–0739–1

The chapter entitled "Laos" is based in part on Roland A. Paul's article, "Laos: Anatomy of an American Involvement," in *Foreign Affairs,* April 1971, copyright by the Council on Foreign Relations, Inc., New York.

Toward a better public understanding of foreign policy

Contents

	Foreword	ix
	Acknowledgments	xi
I	What Is a Commitment?	3
II	Major Written Commitments	14
III	Nationalist China	30
IV	Japan and Okinawa	39
V	Laos	53
VI	The Philippines	79
VII	South Korea	93
VIII	Thailand	105
IX	North Atlantic Treaty Organization	128
X	Greece and Turkey	163
XI	Spain and Portugal	175
XII	Ethiopia and Morocco	185
XIII	Some General Observations and Conclusions	194
	Appendix A	207
	Appendix B	211
	Bibliography	215
	Index	223

Foreword

This book is based mainly upon my experience as counsel to the Subcommittee óf the Senate Foreign Relations Committee on United States Security Agreements and Commitments Abroad. The chairman of the subcommittee was Senator Stuart Symington, and the chairman of the Foreign Relations Committee was Senator J. William Fulbright. To both of these men I owe a deep debt of gratitude.

The subcommittee, which I sometimes refer to in this book as the Symington Subcommittee or as the Subcommittee on Commitments Abroad, was created on February 3, 1969, and issued its report on December 21, 1970. The aims and purpose of the subcommittee were stated in the press release announcing its creation:

> The purpose of the Subcommittee will be to make a detailed review of the international military commitments of the United States and their relationship to foreign policy. It is hoped that this review will result in constructive recommendations concerning the involvement of United States armed forces abroad, the impact of United States overseas commitments, and the relationship between foreign policy commitments and the military capacity to honor them. The situation in Vietnam is excluded from the scope of the Subcommittee's study, because it raises a number of complicated and unique questions which will continue to receive the close attention of the full Committee.

The subcommittee held thirty-eight days of hearings, all in executive session, on NATO and fifteen specific countries in the Far

East, Europe, and Africa where American forces are stationed. The
countries, dates, and principal witnesses (excluding those specifically devoted to intelligence operations) are listed in the appendix.

To provide a basis for these hearings and to supplement the in-
formation received in them, the subcommittee sent its two-man
staff, Walter Pincus and me, on fact-finding investigations to twenty-
five countries—Belgium, China (nationalist), Ethiopia, France,
Germany (Federal Republic), Greece, Iceland, Iran, Israel, Italy,
Japan, Laos, Lebanon, Libya, Morocco, Norway, Okinawa, the
Philippines, Portugal, South Korea, Spain, Thailand, Turkey, the
United Arab Republic, and the United Kingdom.

In each country we met with the chief American diplomats and
military officers. We also talked with many other people within
and outside the official American community in an effort to check
that which was given to us on an official basis. All this was done
under the aegis of the congressional mandate which we carried.
The present account of American military commitments and the
tentative conclusions I suggest in this book are thus based upon
an investigation more comprehensive and information more precise and reliable than most other sources available to the general
public.

The purposes of this book are (1) to present an accurate sum-
mary of the American military involvement and commitments
abroad; (2) to offer some conclusions based upon that information
in the hope of suggesting some courses for foreign policy in the
coming years; and (3) to provide some insight into the processes
by which foreign policy is made, and the ways Congress and the
executive branch deal with each other in this field.

The study made by the subcommittee and presented in this book
deals with commitments in those countries other than Vietnam
where the United States has stationed large numbers of its forces.
Accordingly, two important areas of the world, the Middle East
and Latin America, are not treated in detail here.

Acknowledgments

The senators on the Foreign Relations Subcommittee on United States Security Agreements and Commitments Abroad in 1969–70 were among the most distinguished members of the Senate. They were Stuart Symington, Chairman; J. William Fulbright; John Sparkman; Mike Mansfield; George D. Aiken; John Sherman Cooper, and Jacob K. Javits. They all participated in the work of the subcommittee with keen judgment and strong devotion.

The military and diplomatic witnesses before the subcommittee and the other officials with whom we met were all loyal, conscientious, and intelligent public servants. For their dedication, knowledge, and judgment on behalf of this country, they deserve much public appreciation.

To place the information which the subcommittee was receiving in perspective, I held extended conversations with some of the most brilliant analysts of and commentators on foreign policy, military affairs, and international financial matters. To them I owe a special appreciation for helping me to render significant and coherent what would otherwise be a tremendous amount of disjointed information. They included Gardner Ackley, Max Beloff, Zbigniew Brzezinski, William Bundy, François Duchene, Alain Enthoven, Edward Fried, Roswell Gilpatric, Morton Halperin, Herman Kahn, William Kaufmann, Carl Kaysen, Hans Morgenthau, Henry Owens, Edwin Reischauer, Robert Roosa, Charles Rossoti, Charles Schultze, Theo Sommers, Henry Wallich, Paul Warnke, Adam

Yarmolinsky, and Kenneth Young. Needless to say, they presented a wide range of views; and the opinions and conclusions in this book are mine, not theirs.

To my wife, Barbara, my loving gratitude for accepting and understanding the long trips and extended hours which the work of the subcommittee necessitated. Literally, this book would never have been published without her inspiration.

Finally, I want to thank Angela Morris, Katheryn Smith and Ruth Lutz not only for typing the manuscript of this book but also for performing with a sense of mission and purpose those countless other administrative duties which large projects always entail.

American
Military
Commitments
Abroad

I

What Is a Commitment?

Ever since the early days after World War II, when the wartime alliance between the United States and the Soviet Union broke up on the shoals of communist expansion in Europe and Asia, the United States' foreign policy has centered on the concept of containment of further communist advance around the world. In 1947 the Truman administration put this policy into practice in the Marshall Plan and the Truman Doctrine, and George Kennan conceptualized it in his famous article in the July issue of *Foreign Affairs*.

Since then American soldiers have fought in Korea, the Dominican Republic, and Vietnam, and others have been dispatched urgently to points as distant as Lebanon, Berlin, and Thailand, all in furtherance of this policy. It has likewise been the basis for much of the American military assistance program around the world and one of the justifications for economic assistance.

To say that American policy has been that of containing the advance of communism is not at all to suggest that the policy is tantamount to a simple brand of ideological anticommunism. This has not been the case for at least the last dozen years. Instead,

American policy has been based essentially upon the traditional fear that one great power has of another in a demonstrably antagonistic position, heightened now by the immense dangers of weapons of mass destruction. This, in turn, has led to a belief that a world peaceful enough to provide a reasonable margin of security for the United States itself requires continual belief in the relevance of American power. The policy has hardly been one of opposition to communism as a form of social, economic, and political ordering. Notice, for instance, the official American acquiescence in the establishment of the Allende regime in Chile and President Nixon's trip to communist China. Thus understood, this country's policy in Cuba in 1962 was different from its policy in Vietnam in 1965 more in degree than in kind.

As part of its general program of deterrence and defense the United States has constructed a series of alliances with Western European countries, Japan, the other nations of the Western Hemisphere, and a number of other less developed countries. As part of the policy, and particularly as a result of these alliances, American servicemen stand guard in places as diverse as the Palatinate of Germany and the crescent of Asia.* The purposes served by these alliances and deployments have been (1) to deter attack by indicating with a high degree of certainty that such an act would engage enormous American military power; (2) to bolster friendly countries in continuing their support for American policies and interests by assuring them of American willingness to use force in their defense; and (3) to provide territory and forces far enough forward to defend the interests of the United States with a minimum of risk to the American homeland.

Too many commentators use terms such as "American interests

* Contrary to popular belief, there are only four countries where the United States has major military facilities not covered by a treaty alliance. One is Spain, which both the State Department and the Spanish government publicly avow should be in NATO. The other three, with one facility each, are Ethiopia, Morocco, and Cuba.

abroad" without making clear what they mean. Of course, the United States has a variety of interests abroad. In the context of this study, the most important is to prevent important countries or regions from becoming hostile to this country and thereby increasing danger to the United States in two dimensions. The first dimension is nuclear: nuclear proliferation, nuclear blackmail, and even the danger of actual nuclear engagement. The second is the risk of serious internal problems of a psychological and conceptual nature within the United States itself. One must not overlook the danger to this country's democratic institutions that can come about through fear of and anxiety over a hostile environment beyond its borders.

This has been American policy and posture for the past quarter-century. Its successes should be noted. Peace has been maintained in a number of places in the world where, under an opposite policy, this would not have been possible. Moreover, the United States has enjoyed the physical and moral security of being in a world a large part of which is congenial to its interests, aspirations, and way of life.

This international ordering, however, has brought with it certain difficulties and sacrifices, some more relevant or obvious today than when the system was being constructed. First, these alliances and other commitments serve as the spoken justification for a large American military presence abroad, costing the taxpayer heavily and contributing to the American balance of payments problem. Second, these commitments sometimes have had to be met at enormous cost in American lives and treasure. Third, in some instances this posture may interfere with better relations between the United States and its chief adversaries, the Soviet Union and communist China, and thus prevent a more stable and lasting peace than we now enjoy. Reasonable steps toward *détente* may well go untaken because of the rigidity of the American defense pattern and its threatening appearance. This is, by no means, to say that the United States should dismantle its defenses abroad. There is still no assuring evidence that its opponents have forgone a policy of extending their influence and power through the use of arms or the implied threat of their use.

The National Commitments Resolution, S. Res. 85, adopted by the Senate on June 25, 1969, defines a national commitment as ". . . the use of the Armed Forces of the United States on foreign territory, or a promise to assist a foreign country, government, or people by the use of the Armed Forces or financial resources of the United States, either immediately or upon the happening of certain events. . . ." Although this is perhaps not a very precise or scholarly way to define the term "commitment," it is a helpful starting point for any analysis of American defense policy abroad. A more useful definition of the term may be: any preexisting relationship between this country and another that would significantly tend to lead this country toward the use of force even if, at the moment of crisis, it were not otherwise American policy to use it.

One of the great difficulties in any discussion of commitments is that the term connotes quite different things to various people. State Department representatives often maintained in the hearings in 1969–70 before the Senate Foreign Relations Subcommittee on United States Security Agreements and Commitments Abroad * that commitments were only those obligations expressed in defense treaties. Others have used the term to include the current dispatch of military personnel even if there were no implication in that act for the future. Under the latter use of the term any military base abroad is itself a commitment. Still other persons broaden the term to include the expenditure of funds, even if essentially no American personnel are involved. Thus, all military assistance is a commitment in this sense whether that assistance can tie the United States into sending troops later or not.

* Referred to herein as the Subcommittee on Commitments Abroad or the Symington Subcommittee from the name of its chairman, Senator Stuart Symington of Missouri.

All of these uses of the term are respectable when placed in the proper context and applied with clarity to indicate the meaning intended. But how difficult it is to discuss an important issue of foreign policy when a term such as "commitment" is being used loosely. For instance, in commenting on whether the Congress in 1970 should have authorized a supplemental appropriation of $255 million for Cambodia, journalists and others constantly raised the question whether a commitment was being made to Cambodia— without ever indicating which meaning of the term was intended.

When a commitment is being honored, in the sense of a previous relationship's necessitating some military fulfillment, that fact is often obscured by the coinciding fact that such action happens also to be what American policy and interest would call for even in the absence of such a commitment. For example, the report of the Foreign Relations Committee on the North Atlantic Treaty in 1949 states that the action provided for by the treaty "is substantially that which the United States would follow without the treaty." If the action called for by a treaty were not consistent with American policy at the time of the signing of the treaty (and in most cases it is fairly ambiguous what action is called for), presumably the treaty would never have been signed. Sometimes, however, a commitment can result in this country's becoming involved in the defense of another even if, at the moment of crisis, it may not otherwise be American policy or inclination to become involved. It is with the passage of time that the treaty commitment and the country's policy may diverge.

The distinction between action in fulfillment of a commitment and action pursuant to current American policy may be illustrated by a hypothetical renewal of hostilities between North and South Korea. The United States might have a number of reasons for intervening in such a conflict. It might choose to do so in order to keep communist forces away from Japan. Such action would have a basis in current policy. This country might also intervene to preserve the noncommunist system in South Korea, already preserved at great American sacrifice in the Korean War of 1950–53. This basis for action rests on the line where commitment and interest blend and become almost indistinguishable. Finally, the United States might choose to become involved to fulfill the obligation perceived in the Mutual Defense Treaty with South Korea. This would be action based upon a preexisting commitment.

SEVEN TYPES OF COMMITMENTS

So what forms do American commitments take? Some of them are certainly embodied in written treaties. This country has eight security treaties binding the defense of forty-three other countries to its own. The operative language in each of these treaties is, however, far from clear as to what action would be required in the event of a crisis.

Besides making these eight treaties, the United States government has also entered into several security agreements that have never been ratified as treaties. Most notable among these are the Agreements of Cooperation signed in 1959 with the parties to the CENTO treaty and the successive defense agreements signed with Spain.

Unilateral government declarations form a third type of commitment. These may take the form of congressional resolutions or statements by high American officials. They, too, are invariably general and ambiguous, but nonetheless obligating. In this regard, as Counsel to the Symington Subcommittee I asked Under Secretary of State U. Alexis Johnson the following question in the course of his appearance before the Subcommittee during its hearings in January, 1970, on Japan:

You are suggesting, are you not, that commitments by governments are embodied in public declarations made by their leaders?

He responded:

Yes; I think certainly they can be, certainly they can be. We often use that form ourselves.

Since treaty commitments are ambiguous on a number of points, subsequent declarations are highly important in clarifying, crystallizing—and, in some instances, complicating—the manifest intention expressed in the treaty.

A fourth form which security commitments take is the stationing of American troops in another country. As General Earle Wheeler, then the chairman of the Joint Chiefs of Staff, informed the Spanish in November, 1968: "By the presence of United States forces in Spain, the United States gives Spain a far more visible and credible security guarantee than any written document." Even though the United States has treaty commitments with West Germany and South Korea, it is common knowledge that both of those countries are very eager to have a substantial American military presence within their borders as earnest for the promise to come to their defense.

The commitment through the presence of troops rests upon two fairly straightforward propositions. If American forces are attacked, some American servicemen will be killed and others will be endangered. National dignity is likely to demand that those killed be vindicated and those endangered, saved. The second and related proposition is the belief that American forces once deployed cannot, for the sake of national honor and prestige, be withdrawn in the face of a direct challenge by an acknowledged opponent of this country. President Kennedy summed up this proposition well in the context of the Cuban missile crisis, when he said:

They [the Russians] no more than we, can let these things go by without doing something. They can't, after all their statements, permit us to take out their missiles, kill a lot of Russians, and then do nothing.*

This same phenomenon can be seen today in Soviet policy in the Middle East. Having been unable to save their clients from humiliating military defeat in 1967, the Soviets have, rather cautiously,

* Quoted in R. F. Kennedy, *Thirteen Days, A Memoir of the Cuban Missile Crisis* (New York: W. W. Norton & Co., 1969), p. 36.

developed a military capacity in that area and on the Mediterranean Sea in the hope of averting such a calamity for the Arabs and for themselves in the future.*

These dynamics sometimes operate when even a small American military presence is involved. The firing upon two American destroyers in the Gulf of Tonkin in August, 1964, the seizure of the intelligence ship *Pueblo* in January, 1968, and the shoot-down of the EC-121 reconnaissance aircraft over the Sea of Japan in April, 1969, all tended toward a greater and more belligerent involvement on the part of the United States.

A fifth category consists of what are often called moral commitments. They arise from past sacrifices made or risks incurred by other countries on behalf of the United States or from reliance placed upon its apparent intentions. It has been said, for instance, that the United States may have a moral commitment to defend Thailand in return for the use of its territory as a base from which to bomb in Vietnam. Likewise, such a commitment could well have arisen when President Johnson privately informed the Israeli foreign minister at the end of May 1967, as war clouds darkened once again in the Middle East, that, in the words of the President, "Israel will not be alone unless it decides to go alone." †

A sixth set of commitments is composed of those obligations that arise from a general identification between this country and the

* A distinction should be noted between traditional Soviet behavior and that of the United States. Whereas this country is prone to face every confrontation, the Russian national character is more attuned to stepping down in such situations and negotiating out of them, so long as the Russian homeland is not directly threatened. This attitude on the Soviet Union's part was evident in the Cuban missile crisis, the Six Day War, the Jordanian civil war of 1970 and the mining of North Vietnamese harbors in 1972, However, some changes in both countries' characteristics seem to be emerging as each perceives the consequences of its behavior, the Soviet Union in the instances mentioned and the United States in Vietnam.

† L. B. Johnson, *The Vantage Point, Perspectives of the Presidency 1963–1969* (New York: Holt, Rinehart and Winston, 1971), p. 293.

governing order, broad political programs, or society of another country. In one sense, all commitments, whether they arise from a specific treaty or declaration or otherwise, are based upon an identification between this country and another, but in this attempt at analysis, this sixth category is intended to refer to those broader and more amorphous types of identification not covered by the five preceding categories.

This level of commitment blends almost imperceptibly into what is actually current policy. In this category may fairly be included the commitment to Korea engendered by American sacrifices to save that country in the Korean War and our evident pride in its achievements, with United States support, thereafter; the enthusiastic American adoption, in the eyes of the world, of the post-Diem regimes in Vietnam; and the close American tie with Israel ever since its creation in 1947.

A seventh type of commitment includes those that arise over the course of time as a result of the accumulation of many small contributions to the defense, survival, or well-being of another country. When matters come to a choice between expending a little more effort and seeing all of one's past effort come to nought, one tends to choose the "little more effort."

There are certain thresholds in warfare, however, that tend to be breaking points in this seductive pattern. The most clear-cut is between nuclear and nonnuclear war. At a somewhat lower scale of violence is the more or less definite threshold represented by the deployment of large units of combat forces of various types. Those who believe that the natural consequence of American military assistance or participation in aerial warfare is the later involvement of large numbers of ground combat units overlook the presence of such breaking points. That is not to say that such assistance or fighting will never lead on to greater involvement and casualties if they fail, but it is to say that there are ways to design military assistance programs and even limited participation in actual conflict to minimize the likelihood of their leading to overinvolvement.

The foregoing list of kinds of commitments may well not be comprehensive. The ways of nations are only partly discernible, and the manner in which one nation involves itself in the defense of another is difficult to perceive, especially in advance. Even with the benefit of hindsight, historians continually debate the causes of wars.

AMERICAN FORCES WORLDWIDE

The size of the American military presence abroad is enormous. Until the withdrawal of ground forces from Vietnam got under way, the United States had more than 1,000,000 men stationed overseas. In 1970 about 400,000 of them were in Vietnam and military dependents abroad totaled about 330,000. The worldwide overseas figures for 1960, 1965, and 1970 are as follows:

	1960	1965	1970
Military personnel	665,954	745,708	1,032,620
Military dependents	460,789	474,295	332,026

In 1970 these military forces were serving on 373 major facilities (not including those in Vietnam) and more than 2,000 minor installations. Operating costs for these facilities, excluding major procurement items such as aircraft, totaled $12 billion in the fiscal year 1970. Foreign exchange expenditures totaled $5 billion.

Army and Marine Corps divisions stationed overseas in 1960, 1965, and 1970 were as follows:

	1960	1965	1970
Europe	5	5	4⅓
Korea	2	2	2
South Vietnam	–	1	6⅓
Okinawa	1 (minus elements)	1 (minus)	1 (minus)

(In 1965 the Marines also had three detached brigades in the Dominican Republic, Okinawa, and Vietnam.)

The Air Force had the following number of aircraft assigned overseas in 1960, 1965, and 1970:

	1960	1965	1970	
Europe	1,350	1,050	800	
Pacific	800	800	2,200	(of which 1,600 were in Southeast Asia)

The Navy had the following number of vessels sailing abroad in 1960, 1965, and 1970:

	1960	1965	1970
Atlantic	119	121	97
Pacific	148	158	119
Mediterranean	30	18	28
Caribbean	10	11	11
Other	4	3	4
Total	311	311	259

Of these totals aircraft carriers numbered 24 in 1960, 26 in 1965, and 20 in 1970.

II

Major Written Commitments

The United States has eight mutual security treaties with forty-two other countries, plus South Vietnam as a protocol, nonsignatory country under SEATO. These treaties and the parties to them are as follows:

1. The Inter-American Treaty of Reciprocal Assistance, signed in 1947 (the Rio Treaty), and the related Charter of the Organization of American States, signed the next year by the United States and the following other countries:

Argentina	Haiti
Bolivia	Honduras
Brazil	Mexico
Chile	Nicaragua
Colombia	Panama
Costa Rica	Paraguay
Dominican Republic	Peru
Ecuador	Trinidad and Tobago
El Salvador	Uruguay
Guatemala	Venezuela

2. The North Atlantic Treaty, signed in 1949, with the following members today, besides the United States:

Belgium	Italy
Canada	Luxembourg
Denmark	Netherlands
Federal Republic of Germany	Norway
France	Portugal
Greece	Turkey
Iceland	United Kingdom

3. The Mutual Defense Treaty between the United States and the Philippines, signed in 1951.

4. The Security Treaty among Australia, New Zealand, and the United States, signed in 1951 (the ANZUS Treaty).

5. The Treaty of Mutual Cooperation and Security between the United States and Japan, signed in 1960, superseding a similar treaty signed in 1952.

6. The Mutual Defense Treaty between the United States and South Korea, signed in 1953.

7. The Southeast Asia Collective Defense Treaty, signed in 1954 (the SEATO Treaty), with the following membership, in addition to the United States: Australia (also under ANZUS), France (also under NATO), New Zealand (also under ANZUS), Pakistan, Philippines (also under a bilateral treaty), Thailand, and the United Kingdom (also under NATO). (The free territory under the jurisdiction of the State of Vietnam, i.e., South Vietnam, is covered by the security guarantee of SEATO as a protocol country.)

8. The Mutual Defense Treaty between the United States and the Republic of China [nationalist], signed in 1954.

The fundamental commitment in all of these treaties is to resist an armed attack. With respect to this commitment the language used in these treaties falls into two categories.

The North Atlantic Treaty provides:

An armed attack against one or more of [the Parties] in Europe or North America shall be considered an attack against them all; and consequently they agree that, if such an armed attack occurs, each of them . . . will assist the Party or Parties so attacked by taking forthwith, individually and in concert with the other Parties, such action as it deems necessary, including the use of armed force, to restore and maintain the security of the North Atlantic area.

Article 3 of the Rio Treaty, in slightly different language, is to the same effect with respect to an armed attack in the Western Hemisphere.

The later six security treaties provide, in almost identical language:

Aggression by means of armed attack in the treaty area against any of the Parties would endanger [each Party's] own peace and safety, and [each Party] agrees that it will in that event act to meet the common danger in accordance with its constitutional process.

This difference in language among the treaties was probably not intended to create a difference in the degree of commitment conveyed. The main reason for the change in phrasing between the earlier Rio and North Atlantic Treaties, on the one hand, and the Pacific area treaties, on the other, was Secretary Dulles' attempt in these latter treaties to avoid a dispute with Congress over the question whether its constitutional right to declare war had been preserved. The Secretary of State told the Senate Committee on Foreign Relations in its hearings on the Southeast Asia Collective Defense Treaty in 1954:

It seemed to me that the practical difference between the two [NATO and SEATO] from the standpoint of its giving security to the other parties was not appreciable. . . .

I think that the difference practically is not great, but that the present formula does avoid at least a theoretical dispute as to the relative powers of the President and the Congress under these different formulas. . . .

In a sense, it is perhaps not quite as automatic as the other, but that would depend on circumstances.

In two of the treaties, the Rio Treaty and the SEATO Treaty, there is positive language with respect to the possibility of an internal insurgency. These treaties announce in slightly varying language:

If . . . the inviolability or the integrity of the territory or the sovereignty or political independence of any Party . . . is threatened in any way other than by armed attack or is affected or threatened by any fact or situation which might endanger the peace of the area, the Parties shall consult immediately in order to agree on the measures which should be taken for the common defense.

Thus, the only obligation with respect to insurgency is consultation. The other treaties do not contain affirmative language dealing with the situation of a strictly internal insurgency, but the result would be the same because such an occurrence would not come within the meaning of the term "armed attack."

Two other dimensions of the explicit commitment in these treaties should be mentioned. The SEATO Treaty specifically limits the United States' obligation (beyond mere consultation) to situations involving communist attack. Thus there is no American treaty obligation to come to Pakistan's aid in recurring wars with India. The words of the other treaties do not distinguish between communist and noncommunist attack. In the case of the bilateral treaty with the Philippines, this omission raised an awkward question during the confrontation among the Philippines, Malaysia, and Indonesia over the territory of Sabah on the island of Borneo in 1964–68.

The NATO and ANZUS treaties and the treaty with the Philippines, unlike the others, define an attack to include an attack upon the armed forces, public vessels, or aircraft of the parties. This distinction has significance for the American commitment where allied forces are deployed beyond the borders of the countries that are members of the alliance, for instance Australian forces in Malaysia. Similarly, this provision extends NATO's protection to the occupation forces in Berlin.

It also, of course, bears on our allies' obligation toward us. The State Department informed the Symington Subcommittee with respect to this provision in the treaty with the Philippines:

The available legislative history makes it clear that the obligation of the Philippines extends to attacks against U.S. forces in Japan. And this history, while less clear, suggests that Viet-Nam and Korea are included as well in the term "Pacific area" as it is used in this treaty.

To look only at the bare words of a defense treaty, however, is to perceive only part of the commitment represented by the document. Recall that in the context of this book "commitment" is defined to mean any relationship that has a significant propensity to bind this country to military action in the future. The reason that the literal words do not fully disclose the extent of the commitment is not hard to understand, although many people seem to miss the point. In the interpretation of international commitments, unlike that of ordinary contracts, there is no disinterested judge to decide the rights and obligations of the parties and no effective law enforcement agency standing ready to see that all comply with the decision. Instead, agreements such as defense treaties between sovereign countries are "enforced" only by the sense of comity and fair play that exists, to some extent, among nations and the concern which each country has for the interpretation placed upon its words and actions by other important countries. This means that the overtones and implications of such an international agreement are often more important than the actual words in determining a party's course of conduct. It also means that sometimes the opinion of a country not a party to the agreement is by far more significant than is the judgment of the other party to the accord. Finally, it means that to the extent the language of the treaty is ambiguous—and often it is very ambiguous—each party can construe the words to favor its own interests.

Four authorities on foreign policy have made this same point. McGeorge Bundy, writing in the January, 1967, issue of *Foreign Affairs,* stated: "The true value of the United States as an ally and friend rests not on the language of treaties which always have escape clauses. . . ." Richard Goodwin in his book *Triumph or Tragedy: Reflections on Vietnam* wrote:

The language of the treaty [SEATO] itself is imprecise. In case of "armed attack" we agreed only "to meet the common danger in accordance with [our] constitutional processes." No nation is specifically required to go to war, although it is true that a skilled lawyer could interpret the language as a commitment or as an excuse for inaction, depending upon his instructions.

George Ball, in his book *The Discipline of Power,* wrote:

No one has yet devised a graceful means by which a great nation can formally disengage from assurances it has given without undermining other assurances it would like to maintain, although in practice . . . there is normally some wiggle room for interpretation.

And U. Alexis Johnson, before the Symington Subcommittee in its hearings on Japan stated: ". . . what is usually most important is not the fine print of contracts or treaties or agreements, but the attitude of governments. . . ."

To illustrate the point, the literal language of the SEATO treaty may well not have required the American action in South Vietnam that took place in 1965; the communist forces operating in that country then were mainly indigenous South Vietnamese. Nevertheless, the treaty was one expression of the importance the United States attached to South Vietnam in the eyes of the world. Among the variety of reasons, therefore, that led the United States to take the fateful step it did in 1965 was a belief that failure to aid this treaty ally in its hour of desperation could have been interpreted to America's disadvantage by several important nations.

In short, these treaties do represent an obligation, or commitment, on the part of the United States. But what the extent of that commitment will be, for all practical purposes, depends upon the very complicated interaction of numerous factors, including the language of the treaty, the need for credibility, common decency and fair play, the various competing interests of the United States, the history of its relationship with the particular treaty partner, and other conditions and circumstances existing at the time the commitment is called.

Looking at some of the ambiguities in these treaties, we see first that none of these agreements specifies the type of forces which any country must provide for the common defense. The choice of weapons and amount of effort are left to the individual members of the alliance to decide for themselves. With such latitude of choice reserved, it becomes obvious that the practical effect of the literal words of the treaty, as contrasted with its implications and symbolic significance, is substantially diminished.

We could try to parse the sentences of the various treaties in the hope of finding what sort of defense the United States is obligated to undertake. We may be struck by the words of the North Atlantic Treaty, which require action "to restore and maintain the security of the North Atlantic area"; whereas the Pacific treaties require the parties only "to act to meet the common danger." But any practical significance in this difference in phraseology is illusory. The degree of obligation above a bare minimum common to all these treaties depends in each case upon a perception of where American interests lie at the time. The State Department said just that, in a statement to the Subcommittee on Commitments Abroad:

In reality, the distinction between the obligation of the United States under the North Atlantic Treaty and the obligation under the Southeast Asia Collective Defense Treaty is more a textual than a practical matter. The Department of State has stated on several occasions that the difference is "not appreciable." . . .

While the language of the North Atlantic Treaty regarding the use of armed force is somewhat more specific and direct than that of the other treaties, the response of the United States in every case, regardless of the particular treaty creating the commitment, would depend upon the requirements arising from the situation.

Some State Department witnesses before the subcommittee interpreted the phrase in the Pacific treaties "to act to meet the common danger" to mean that the United States has an obligation to see that an armed attack is defeated, but others conceded that this is not so clear. Several agreed that an appropriate response "might range from effective diplomatic action, to economic assistance, to the provision of equipment and logistics support, to combat operations."

It is worth noting in this regard that in Laos in 1962 the United States accepted a political settlement, the Geneva Accords, that fell considerably short of victory over the opposing side, and acquiesced in the continued presence in that country of 6,000 North Vietnamese troops, even though up to that time Laos was a protocol state under the protection of SEATO.

The assistance the United States is providing to Laos and Cambodia today, two countries not covered by any American security treaty, falls into this category of limited help without all-out commitment. These two cases may be highly informative for ordering our commitments elsewhere, especially when they are compared with our excessive involvement in Vietnam.

Looking for other ambiguities in these defense treaties, we see that they do not specify whether the term "armed attack" includes an internal insurrection supported by outside assistance such as armed "volunteers." This ambiguity likewise gives a latitude to the individual members to determine their own respective courses of action. The Foreign Relations Committee's report on the North Atlantic Treaty states:

Obviously, purely internal disorders or revolutions would not be considered "armed attacks" within the meaning of article 5. However, if a revolution were aided and abetted by an outside power such assistance *might possibly* be considered an armed attack. (Emphasis added.)

Still another area of uncertainty lies in a situation where the member attacked may have been responsible for provoking the attack or may in some other way have acted contrary to the best interests of the alliance as a whole. If, for instance, one member of the alliance attacks another, it may thereby forfeit its own protection under the treaty. This question arose at the time of German entry into the North Atlantic alliance. In response to French concern over a possible attack by Germany, the United States and the United Kingdom joined with France in announcing, on October 3, 1954, during the London conference, that in the event of any use of force by a member nation threatening the alliance itself:

. . . the three Governments, for their part, will consider the offending government as having forfeited its rights to any guarantee and any military assistance provided for in the North Atlantic Treaty and its protocols.

The question came up again in connection with the confrontation between Greece and Turkey in 1964. In a letter to Prime Minister Inonu of Turkey on June 5, 1964, President Johnson informed the Turkish government that the United States would not consider itself bound by the North Atlantic Treaty to come to Turkey's defense if, by attacking Cyprus, Turkey should provoke an attack upon itself by the Soviet Union. This letter is an important item in the recent history of American foreign policy, indicating the true nature of the United States' relationship with its allies.

The obligation of the United States under the literal language of these treaties may be further attenuated by the stated limitation that action is to be taken only "in accordance with . . . constitutional processes." In the North Atlantic Treaty this limitation was preserved almost as an afterthought in Article XI. In the Pacific treaties this language appears more prominently. As a matter of constitutional law, the provision would apply whether it was stated explicitly or not. Whether it has any practical force in preserving the war-making powers of the Congress as an effective part of our governing procedures is another matter. Such power has not been formally exercised now for thirty years, even though the United States has been engaged in two major wars and several lesser conflicts in the meantime without benefit of a declaration of war (unless one is prepared to equate a congressional resolution with such a declaration). To the extent that this right continues in the Congress, it serves as a limiting factor on the American obligation; it at least requires the judgment of an independent deliberating body, in addition to a determination by the President, in arriving at an answer to the question whether the United States' treaty obligation could be fulfilled short of war.

In some cases treaty relationships contribute substantially to American security. In other instances, however, American treaty commitments are more a result of outmoded strategy, misconceived mission, or historical circumstances that are no longer relevant. The United States has treaty commitments with some countries whose security is probably less significant in terms of America's own security than is the security of other countries with which it has no treaty commitments. If the choice were presented today whether to enter into some of these treaties for the first time, it is doubtful that this country would choose to do so.

Nevertheless, to renounce formally any of these treaties at the present time would probably, on balance, be worse than to continue them. Through an awareness of the limited commitment which the language of the treaties actually conveys, some of the exaggerated implications and overtones can be deflated, and the United States can gain the flexibility which it should have to avoid unnecessary involvement. A formal renunciation, on the other hand, might appear so radical a step as to invite aggression from abroad or civil disorder from within for the other country involved; it would unnecessarily shake the confidence of other countries that rely upon American good faith; and it might even engender unfortunate problems of morale and political perspective within the United States itself.

The most recent official elaboration on these treaties was contained in President Nixon's Guam Doctrine, first announced on his visit to that Pacific island on July 26, 1969, and subsequently refined and restated on February 18, 1970, in the President's Report on Foreign Relations, as follows:

—The United States will keep all its treaty commitments.

—We shall provide a shield if a nuclear power threatens the freedom of a nation allied with us, or of a nation whose survival we consider vital to our security and the security of the region as a whole.

—In cases involving other types of aggression we shall furnish military and economic assistance when requested and as appropriate. But we shall look to the nation directly threatened to assume the primary responsibility of providing the manpower for its defense.

In this pronouncement, the President seems to be saying—quite rightly—that treaty commitments can be fulfilled without an all-out military effort on the part of the United States; that the American treaty commitment is one of assistance, not guarantees, even if this assistance should prove inadequate to achieve victory or merely a stalemate.

If so, however, in assuring the countries of Asia that the United States will provide a shield if a nuclear power threatens them, the President has gone beyond what the treaties require in that particular type of situation.

This historic pronouncement left other questions unresolved as well, such as what constitutes the "primary responsibility" for providing manpower. It is possible that the President is saying that if the local country commits its manpower fully, the United States will also commit some of its ground combat forces; but this interpretation is doubtful.

The major concern about the Guam Doctrine, however, does not lie in the fact that it left some questions unanswered or ambiguous. On the contrary, the pronouncement may have too clearly implied to would-be aggressors that the United States would not intervene militarily to oppose their attack. One need only recall the much debated origins of the Korean war to be wary of too much specificity in official declarations of policy.

As mentioned above, the United States has entered into commitments not only by treaty but also through other documents and expressions of national intention—congressional resolutions, executive agreements, and declarations by high officials.

Congress has adopted five resolutions, dealing with Formosa, the Middle East, Cuba, Berlin, and Vietnam (the Gulf of Tonkin resolution), the last of which was rescinded on January 13, 1971. Each of these purported to authorize the use of American armed forces in the area and circumstances referred to in that particular resolution. The relevant portion of each resolution is set forth in Appendix B.

There are also numerous written and oral statements made by the executive branch without explicit congressional approval that tend to commit the United States to the defense of another country. In some cases these expressions purport to be reaffirmations or clarifications of underlying treaties, but in the reaffirmation or clarification an ambiguous treaty commitment is made more certain.

Other executive agreements and declarations serve in lieu of treaties. They exist with countries that for one reason or another fail to receive a treaty commitment from the United States but whose defense is thought important by the executive branch.

Among the most significant commitment-making documents entered into by the executive branch without specific Senate ratification were (1) the Declaration of June 19, 1968, in the U.N. Security Council with respect to safeguarding nonnuclear-weapon states that ratify the Nuclear Non-Proliferation Treaty, and (2) the Declaration of July 28, 1958, and the Agreements of March 5, 1959, by which the United States associated itself with the Central Treaty Organization, or CENTO.

The nuclear declaration made in the Security Council could well be the most important foreign commitment ever made by the United States. It states:

Aggression with nuclear weapons, or the threat of such aggression, against a non-nuclear-weapon State would create a qualitatively new situation in which the nuclear-weapon States which are permanent members of the United Nations Security Council would have to act immediately through the Security Council to take the measures necessary to counter such aggression or to remove the threat of aggression in accordance with the United Nations Charter. . . .

The United States reaffirms in particular the inherent right . . . of individual and collective self-defense if an armed attack, including a nuclear attack, occurs. . . .

Identical declarations were made the same day by the Soviet Union and the United Kingdom. Many publicists have tended to deemphasize the gravity of this American declaration. It has been said that it means little because it requires action through the Security Council and everybody knows that the Soviet Union would veto any action of which it disapproved, thus effectively letting the United States out of its commitment. But what if the Soviet Union only abstained instead of vetoing reprisals against, say, communist China. The Soviet Union could probably ignore any mandate by the U.N. to use or threaten to use nuclear weapons against China. But could this country?

In terms of legislative-executive branch relations, the American declaration presented something of a dilemma for the Senate Foreign Relations Committee. It was a highly pertinent part of the legislative history of the Nuclear Non-Proliferation Treaty. The committee was very sympathetic to the treaty, but did not quite know how to deal with this declaration made by the executive branch. To repudiate it could well have undermined the prospect of other countries' signing the treaty. On the other hand, it did not seem appropriate for the committee to recommend senatorial ratification of the declaration, especially since at the time there was great public opposition to entering into further commitments. The committee's answer was a bit ambiguous:

The committee, therefore, records its firm conclusion, reached after extensive testimony, that the Security Council resolution and security guarantee declaration made by the United States in no way either ratify prior *national* commitments or create new commitments.

Under normal charter procedures, the United States had the *option* of calling the attention of the Security Council to a case of aggression or threat of aggression. Now that option has apparently become an *obligation. . . .*

The change here is a subtle one that has no bearing on the committee's judgment that the Senate's approval of the treaty is not to be construed as approval or disapproval of the administration's security guarantee measures, or the committee's further judgment that these actions in no way either ratify prior national commitments or create new commitments. The committee only wishes to point out that in its view the administration has surrendered some of its diplomatic flexibility in hopes of creating a framework for United States-Soviet cooperation in the United Nations.

The United States did not sign the CENTO Treaty. The parties to the treaty were Iraq (which withdrew in 1959), Turkey, Iran, Pakistan, and the United Kingdom. Among the main reasons that the United States did not become a full member was that it did not wish to become an ally of Iraq, a country then technically at war with Israel. The operative language of the treaty merely states that the parties "will cooperate for their security and defense. Such measures as they agree to take to give effect to this cooperation may form the subject of special agreements with each other."

The 1958 declaration by the United States announced:

. . . the United States, in the interest of world peace, and pursuant to existing Congressional authorization, agrees to cooperate with the

[CENTO members] for their security and defense, and will promptly enter into agreements designed to give effect to this cooperation.

The agreements to implement this declaration stated:

In case of aggression against [Iran, Pakistan, or Turkey], the Government of the United States of America, in accordance with the Constitution of the United States of America, will take such appropriate action, including the use of armed forces, as may be mutually agreed upon and as is envisaged in the Joint Resolution to Promote Peace and Stability in the Middle East, in order to assist the Government of [Iran, Pakistan, or Turkey] at its request.

Under these accords the United States now participates in CENTO planning, some of its exercises, and certain of its military committees. At the CENTO headquarters in Ankara at this writing are twenty-two Americans, including two generals, one of whom is the chief of staff of the treaty's Combined Military Planning Staff.

When one compares the language of these documents with the language of American treaties in the Pacific, it is hard to discover any significant difference in the level of commitment conveyed. The chief difference between the CENTO obligation and the Pacific treaty obligations, therefore, rests simply in the fact that the Pacific treaties are treaties and the CENTO documents are not. This distinction gives the United States slightly more flexibility to avoid engagement in Iran * than in situations involving its Pacific treaty partners.

The American participation in CENTO presents some difficulties. It does not seem good policy for the United States to be increasing its commitments in places such as Iran, which would be the case if the Senate ratified the CENTO declaration and agreements as a treaty. On the other hand, an explicit Senate repudiation of the CENTO arrangements would have unfortunate effects on American relations with the countries involved and with others. But the

* All the other members of CENTO are full-fledged allies of the United States under other defense treaties.

present situation, too, is unsatisfactory from a constitutional point of view, since international agreements should be submitted to the Senate for its advice and consent. Perhaps the least unsatisfactory course is to allow these agreements to fall into silent oblivion.

The following chapters describe the American military presence in those countries in the Far East, Europe, and Africa concerning which the Symington Subcommittee held hearings in 1969–70 and the military and political context surrounding that American presence in each country.

Nationalist China

The United States assumed its present role in the defense of nationalist China on Taiwan through the declaration of President Truman on June 27, 1950, at the outset of the Korean war, that he was interposing the Seventh Fleet in the Taiwan Strait to preclude communist Chinese conquest of the island and calling upon the nationalists to desist from operations against the mainland. The United States thereupon resumed the military assistance to nationalist China which it had stopped six months earlier in connection with the then announced American policy of neutrality with respect to Taiwan. In February, 1953, shortly after President Eisenhower came to office, he announced that the Seventh Fleet would "no longer be employed to shield communist China." This was done in the hope of inducing a settlement to the Korean war.

Following prolonged communist attacks against nationalist forces on Quemoy and the Tachens and the massing of communist forces on the mainland opposite the Taiwan Strait during August and September, 1954, this country strengthened its own defense ties with nationalist China on December 2, 1954, by joining in a Mutual Defense Treaty similar to the others then being negotiated in the

Pacific. By an exchange of notes on December 10 of that year, Secretary of State Dulles and Foreign Minister Yeh agreed that the use of force from Taiwan or the Pescadores Islands would be a matter of joint agreement, except for emergency steps taken in self-defense. Following communist attacks on nationalist positions on the offshore islands in November, 1954, and January, 1955, Congress by a joint resolution on January 29, 1955, authorized the President to use armed force to protect Formosa and the Pescadores and also, if necessary as part of the defense of those islands, to protect the offshore islands of Quemoy and Matsu. On March 12, 1970, however, the State Department informed the Senate Committee on Foreign Relations that, because this resolution was then over fifteen years old, the Administration would not consider it a source of congressional authority for action in the event of a new crisis in the Taiwan Strait. And on September 21, 1971, the Senate Foreign Relations Committee recommended repeal of the resolution itself.

There are several things that the American obligation under the treaty with Taiwan does not require. It does not obligate the United States to station forces on Taiwan. It does not affect the legal status of Taiwan, which has never been settled since World War II except for the relinquishment of Japanese sovereignty. It does not oblige the United States to defend the offshore islands for their own sake. Furthermore, it does not require this country to come to the defense of Taiwan in the event of an attack provoked by action taken by nationalist China, a fact of which the nationalists are quite aware.

Until the Vietnam War, the American military presence on and around Taiwan was small. There was the Taiwan Strait patrol composed of a small number of destroyers and a unit of maritime patrol aircraft. Recently, however, the destroyers were removed as an economy measure. About sixty American naval vessels came through the Taiwan Strait for various purposes in 1969; and similar transiting vessels will constitute the vessels of the Taiwan Strait patrol hereafter.

A military advisory group, now with a strength of 485 personnel and a major general at its head, was established to administer the military assistance program. In 1952 the United States also created the Taiwan Defense Command, a planning staff now numbering 190 American personnel and commanded by a vice admiral. The only American combat units on Taiwan were some Matador missiles, which were removed a few years ago, and a small unit of fighter aircraft, which came in 1962 and are still there.

Before the buildup in connection with the Vietnam war, there were about 3,700 American servicemen on Taiwan. The number increased to about 10,000 during the war. In January, 1966, with nationalist consent, the Ching Chuan Kiang Air Base was upgraded and a wing of C-130 airlift aircraft and a squadron of KC-135 tankers were stationed there to support Southeast Asian operations. In addition, the base serves as a B-52 weather refuge in the event of typhoons affecting the regular base for these aircraft on Guam.

Following the shoot-down of an EC-121 reconnaissance plane by North Korean forces in April, 1969, the United States stationed an air defense fighter unit on Taiwan to provide cover for American reconnaissance aircraft transiting the Taiwan Strait. Also, according to articles in the *New York Times* and *Foreign Affairs Quarterly,* the United States stores some nuclear weapons on the island and operates an intelligence operation at the Shulinkuo Air Base on the northern end of Taiwan. Total American personnel are now 8,600 (with 6,000 dependents). Operating costs are $85 million and foreign exchange costs are $81 million.

The People's Republic of China continues to claim Taiwan as an integral part of its country and to avow its intention of "liberating" it. However, neither the communists nor the nationalists have risked large-scale hostilities since the Taiwan Strait crisis of 1958. Since 1964 both sides have engaged in alternate-day firing of propaganda leaflet shells between the mainland and the offshore islands, the closest communist territory to Quemoy being only 2,000 yards away.

Communist China has an estimated army of 2,400,000 troops—about as many men under arms as the United States has—organized into 164 tactical divisions; it has more than 3,000 combat aircraft. The Navy is essentially a coastal defense force composed of 47 major ships. The Air Force is composed mainly of Korean war vintage MIG-15s, some MIG-17s and 19s, and a few MIG-21s. Thus, the communist Chinese have a very limited conventional overseas capability with which to challenge Taiwan. They do have a growing nuclear stockpile and are progressing in missile development.

The nationalist Chinese have a force of 592,000 men. Their Army totals more than 336,500. Their armed forces are small compared to those of mainland China but they do constitute 4.2 percent of the total population of Taiwan, which is far above the percentage in other countries in the area such as Indonesia, Japan, Korea, and the Philippines. Also nationalist Chinese defense expenditures run nine to ten percent of GNP and more than fifty percent of the combined central and local government budgets on Taiwan, also extremely high for countries of that region.

Besides these statistics, other facts indicate a continued intention, or hope, on the part of the nationalists to return to the mainland by force. The nationalist Chinese armed forces are larger than the force level recommended for that country by the American military advisory group. The nationalists maintain special forces groups and airborne infantry brigades, some of which the United States supports through military assistance. They have an inordinate number of small landing craft in comparison with South Korea. Among other exercises, each year the nationalists conduct a large-scale exercise, drilling techniques for making a Normandy-type invasion from the sea.

The nationalists claim that their ambition for returning to the mainland is seventy percent political and thirty percent military, by which they say they mean an expectation of an internal revolution on the mainland in which they will be invited to participate. This continued theme of returning to the mainland helps to justify the

nationalists' control of Taiwan and to deny the indigenous population effective representation in the government of the island.

Over the last five years the nationalists have been much more
active than the communists in conducting small-scale military operations against the other side, including reconnaissance flights and
maritime raids. A portion of these raids have been conducted by
the National Salvation Force stationed on Matsu, about which
neither the U.S. ambassador nor the American commander of the
Taiwan Defense Command claims to know very much, even though
it has been in existence since 1950.

On July 2, 1969, one such raid was conducted in the Min River
estuary near Matsu. The raiders destroyed a few small boats of the
communists. On Taiwan, however, the raid was publicized as a
much larger operation. Until American participation in the war in
Vietnam, the United States had been very indulgent of such minor
raids. But because of the war, this country became concerned that
such hostilities might serve as provocation for the communist
Chinese to intervene in the war itself, and strongly protested the
Min River raid. Since then there have been no such occurrences.

Likewise, this country declined nationalist China's informal offer
to send combat troops to Vietnam because of concern that this too
might induce the communist Chinese to become involved in the
war. A thirty-one-man psychological warfare team from Taiwan
was accepted.

According to reports from Peking, the United States continues to
fly reconnaissance drones over the mainland. They claim to have
shot down nineteen such drones since 1964. The communists also
view American reconnaissance flights along their coast and the
American military presence on Taiwan as especially hostile toward
them.

Another instance of such antagonism is the joint American-
nationalist military exercise Forward Thrust, which has been conducted annually for the last ten years. This exercise is designed to
train Chinese and American special forces in unconventional war-

fare and to train some Chinese units in conventional warfare. The scenario of the exercise focuses on parachuting special forces personnel, and landing other troops, in occupied territory for the purpose of linking up with insurgent forces already operating there. The exercise drills in guerrilla, infiltration, and civil affairs techniques as well. The United States provided about 500 personnel for the most recent exercise and a number of aircraft.

Also until 1969 this country was participating with the nationalists four times a year in another unconventional warfare exercise known as Fond Memory, each involving twelve American special forces personnel. The Embassy at Taipei and the commander of the Taiwan Defense Command knew very little about this exercise.

Another curious step taken by the nationalist Chinese in recent years was the enlarging of certain airfields at a cost of several million dollars. At least one of the purposes for which this was done was to make these airfields available for supporting American B-52s should the United States choose to relocate such aircraft from Okinawa. American officials seem to have acted with inconsistency in this matter, some encouraging the Chinese to make the effort, others willing to discourage them. Stationing of B-52s on Taiwan would be a further provocation to the communist Chinese, even though the main mission for such aircraft would probably be in connection with the war in Vietnam. The United States has no present intention of making such a deployment.

Although the ordinary American military assistance program to nationalist China has been declining in the last few years, the United States has been providing that country with a very large amount of excess military equipment. In the fiscal year 1970 it provided the nationalist Chinese in excess equipment more than thirty-five F-100 aircraft, over twenty F-104 aircraft, more than thirty C-119's, more than fifty medium tanks, some howitzers, and thousands of M-14 rifles. Also at about this time the United States sold them five destroyers and provided them the equipment for a Nike Hercules battalion. Excluding the last two items, this excess equipment had a current utility value of $35,989,000, more than $10 million greater than the regular congressionally approved military assistance program of $25,003,000.

During the Symington Subcommittee's hearings in November, 1969, on nationalist China, the State and Defense witnesses failed to disclose that this country was providing those F-100 and F-104 fighter aircraft, even though Senator Fulbright asked these witnesses a specific question as to the extent and nature of excess equipment being provided to nationalist China. Their testimony disclosed only that the United States was providing some outmoded wheeled vehicles to China under this program.

Also at about that time Congress was considering authorizing $54 million to procure a squadron of F-4 aircraft for China. Congress was not informed that these other aircraft were being made available to that country.

Another instance of an attempt to enhance nationalist China's offensive capability was an effort to obtain congressional approval for the loan of three submarines. These would have had greater implications for offensive tactics and raids than for the defense of Taiwan, in view of the very limited naval capability of the communist Chinese. The United States is also lending the nationalists $20 million to start a helicopter construction program of their own.

Nationalist China maintains a police state on Taiwan. Martial law is in effect and severe penalties are meted out for activities considered subversive, whether pro-communist or not. Rule on the island was exceptionally brutal when the nationalists first came to the island at the end of World War II. In February, 1947, the government quelled an insurrection, in which action 10,000 to 20,000 people were killed.*

Today, the indigenous Taiwanese are effectively denied political

---

* In testifying before the Symington Subcommittee, the U.S. Ambassador, Walter P. McConaughy, had great difficulty remembering these numbers although he had devoted most of his career to that part of the Far East.

representation proportionate to their presence on the island. They constitute eighty-four percent of the total population of 14,000,000 but have only minor representation in the national assembly. Most military officers in the nationalist army are mainlanders but ninety-five percent of the draftees are Taiwanese. Over sixty percent of the only political party, the Kuomintang, are now Taiwanese, but only three of the sixteen county chairmen of the party are Taiwanese. There is also discrimination in the higher offices of the government monopolies and in government service, and the public sector accounts for almost one-fourth of the GNP.

Taiwan is, however, a prosperous member of the world community, having graduated from American economic assistance in 1965. The country has accomplished a very successful land reform program, and the indigenous Taiwanese have participated on about an equal basis in this growing prosperity and in the educational system.

Chiang Kai-shek was eighty-six years old in the spring of 1972. Little is expected to change on Taiwan when he dies. The Taiwanese generally believe that, because of their preponderant numbers, time will eventually permit them to prevail. They would dread a communist takeover of the island almost as much as would the mainlanders on Taiwan.

It is United States policy to favor greater participation by the Taiwanese in the government of the island, but the American government also takes the position that basically it is a matter for the people of the island to determine. Likewise, it is American policy that the international position of Taiwan should be decided peacefully by the "Chinese."

Over the last several years, the number of United States allies with increased contacts with the People's Republic of China continued to grow. On October 14, 1970, Canada became the first non-communist country in the Western Hemisphere to recognize the government in Peking. Then, America's own posture toward the People's Republic underwent a great change with the startling announcement on July 18, 1971, of the secret visit to Peking by President Nixon's Special Assistant Henry Kissinger, the visit to China by Mr. Nixon himself in February, 1972, and the U.S. support of communist China's membership in the United Nations. These events accelerated trends already evident toward some *détente* between the United States and the People's Republic. However, the full consequences of these changes for the two countries as well as for nationalist China and Japan cannot be assessed for some years.

IV

Japan and Okinawa

JAPAN

The security relationship between the United States and Japan grew out of the American military occupation at the end of World War II, passed through the period covered by the Security Treaty of 1952, which was signed at the same time as the Treaty of Peace, and now rests on the Treaty of Mutual Cooperation and Security entered into in 1960. This treaty is similar to our other five security treaties in the Pacific.

Another significant document in the evolution of this relationship was the joint communiqué of November 21, 1969, announcing the reversion to Japan of administrative rights over Okinawa. In this declaration the Japanese government acknowledged for the first time, publicly and authoritatively, "that the security of Japan could not be adequately maintained without international peace and security in the Far East and, therefore, the security of countries in the Far East was a matter of serious concern for Japan." Although this may sound rather nebulous to American readers, it reflects a very important change of attitude on the part of the Japanese, a new willingness to participate in the security of the region as a whole.

39

The Japanese Prime Minister specifically stated in the communiqué that "the security of the Republic of Korea was essential to Japan's own security" and "security in the Taiwan area was also a most important factor for the security of Japan." In his speech to the National Press Club following the issuance of the communiqué, Prime Minister Sato went even further by saying that this accord marked the "transition from a 'closed' relationship between Japan and the United States, confined to the solution of bilateral problems which concern the two countries alone, to an 'open' relationship." Elsewhere in his speech he described this new relationship as "a great historical experiment in working together for a new order in the world, on a dimension that transcends a bilateral alliance."

Prime Minister Sato's policy, reflected in these statements, and his commitment to continue the Security Treaty, were approved on December 27, 1969, in an election in which his Liberal Democratic Party won the largest majority of seats in the Diet that it had had since 1960. Following that, there was little difficulty continuing the treaty past June 23, 1970, the date on which, by its terms, the treaty became subject to renunciation. The relative calm with which the Japanese people accepted the coming of that date was in marked contrast with the public outcry in Japan against the adoption of the treaty ten years before.

In 1970 the United States had 125 military installations in Japan, of which thirty-two were classed as major facilities. These included six airfields, two naval bases, two bombing ranges, six ammunition depots, and a maneuver area. Operating costs in the fiscal year 1970 were $550 million. American military-related foreign exchange expenditures in Japan, which involved procurement and services for Vietnam as well as operation of the American bases, totaled $613 million.

There were in 1970 about 40,000 American military personnel in Japan, with about the same number of dependents. They were enjoying ten golf courses and a downtown Tokyo hotel, all reserved for their exclusive use. Seventy percent of the bases, by area, and seventy-seven percent of American military personnel were located at that time within sixty miles of Tokyo. Over the years almost all of the bases have been subjected to numerous complaints and demonstrations concerning noise, congestion, and other problems. Aircraft and military train accidents caused a number of such protests, such as aircraft accidents at Itazuke and the petroleum car derailment at Shinjuku Station in Tokyo in 1967.

All major American naval facilities had had their problems with community relations. There was always pressure for the return of at least one of the two major naval bases, Yokosuka or Sasebo. For several years the Atsugi Naval Air Station was creating a serious noise problem with its landing field and testing facility for an adjoining Japanese commercial enterprise in the business of overhauling American aircraft. The base's only other substantial function was to support fifteen reconnaissance and transport aircraft. Kamiseya Naval Facility, a communications installation near Tokyo, effectively deprived thirteen small nearby communities of television reception. For this inconvenience, the Japanese government regularly provided the residents of these communities with a specified amount of monetary compensation. Yokosuka Naval Base, just below Tokyo, had once been one of the largest Japanese naval bases. In recent years, however, with the Americans using most of the facilities, the headquarters of the Japanese naval contingent there had to be relegated to a former warehouse.

Among the six air bases in Japan, only Misawa, at the northern end of the central island of Honshu, and Iwakuni, at the southern end, were relatively free from opposition. Yokota, thirty-five miles from Tokyo, a highly urbanized and congested part of Japan, was serving in 1970 as the base for a wing of F-4 fighter-bombers and as a large transport terminal for American personnel going and coming between the United States and Southeast Asia. Here, also, the Japanese government had to pay nearby residents compensation for the noise and other inconveniences which the air base was causing them.

Tachikawa Air Base, located near Yokota, had caused so much protest that it had to cease air operations in December, 1969. For years, protesting students literally camped at the end of its runway in pitched tents with hundreds of banners flying. Then, since the runway was not being used, the Japanese government suggested that Tachikawa be returned to Japan.

Itazuke Air Base, near the city of Fukuoka, had also incurred such strong opposition that it had had to reduce its air operations to a minimum. To quiet this discontent the United States kept paying all the costs for operating the facility, although it was serving as Fukuoka's civil airport and sixty-three percent of its air traffic was commercial. In 1970 there were 880 American personnel there. Of these, 184 were operating the long distance communications link with South Korea. The rest were there to service a few EC-121 aircraft and to support Itazuke as a contingency, i.e., standby, base, even though the facility was a fully functioning civil airport. Operating costs at Itazuke were running $12.4 million in 1968 and $16.9 million in 1969.

Perhaps the most provocative of the American facilities was the Mito Bombing Range, located only 2.6 miles from a plutonium research and development laboratory of the Japan Atomic Fuel Corporation and only two and one-fifth miles from one resort beach and three miles from another. Accidental releases of training munitions off the range were not unknown, and for many years the Japanese had been asking to have the range back. In 1968 and 1969 the tactical squadrons at Yokota Air Force Base, the primary users of the Mito range, were able to take seventy percent of their gunnery training in Korea. The flying time from Yokota to the alternative bombing range that serves Misawa Air Base was forty-four minutes. To comply with proficiency standards, each F-4 pilot is required to participate in forty-eight range events twice a year.

Other instances were hardly less striking. In 1970, the U.S. Marine Corps maintained a 45,000-acre maneuver area at the foot of Mount Fujiyama, two hours away from Tokyo by ground transportation;

this in addition to two other maneuver areas on Okinawa, each approximately 20,000 acres in area. On one of these two Okinawa maneuver areas, the Marines could employ virtually every tactic for which they were using the Fujiyama maneuver area, including the firing of live artillery ammunition (although it was more difficult to score such firing on Okinawa because of the jungle canopy).

A large amount of land was retained also by U.S. forces for recreational purposes. Ten golf courses covered 800 acres. One ammunition depot, Tama, covering 492 acres, was being used only for recreational purposes. Four of the golf courses and Tama were in the highly urbanized Kanto Plain area surrounding Tokyo. The Japanese government also provided the American forces with a hotel in downtown Tokyo. Also in the Tokyo metropolitan area was the Tokorozawa Logistics Depot, which comprised 737 acres of largely open space, much of which was being held for contingency purposes.

The United States had thirty-seven naval vessels home-ported in Japan, of which nine were destroyers, frigates, and a cruiser. Ten others were minesweepers. To improve morale and save costs, the Navy has been experimenting with the possibility of increasing the number of vessels home-ported in Japan. This means locating the seamen's dependents in that country.

A Japanese commercial concern operated and maintained the landline communications system in Japan for our forces. The troposcatter and other tactical communications used by the American forces were operated by U.S. personnel.

Over the years the United States had always taken the position that it was willing to relocate virtually any of its facilities in Japan if the Japanese government would provide, at its expense, equivalent facilities elsewhere. In a much-heralded proposal in 1968 the United States offered to turn back to the Japanese or relocate fifty-four facilities subject to such a condition. A year later twenty-three of these facilities had in fact been returned to the Japanese, but they represented only two and one-half percent of the total area of the bases covered by the proposal.

By 1970 it had become increasingly obvious that the United States had far too many active bases in Japan for this relatively quiet period in that part of the Far East. If the Japanese or some other foreign power had had forces in the United States equivalent to those the United States had in the Tokyo area that year, it would have been as if there were in the New York metropolitan area 30,000 foreign troops and their dependents on seventy foreign military facilities, including three air bases, one naval base, three large depots, four golf courses reserved for foreign military personnel, and an exclusive downtown hotel.

Finally in December, 1970, the two governments announced plans to reduce the American military presence by 12,000 men and to turn over to Japan a number of major bases, some entirely and some only in part. Most of the American air bases are affected by this decision. Two of the three F-4 squadrons at Misawa will go to South Korea and the other one will return to the United States, greatly reducing American air operations at that base. The F-4 wing at Yokota will relocate to Kadena Air Base on Okinawa. The Southeast Asia air transportation terminal at Yokota will, however, continue there, and the facility will stay as an American base. With the relocation of Yokota's F-4s the Mito Bombing Range will doubtless revert to Japan. Itazuke Air Base will cease being an American air base. Operations at Atsugi Naval Air Facility will become predominantly Japanese. Repair work on American aircraft there will continue.

The naval facilities will also be greatly affected. The United States will cease to use Yakosuka as a naval base, moving the Seventh Fleet headquarters formerly there to Sasebo. It will also change its exclusive rights to the ship repair facilities at Yakosuka to those of priority use in times of emergency. This relocation away from Yakosuka will also eliminate much of the need for the large

American housing facilities at nearby Yokohama. It is likely that the Kamiseya communications facility will also revert to Japan.

Thus, many needed changes are now in progress. However, other similar steps might also be fitting, including reversion of Tachikawa, the Fuji Maneuver Area, Tama Ammunition Depot, Tokorazawa Logistics Depot, and Yokota Air Base.

The use of United States bases has been the subject of continual dialogue with the Japanese. Under an exchange of notes at the time of the signing of the 1960 Security Treaty, the United States agreed to "prior consultation" (which is understood to be tantamount to a Japanese veto) before making any major change in the deployment of American forces in Japan, introducing nuclear weapons there, or launching combat operations from there. A major change in deployment would probably be the introduction into Japan of an Army division, a naval task force, or an air wing. The launching of a combat operation would include the launching of aircraft on bombing missions but would not include the prompt dispatch of American warplanes to protect a reconnaissance vessel or aircraft threatened or attacked by enemy forces, as happened to the USS Pueblo in January, 1968, and to an EC-121 reconnaissance aircraft over the Sea of Japan in April, 1969.

In the Okinawa communiqué and Prime Minister Sato's contemporaneous speech in November, 1969, the Prime Minister made reasonably clear that the Japanese government would respond favorably to a United States request for permission to use its bases in Japan to repel an attack upon South Korea. He also indicated sympathetic consideration for the use of such bases to repel an attack against Taiwan. However, there have been some official Japanese statements following President Nixon's announcement of his trip to communist China indicating that the Japanese may be reconsidering this position.

There is no doubt that Japan is entering a new chapter in its history. American relations with it, therefore, must also enter a new phase. Japan's GNP reached $200 billion in 1970, tripling in real value over the decade of the 1960s and bringing her today to second place in the free world's economy. Analysts see no reason why her GNP will not double or triple again in the 1970s. That would mean the growth of an economy already large to one of gigantic proportions. The implications of this economic power will go far beyond the fields of finance and commerce into the realm of the political and the strategic.

The Okinawa communiqué and Prime Minister Sato's other statements in Washington in November, 1969, clearly indicated that Japan expects to play a larger role in the Far East than it has in the past. Its booming economy and reviving national pride are definite factors in this trend. Japan has already expressed a willingness to participate in an international peacekeeping operation in Southeast Asia after the Vietnam war, if one is established. Also significant is Japan's continued reluctance to ratify the Nuclear Non-Proliferation Treaty.

Having lived long under the trauma of defeat, the Japanese people are just now becoming aware of the position in the world to which their inherent strength and energy entitle them. Secure in their insular position and protected by the American nuclear umbrella for the last twenty-five years, they have had, in the words of one authority, virtually no foreign policy at all—and hardly any defense budget.

The reawakening of a spirit of nationalism in Japan is evident in a number of ways, the new "open relationship" announced in the Okinawa communiqué, their slowness in signing, and their continued reluctance to ratify the Nuclear Non-Proliferation Treaty being but two instances. Upon his return from a trip to Japan in January, 1970, Senator Javits informed the Subcommittee on Commitments Abroad "that they [the Japanese] have finally awakened to the fact that they are a lot closer to us." By this statement, the Senator meant the Japanese seemed to be more in accord with

United States policies and presence in the Far East than they had seemed to be a few years before.

Because of what Japan is today, and even more because of what she will be during the next decade, that country is far more important in determining American foreign policy in the Far East than any other country in that area of the world with the possible exception of communist China. Two men quite familiar with Japan, Under Secretary of State U. Alexis Johnson and Dr. Edwin Reischauer, both former ambassadors to Japan, consider our relationship with Japan to be, in Mr. Johnson's words, "the single most important element in the preservation of American security west of Hawaii." * A very important factor in this equation is the awareness, in Under Secretary Johnson's words before the Symington Subcommittee, "that a likely alternative to a strong U.S.-Japan security relationship might well be the development of a unilateral Japanese strategic [i.e., nuclear] military force," a consequence the Soviet Union appreciates as well as the United States.

American recognition of Japan's importance to the United States is reflected in the Security Treaty and in the presence of American forces in Japan, as well as in Korea and Okinawa, to some extent. It is also evidenced in the language of the communiqué on the reversion of Okinawa and in the existence of the U.S.-Japanese Joint Security Consultative Committee that regularly reviews the defense relationship between the two countries.

The Okinawa communiqué was a remarkable document. In graciously accepting the inevitable, the return of Okinawa to Japan, we achieved by the same stroke a Japanese commitment toward closer defense ties with this country, what Prime Minister Sato characterized as an "open relationship" "that transcends a bilateral alliance." This bent in Japanese policy was strengthened by the election victory of Prime Minister Sato's Liberal Democratic Party

* Statement by Mr. Johnson to the Symington Subcommittee on January 26, 1970. Dr. Reischauer is quoted to the same effect in the *New York Times,* November 23, 1969, p. E4.

that followed his return from Washington. It is of more than passing significance that this was the first Japanese election since World War II in which the governing party ran on a foreign policy platform. In this same direction of closer security relations with the United States, Yosuhiro Nakasone, when he was director of the Japanese Defense Agency and an influential political figure in his own right, proposed that the American membership on the Joint Security Consultative Committee be elevated from the Ambassador and CINCPAC * to the Secretaries of State and Defense.

The pledge to return Okinawa to Japan was a step toward that self-respecting status which Japan deserves and that harmonious partnership which both countries must have. The December, 1970, announcement of substantial reductions in the American base presence in Japan was another step in that direction.

Nevertheless, as Japan grows in power and importance in the next decade, the large number of American military bases remaining in Japan, particularly in the Tokyo area, will be increasingly viewed as affronts to Japanese dignity and sovereignty. Both Americans and Japanese consider these bases to be there not to protect Japan directly, but to support American military commitments elsewhere in the Far East. It is fortunate that the Japanese acknowledged in the Okinawa communiqué that their security is indeed tied to the security of the other parts of the Far East. Still, the American base structure in Japan and Japan's own defense efforts do not yet evidence a fully cooperative, truly mutual defense arrangement for the achievement of common ends. Unlike the closeness in purpose Americans have with the Germans and the Koreans as far as United States troops on their soil are concerned, the Americans appear to many Japanese to have seized bases in their country through conquest, and to hold them stubbornly for purposes not entirely consistent with their own aspirations and policy. In return the U.S. provides them security in the form of a nuclear

* Commander-in Chief, Pacific.

umbrella and the Seventh Fleet but against a threat they some-times have difficulty in perceiving. The relative reticence of Japa-nese officials on this matter could well have stemmed from their desire to do nothing to interfere with the reversion of Okinawa. Now this factor is no longer relevant. The recent call by the Japa-nese defense minister for the conversion of all the American bases to a joint-use status to be shared by Japanese and American forces may well be a precursor of the coming change in Japanese policy.

A total withdrawal of American military personnel from Japan would not be wise, as such a step might cast doubt upon the credi-bility of the American nuclear guarantee for Japan and needlessly unsettle many other countries in the Far East. However, a further thinning out of the military presence in Japan is quite a different matter. The American military presence should gravitate toward the ends of the home islands and Okinawa instead of toward the bright lights of Tokyo, as in the past.

As far as Japan's own military efforts at present are concerned, its defense budget, currently totaling $1.6 billion, has been less than one percent of the country's GNP for the last several years. Never-theless, the Japanese Self-Defense Forces, composed of 240,000 men, thirteen divisions, a 210-ship navy, and an air force of 960 aircraft, including fifteen jet fighter squadrons, provide the entire conven-tional peacetime defense of the Japanese home islands. No Ameri-can units in Japan are devoted primarily to the direct defense of the Japanese homeland. Because of Japan's insular position, the very limited overseas capability of the communist Chinese armed forces and the continued credibility of the American nuclear guarantee, the Japanese see very little threat to their country. The greatest source of what threat there may be lies in the tensions existing on the Korean peninsula.

With respect to foreign aid, in 1968 the rate of United States governmental assistance to Far Eastern countries (excluding mili-tary assistance to Vietnam), as a percentage of our GNP, was more than twice that of equivalent Japanese assistance to these countries. Many Americans feel shortchanged when they compare the Japanese defense budget and Japanese foreign aid with American efforts in these fields. Since the Japanese already provide the conventional defense for their homeland, further Japanese security efforts would have to relate to the defense of the region as a whole instead of to the home islands alone. Certain steps in this direction can be made without unduly alarming the other countries of the Far East, which still remember World War II. For instance, the Japanese could give more military and economic assistance in the form of equipment and training, operation of the military communications system in Japan, electronic intelligence gathering, and perhaps tripartite military planning with the United States and certain of Japan's neighbors in the Far East.

OKINAWA

The United States has used Okinawa as a stationing, training, and logistics base ever since World War II. American authority there, which ended May 15, 1972, derived not from the Mutual Security Treaty with Japan but from the provision in the 1952 Peace Treaty that gave the United States the "powers of administration, legislation and jurisdiction" over the Ryukyu Islands. Such authority has now ceased, and the American military presence on Okinawa will be governed by the Mutual Security Treaty just as the bases in Japan proper are today.

The November, 1969, communiqué of President Nixon and Prime Minister Sato on the reversion of Okinawa stated:

. . . the two governments would immediately enter into consultations regarding specific arrangements for accomplishing the early reversion of Okinawa without detriment to the security of the Far East including Japan. They further agreed to expedite the consultations with a view to accomplishing the reversion during 1972 subject to the conclusion of these specific arrangements with the necessary legislative support.

The communiqué added in effect that nuclear weapons would not be stored on Okinawa without prior consultation with the Japanese government (which, as mentioned above, is tantamount to requiring its consent). The document further stated, however, that reversion would not interfere with the United States' use of its bases on Okinawa for carrying on the war in South Vietnam, and implied that most of the bases there could remain.

The gradual Japanese assumption of responsibility for the immediate defense of the Ryukyus after reversion will include internal security, air defense, coastal surveillance, and sea lane security, for all of which in the home islands the Japanese are now responsible.

In 1970 the United States had 120 military facilities in the Ryukyu Islands, of which nineteen were classed as major, including three air bases, two maneuver areas, two Marine Corps camps, a very large logistics depot and adjoining port facility, and a small naval base. American military installations occupied twenty-six percent of the entire area of Okinawa. Stationed at Kadena Air Base, one of the largest bases in the world, were tactical aircraft, B-52 bombers and KC-135 aerial refueling tankers. Upon reversion the Japanese took over the Naha Air Base on Okinawa for their Air Self Defense Forces on the island. American operating costs on Okinawa in the fiscal year 1970 were $538 million. Foreign exchange costs were $261 million. Stationed on Okinawa in 1970 were almost 45,000 American servicemen with almost 30,000 dependents. These servicemen included about 19,000 Marines, comprising two Marine regiments and some of their support units.

Some of the first American units to deploy to South Vietnam in 1965 were based on Okinawa. Other units sent to Vietnam during that period were supplied with equipment pre-positioned on Okinawa. This was one of the first significant demonstrations of the effectiveness of the pre-positioning concept under wartime circumstances.

The reversion to Japan of the administrative rights over the Ryukyus, as an amendment to an existing treaty, the Peace Treaty of 1952, was properly submitted to the Senate for its ratification, and the Senate quite properly voted for the reversion. Japan is too important to this country and the diminution in military value of Okinawa under reversion is too insignificant for such an issue to divide the two countries.

The absence or presence of nuclear weapons on Okinawa has little bearing on the strategic value of American installations there. Lieutenant General James B. Lampert, the High Commissioner of the Ryukyu Islands, testified before the Symington Subcommittee:

Reversion itself will not basically alter the strategic importance of our Okinawan bases which are a tremendously valuable investment of the United States. Our Okinawan bases will continue to be a key element in the deterrence of aggression.

In view of the relative importance of Japan in comparison with other American interests in the Far East, there should be no discontent over the requirement for prior consultation with the Japanese before launching military operations from bases on Okinawa and before making major changes in the American military presence there.

V

Laos*

In 1961–62 there were in Laos almost 700 American soldiers, of whom more than half were members of the Special Forces. A force of about 500 Soviet troops was also there providing logistical support for the local communists—the Pathet Lao and their North Vietnamese allies.

Neither the United States nor the Soviet Union was anxious to continue this confrontation in that remote country, so both sought to disengage. Negotiations ensued at Vienna, at Geneva, in Laos, and elsewhere. The result was the ambiguous compromise set forth in rather unambiguous language in the Declaration on the Neutrality of Laos and the Protocol to that Declaration, signed by thirteen communist and noncommunist countries in July, 1962, and commonly known as the Geneva Accords of 1962.

Under the mantle of this agreement, the Laotians themselves established a tripartite government composed of right-wing royalist elements under General Phoumi Nosavan, neutralist elements under Prince Souvanna Phouma, and communist elements whose

* Part of this chapter appeared as an article in *Foreign Affairs*, April, 1971.

nominal leader was Prince Souphanouvang (Souvanna Phouma's half-brother).

The Geneva Accords themselves required Laos to dissociate herself from all military alliances, including SEATO, prohibited the introduction of foreign military personnel and civilians performing quasi-military functions (except for a small French training mission), precluded the establishment of any foreign military installations in Laos, and forbade the use of Laotian territory to interfere with the internal affairs of another country. Pursuant to this agreement the Americans and Russians withdrew their military personnel. The North Vietnamese, however, failed to withdraw most of their 6,000-man force then in Laos.

Nevertheless, a relative peace settled over the country for about a year, to be shattered in 1963 by an exchange of assassinations. The noncommunist officer Colonel Ketsana was murdered and shortly thereafter the pro-Chinese Foreign Minister Quinim Pholsema was killed. These assassinations once again ignited hostilities, which have raged ever since.

In Laos today not one but two distinct wars are being fought for quite different purposes and to some extent by different forces. The contest waged by the government forces of Laos supported by their American and Thai allies against the communist Pathet Lao and their North Vietnamese allies for political control of the kingdom is carried on in northern and central Laos and, to some extent, in the Mekong River Valley in the western half of the southern Laotian panhandle. In 1970 the noncommunist forces in Laos totaled between 95,150 and 97,650, a large portion of which were in northern Laos. The communist forces in northern Laos totaled 43,400 (comprised of about 23,400 Pathet Lao and 20,000 North Vietnamese).

The other war involves the efforts of the North Vietnamese to use the network of roads, waterways, and trails in the eastern part of the Laotian panhandle as a corridor for the transportation and provisioning of their forces fighting in South Vietnam and more recently in Cambodia, and the efforts by the Americans to interdict such traffic. (Laotian forces hardly participate in this conflict.) This is the famous Ho Chi Minh Trail, the northern entrance of which is generally considered to be the Mu Gia Pass less than 100 miles north of the Demilitarized Zone between North and South Vietnam. The contest on and over the Ho Chi Minh Trail is actually only an adjunct of the struggle for power in South Vietnam. Communist forces in this part of Laos were estimated in 1970 at about 95,600 (comprised of about 80,000 North Vietnamese and 15,600 Pathet Lao).

In the war in northern Laos the brunt of the battle on the government's side has been borne by the Meo and other montagnard tribes who dwell in the highlands of that region. Hardened by centuries of nomadic life, slash-and-burn farming, and oppression at the hands of their neighbors, historically the Chinese, these 30,000 or so sturdy warriors are sustained and supported by the U.S. Central Intelligence Agency. Under the leadership of Meo General Vang Pao, they constitute the bulk of the government's paramilitary forces and are by far its most effective fighters. Designated by American military planners as the BGs (*Bataillons guerriers,* and formerly known as the *Armée clandestine* or the Special Guerrilla Units), these forces do most of the patrolling, ambushing, and attacking done on the government side. In contrast to the situation in Vietnam, the main force of guerrillas in Laos is on the noncommunist side.

The other Laotians, whether in the government's army or that of the Pathet Lao, are generally poor soldiers. The most effective soldiers on the communist side generally come from North Vietnam. Without this North Vietnamese support the Pathet Lao effort would collapse.

Another significant factor in the fighting is its seasonal pattern. During the dry season that lasts from October to early June, the communists invariably make their greatest advances. In the ensuing rainy season each year, with the communist supply lines clogged, the forces of the central government have been able to recoup most of their losses of the preceding dry season, often with very little opposition.

While Laotians, Vietnamese, Americans, and Thais contest for power in Laos, like a brooding omnipresence in the northernmost provinces of Laos are more than 14,000 Chinese soldiers serving as construction crews and security troops in connection with the extension of two branches of a road originally laid by the Chinese in years past. The road is guarded by 395 antiaircraft weapons and is carefully avoided by most American and Royal Laotian aircraft. One of the ironies in Laos is that the Chinese were first invited into Laos to do road construction in 1962 by Souvanna Phouma as Prime Minister and the right-wing leader Phoumi Nosavan as his Defense Minister.

One of the branches now being worked on extends south into Laos more than eighty miles toward the Thai border. Another branch runs forty miles in a northeasterly direction connecting with Route 19 from Dien Bien Phu in North Vietnam. However, there has been no extension of the road since February, 1970. American policymakers view this present road-building effort with obvious concern, particularly to the extent that it indicates Chinese movement toward the Thai border.

To understand how the United States came to be involved let us turn back to the autumn of 1962, three months after the signing of the Geneva Accords. By this time the United States had come to realize that the North Vietnamese were not going to withdraw their forces from Laos, and the American Government therefore agreed to provide Souvanna Phouma with certain limited amounts of military equipment. This was permitted by the Geneva Accords. To administer this program a small office in the AID Mission at Vientiane was set up under the nondescript title of "Requirements Office" and staffed with retired American military officers. This was of dubious legality under the Geneva Accords. Thus began the American military assistance program to the present regime in Laos.

With the outbreak of serious hostilities in 1963, the United States began to train Laotian pilots and ground crews in Thailand. By the spring of 1964 the war was going badly for the government forces. The communists were able to overrun the remaining government positions on the Plaine des Jarres, the famous, picturesque plateau situated in the center of Laos. In the face of this threat American tactical fighter-bombers began striking targets in northern Laos under what was publicly described as "armed reconnaissance." In that campaign the American participation was small. There were only twenty such sorties in the whole year of 1964. (A sortie is a single mission by a single aircraft.)

The United States also began to provide greater amounts of war materiel and other assistance. To transport Laotian supplies and military personnel, the services of the CIA-sponsored companies Air America and Continental Air Services were made available, both their airplanes and their helicopters.

The communist drive was stopped on the western reaches of the Plaine des Jarres at the town of Muong Soui. Almost invariably journalistic references to the Plaine des Jarres describe it by terms such as "strategic" or "key." This terminology is hardly apt; the plain was to remain in communist hands for most of the next eight years, and meanwhile the Souvanna Phouma government was still able to survive and control about eighty percent of the population.

The government forces launched an offensive in another part of Laos in the summer, the rainy season, of 1964. No American air strikes were provided, but a few American airmen went along with the Laotian forces on the ground to guide Laotian planes to their targets, and eight American soldiers accompanied the Laotian regiments as military advisors.

In the autumn of the same year, at American request, Laotian fighter-bombers began to hit North Vietnamese supply routes along the panhandle of Laos. In 1965, as the war in South Vietnam intensified, American aircraft took over this mission.

The war in Laos has seesawed back and forth ever since. The

government forces made impressive gains in 1967, advancing to within twenty miles of the North Vietnamese border and reaching the outskirts of Sam Neua, the principal town in the communist-held portion of Laos. With substantially increased Soviet assistance in materiel, the communists launched offensives in 1968 and 1969 (the planning for the first of which coincided with the planning for the Tet offensive in South Vietnam). These communist drives in Laos wiped out the gains made by the government forces in the previous year and brought the communists beyond their previously held positions. In June, 1969, Muong Soui fell to them and they encircled the royal capital of Luang Prabang from three sides.* That they did not push on and seize this town is one of the curiosities of the war that may be of more than passing significance.

As the war intensified in these years, so did American involvement. In 1966 about fifty U.S. Air Force officers and enlisted men, technically assigned to the Air Attaché's office, were stationed at the Laotian Air Force bases as advisors. In 1967 about the same number of U.S. Army personnel were deployed to the regional headquarters of the Laotian Army for similar duty.

The Americans who had briefly served with the Laotian forces to guide tactical aircraft to their targets were replaced by Laotians who had been trained to do such work. But then about twenty U.S. Air Force pilots stationed at five bases in Laos and others stationed in Thailand began to serve as airborne forward air controllers in single-engine, slow-moving airplanes for the same purpose.

In connection with the American air war over North Vietnam several navigational aid facilities were installed in Laos to guide American F-4s, F-105s, and other aircraft to their targets. Some of these facilities were manned by U.S. Air Force personnel; others were unmanned. One of the manned facilities was set up at Muong

* The King of Laos resides at Luang Prabang. The administrative offices of Souvanna Phouma's government are at Vientiane.

Phalane in the panhandle. It was overrun by communist forces on Christmas Day, 1967, with the loss of two American lives. In October, 1967, another such facility was placed on a 5,000-foot cliff in northern Laos just thirteen miles from the North Vietnamese border at a place called Phou Pha Thi, then in the hands of friendly Meo tribesmen. This facility functioned for five months and then was overrun by communist forces on March 11, 1968, with the loss of all but a few of the Americans who were there.*

By far the largest American contribution to the war in northern Laos has been the air strikes by American Air Force planes against communist interdiction and close-in targets. By 1969 the level of such strikes had reached more than 100 sorties a day—not including any near the Ho Chi Minh Trail in southern Laos. The increased American involvement in the war in northern Laos can be shown graphically by the rise in the sortie rate over that area:

	Daily Sortie Rate
1964	(20 per year)
1965	12
1966	20
September, 1968	32
December, 1968	52
1969	More than 100

The large increase in 1969 was a result of several factors: the increased intensity of enemy action in northern Laos, the availability of American aircraft following the suspension of bombing over North Vietnam, and the reduced number of targets on the Ho Chi Minh Trail during the rainy season. There has been a decline in the number of sorties since 1969.

There is a significant distinction between American air operations over northern Laos and those conducted over North Vietnam

* An account of the fall of Phou Pha Thi, truly an instance of unheralded bravery in the Vietnam war, was provided to the Subcommittee on Commitments Abroad by one of the survivors, Major Stanley Sliz, on May 8, 1970.

that may explain the greater success achieved in Laos. In North Vietnam the strikes were exclusively against interdiction targets. The enemy controlled all of the ground there. By contrast, operations in northern Laos involve close air support for friendly forces in addition to strikes at interdiction targets. Furthermore, the friendly forces there are indigenous guerrillas, and the enemy is composed of road-bound conventional forces. Thus, in Laos there have been advantages in terms of target acquisition, as well as fairly minimal antiaircraft opposition.

The next most important American assistance provided to the Laotians was the aid the United States has been giving to General Vang Pao's montagnard forces. With CIA and U.S. Army advisors and substantial American logistical support, these forces have been able to bear the brunt of the battle for the Vientiane government. About 150–175 CIA case officers stationed in Laos and augmented by others from the American base at Udorn in Thailand supervise training and supplies and give advice on operations, but do not accompany these Laotian forces on such operations. CIA-chartered aircraft of the Air America and Continental Air fleets shuttle these Americans back and forth from Vientiane, Udorn, Vang Pao's headquarters at Long Tieng and Sam Thong, and other montagnard outposts. These CIA officers operate under the supervision of the CIA station chief on the Ambassador's staff at Vientiane.

Another important American-related contribution to the war in northern Laos is the Thai irregular forces serving under the command of General Vang Pao. Senator Fulbright has publicly estimated that there are as many as 5,000 Thai forces in Laos. This program is also run by the CIA.

The United States Air Force advisors with the Laotian Air Force exercise great influence over their protégés. The American Army advisors, except those with General Vang Pao's forces, have much less influence on the Laotian Army. The Air Force advisors in effect, if not in name, run the Air Force of Laos. That force is small, composed of relatively intelligent officers and men motivated by an esprit and sense of professionalism lacking in most of the other Royal Laotian units. Working with men of this caliber, the American airmen have little difficulty in guiding operations along the lines of their own experience and training. Not so with many of the Laotian Army units. Besides the natural Laotian disinclination for fighting, the Royal Laotian Army and its adjunct the Neutral Laotian Army, known by their respective French names *Force armée royale* and *Force armée neutrale,* are plagued by extreme class distinctions between officers and enlisted men, widespread corruption, an absence of political or ideological motivation, and an awareness from long experience that a live-and-let-live policy is often the wisest. As many as thirty percent of all new recruits desert. Under these circumstances, an American advisor's ability to influence events is often measured more by his personality and his control over American logistical support than by his military knowledge.

The total amount of American military assistance to Laos over the years runs into billions of dollars, but the exact amount remains secret. American support for the regular Laotian forces has grown to more than $230 million for the fiscal year 1971—$162 million in ordinary military assistance and $70 million spent by the CIA. By comparison, the Laotian government's total budget is only $36.6 million. The $230 million American contribution does not include the amount provided to the Thai forces in Laos, nor does it include the very large cost of American air operations in the war.

To maintain a color of compliance with the Geneva Accords, the large American logistical support for the Laotian forces is not administered by a typical military assistance group as in most other countries. Instead, such a group of Americans was assembled in neighboring Thailand under the command of a colonel carrying the deceptive title of "Deputy Chief of the Joint Military Advisory Group for Thailand." This group of supply and training experts does its work for Laos through the small Requirements Office in the AID Mission in Laos and through frequent visits to Laos.

Thus, there are stationed in Laos no more than several hundred Americans who are directly involved in the war. The main American support is furnished by Americans stationed elsewhere, mainly Thailand.

In the winter of 1969–70, the North Vietnamese poured considerably more men into northern Laos, reaching 33,000 men or so, and seemed on the verge of new and ominous gains. They retook the Plaine des Jarres, seized Vang Pao's base at Sam Thong, and threatened his headquarters at Long Tieng. To stop them, the Laotian government forces and their American allies redoubled their efforts, including a series of raids by B-52 bombers over the Plaine des Jarres.

Concerned that the still publicly unacknowledged American role in the war in Laos might escalate beyond bounds, Congress in December, 1969, passed an amendment to the 1970 Defense Appropriations Act which precluded the use of any funds so appropriated "to finance the introduction of American ground troops into either Laos or Thailand." The White House publicly endorsed this legislation as being consistent with its own policy. Identical amendments were attached to the 1971 and 1972 Defense Appropriations Acts thereafter.

As the American effort continued to mount in the early months of 1970, worry persisted in the Congress, in the press, and among the public. Under this pressure, the President felt obliged on March 6 to acknowledge a good deal of what this country was doing in Laos. He went on to say, "We have no plans for introducing ground combat forces into Laos." This presidential disclosure made it possible for the Subcommittee on Commitments Abroad to obtain executive branch consent to the release of a large portion of the testimony which it had taken in October, 1969, concerning the American role in Laos.

With the approach of the rainy season in the late spring, the communists had not yet made the gains expected of them. Vang Pao still held his headquarters at Long Tieng and a new front had been opened elsewhere in Indochina. In April and May, 1970, American and South Vietnamese forces invaded the communist sanctuaries in Cambodia. In the United States, this allied invasion revived public protests against the war. In Laos it caused the communists to increase their activity in the Laotian panhandle but to reduce their operations in northern Laos. When the rainy season returned to northern Laos, the front there stabilized as in past years.

Because of their need for more troops further south, along the Laotian panhandle and in Cambodia, in the 1970–71 dry season, the North Vietnamese reduced their forces in northern Laos to 25,000 to 30,000 men. Their operations during that dry season were not as intensive as those of the preceding several years. However, in the 1971–72 dry season, the North Vietnamese again pressed their offensive in northern Laos, striking hard at General Vang Pao's headquarters at Long Tieng. But, again, when the rainy season returned, Vang Pao still held Long Tieng, a fact hardly noticed in the American press.

From time to time both sides have made proposals for settling the war. The communists did so privately in 1967 and 1969, and they publicly made such a proposal in 1970. This communist plan involves the following five points: (1) a political settlement based upon the Geneva Accords of 1962; (2) free and democratic elections; (3) a withdrawal of United States equipment, advisors, and bombing; (4) the unification of the country based upon consultations among equals; and (5) evacuation of pro-American units from areas they illegally hold. On October 7, 1970, President Nixon, with the approval of the Laotian government, proposed a new peace plan for all of Indochina that called for a cease-fire along the existing battle line. Negotiations have been off and on between the government and the communist forces in Laos on the basis of these proposals ever since.

American casualties in the Laotian war have not been high. Among Americans stationed in Laos, the President has announced, up to 1970 about fifty were lost because of hostile action. The total number of American pilots lost over northern Laos, pilots stationed in Thailand or on the carriers, is hard to come by. Thirteen American crew members were lost there in the period from January, 1970, through April, 1971. American aircraft lost over northern Laos numbered fewer than 100 from 1964 through 1970, and twenty-five U.S. aircraft were reported lost during the period from January, 1970, through April, 1971.

The Laotians themselves, on the other hand, have suffered enormously from this war. They have had more than 600,000 refugees since 1962. By official reports, from 15,000 to 35,000 Laotians have been killed and they continue to lose 120 to 140 men a month. According to former American Ambassador William Sullivan:

It is pertinent to point out that the Lao themselves, a nation of less than three million, have suffered enormous casualties by their standards, . . . a loss that, proportional to the population of Laos, would be considered, I think, larger than the losses sustained by any other country on the face of this earth in that same period.

Perhaps even more poignant was the account of Edgar "Pop" Buell, the AID director for the northeastern region of Laos in the May, 1968, issue of the *New Yorker* magazine:

A few days ago, I was with V.P.'s [Vang Pao's] officers when they rounded up three hundred fresh Meo recruits. Thirty percent of the kids were fourteen years old or less, and about a dozen were only ten years old. Another thirty percent were fifteen or sixteen. The rest were thirty-five or over. Where were the ones in between? I'll tell you— they're all dead.

Although the United States is heavily involved in the fighting in Laos, particularly in the air, it is unlikely for several reasons that American ground combat troops will be sent to defend the Vientiane government. To do so would be contrary to the Nixon Doctrine announced on Guam. It would definitely be against the prevailing mood of the American people growing out of the frustrations of Vietnam. It would also be in violation of the amendments to the Defense Appropriations Acts quoted above—legislation which was publicly endorsed by the White House. The legal effect of any such legislation, however, expires at the end of the period for which the appropriations are provided.

The policy of the present Administration was probably best summed up by a high-ranking official at the Embassy in Vientiane, when he said, "We are not sending in any ground troops. This is not the Embassy's policy, this is the State Department's policy and President Nixon's policy." If further evidence need be adduced, the direct interests of the United States in Laos are small, and this country is no longer using American ground troops in any outright support of the Lon Nol government in Cambodia, which stands in a rather similar relationship to the United States. Nor is any unintentional commitment of ground forces a very likely possibility.

The United States has no defense treaty or other written defense commitment with Laos. Until 1962 Laos was a protocol country under the protection of the SEATO Treaty, but in accordance with the Geneva Accords of that year she dissociated herself from that treaty. Under the Geneva Accords this country is legally obligated to respect the neutrality of Laos, but is under no legal responsibility to come to the defense of Laos in the event that her neutrality is violated by another.

Going beyond the language of the Accords themselves and looking at the more important overtones and implications of this document, one sees that it has never taken on the sanctity of some other international accords that could entangle the United States in the name of national honor. The Geneva Accords have always been considered an unhappy compromise. They were the best bargain that could be struck in a very awkward situation. Their multilateral nature has also tended to diffuse responsibility. No American leader is likely to sound a call to the barricades to preserve the Geneva Accords of 1962.

Another aspect of the American relationship with Laos that might have led to very unfortunate consequences was a series of exaggerated declarations by several American officials. Perhaps the most expansive were the following. In a news conference on March 15, 1961, President Kennedy said: "The security of all Southeast Asia would be endangered if Laos loses its neutral independence. Its own safety runs with the safety of us all. . . ." On June 18, 1964, it was publicly reported that Assistant Secretary of State William P. Bundy had informed a congressional committee that the United States would "put our own forces" in Laos if communist forces got the upper hand there. Two days later, Admiral Harry Felt, the commander-in-chief of our forces in the Pacific, told a press conference in Taipei, Taiwan, that the United States would risk all-out war in Asia because "we believe so strongly that the communists cannot and must not win."

Later the same month, President Johnson, in a speech in Minneapolis, warned that the United States was prepared "to risk war" to preserve the peace in Southeast Asia. And on October 13, 1966, President Johnson informed the press that he had told Souvanna Phouma that "the world must know that aggression will not succeed in Indochina."

The obvious mistake in all of these well-intended statements is that they commit American prestige to the fulfillment of the spokesman's word. When a high government official, especially the President, speaks, he inevitably speaks for the entire country to the ears of the world.

Fortunately in the case of Laos no occasion has arisen that would have required the United States to fulfill the noble sentiments expressed. Unlike radioactivity, the dangerous effects of such emissions are measured in fairly short half-lives. That is why foreign statesmen frequently insist upon a repetition of such expressions. For these declarations on Laos, the change in administrations and the widespread discontent over events in Vietnam, as well as the simple passage of time, have tended to dissipate their meaning and implication. The present Administration has wisely refrained from publicly overstating the importance it attaches to Laos.

Another familiar commitment-making step is the stationing of American forces, especially combat units, at various points around the globe. There are, however, in the embattled areas of Laos very few truly American installations the loss of which would be likely to generate an attitude in this country like the reaction to the loss of Americans at Pleiku or aboard the *Pueblo*. There are some facilities in the Vientiane area that could conceivably belong in this category, but they have remained reasonably secure from attack; and with the attitude of Americans over Southeast Asia being what it is today, it is even unlikely that an attack on one of these places would lead this country to plunge in with ground troops.

American presence elsewhere in Laos is strictly "low-profile" and in most cases ancillary to some more significant Laotion operation. For instance, the American servicemen acting as advisors to the Laotian Army and Air Force are integrated into the operations of these Laotian forces, and, therefore, present no clear-cut American target for the enemy.

There is a fundamental distinction between assaults upon Americans as Americans and upon those who happen to be present when others are being attacked. It is a matter of placement, proportion, and purpose. As regrettable as would be the loss of any Americans in these integrated or ancillary roles, such an event is not likely to contain in it the dynamics that would lead to greater American involvement. There is a difference between a Pearl Harbor situation, on whatever scale, and an intentional exposure of a relatively small number of Americans to hostilities already commenced. This is especially so in light of this country's present mood with respect to Southeast Asia. The distinction that is being suggested here is similar to the one between the attitude in this country over the news that two American ships in the Gulf of Tonkin had been fired upon in August, 1964, and the attitude over the loss of two of the aircraft sent to attack North Vietnam in reprisal. In the first case, the attack was considered unprovoked and unjustifiable, in the second, regrettable but not requiring further reaction.

The loss of the navigational aid facilities at Muong Phalane and Phou Pha Thi should be mentioned in this regard. These were small, but essentially American, facilities overrun by the communists costing some American lives. These were instances, like the aircraft lost over Vietnam, where all concerned realized risks were being assumed, and the loss, though regrettable, was not entirely unexpected or unprovoked.

Although there are a number of sources for moral commitment to the Laotians, none is so great as to compel the United States to send ground troops to defend Laos. These sources of moral obligation include Souvanna Phouma's willingness to allow American aircraft to bomb the Ho Chi Minh Trail in his country, the close American relationship with General Vang Pao and his montagnard forces, the reliance Souvanna Phouma has placed on continued American support when rejecting communist overtures for a settlement, and the contribution to the war in Laos made by the Thais. But these claims upon the conscience of the United States are not as great as they may initially appear. Souvanna Phouma is long familiar with the machinations of power politics. According to former Ambassador William Sullivan, the Laotian Prime Minister is "a man without any illusions." Vang Pao's claim upon the United States may induce this country to assist in the evacuation of his people, if that becomes necessary, but not to fight to save Laos for him. And the Thais are making the contribution they are solely in their own national interest. Any other interpretation would be the height of naïveté.

As to a possible American involvement in the fighting on the ground as a result of some broader and more amorphous identification with the regime in Vientiane, there is a basic difference between the situation in Laos and the situation in Vietnam that led to the American combat role in 1965. In almost every violent contest in the world, it rapidly becomes evident which side the United

States would prefer to see prevail; this is inevitable from the close interrelation of world events and the prominence of this country. There is no escaping that fact, but there is a very significant difference between that and the conduct of American affairs in such a way that the cause of the preferred party becomes the cause of the United States.

Vietnam in the early 1960s grew in America's estimation and avowal to be the great test of communist insurgency, or "wars of liberation." This view of the importance of Vietnam was vividly acknowledged by the presence by the beginning of 1965 of more than 23,000 American military advisors in that country and a stream of visits by high American officials, who would then return home to espouse new concepts as to how "we" could contain the threat there. Counterinsurgency was a new and fascinating phenomenon. With this attitude and hope the United States plunged into the Vietnam experiment with gusto and with little concern for the risks of over-involvement. And its enthusiastic embracing of the post-Diem regimes only served to tie the knot even tighter.

By contrast, the way the United States has "packaged" its position in Laos has been a classic case of low profile. Until recently the operation was an official secret. This secrecy was regrettable from an American constitutional point of view, and after a point should have ceased, but from the point of view of commitment it avoided the Vietnam type of entanglement.

Even when the United States government on March 6, 1970, decided to make a public acknowledgment of its activities in Laos, it did so for the purpose of portraying how little, not how much was being done there. The President said:

In recent days, however, there has been intense public speculation to the effect that the United States involvement in Laos has substantially increased in violation of the Geneva accords, that American ground forces are engaged in combat in Laos and that our air activity has had the effect of escalating the conflict.

Because these reports are grossly inaccurate, I have concluded that our national interest will be served by putting the subject into perspective through a precise description of our current activities in Laos.

Another potential snare is the commitment that could arise simply from the survival of a particular policy. Each year something is expended to support the war effort in Laos. This country has never been confident that it would be sufficient to stave off disaster. But suppose the United States continues to prop up the neutralist government for, say, fifteen more years, and then the communists appear on the verge of destroying that government. The situation as far as an American commitment is concerned would then be significantly different from what it is today. American leaders would say to themselves, and the American public and press might well remind them: "We have cumulatively spent much in tangible assets and intangible effort to keep Laos noncommunist. Are we now prepared to see all of that treasure and effort come to naught?" It is a commitment that could arise simply through the accumulation of a lot of relatively small costs.

This source of entanglement should not be overstated, however. There is nothing inevitable about the outcome of any of these commitment-building blocks, especially this one. The United States expended a great amount of effort to save Chiang Kai-shek from the Japanese. Nevertheless, it could watch, with disappointment but without greater involvement, when he shortly thereafter was driven out by the communists. It was likewise with the French in Indochina in 1954. After the United States provided military assistance to them totaling, by some reports, as much as eighty percent of their total effort there, it could accept their defeat without further direct assistance to them.

The American attempt to provide Laos with substantial assistance without overcommitment will not face the ultimate test, of course, unless the communists press on in an attempt to take over the entire country. Only then could it be known for certain whether the United States had ordered its affairs so that even a collapse of the noncommunist forces would not compel it to send combat troops into Laos.

This raises the highly puzzling question why the communists have apparently not attempted to take over the entire country. Recall, for instance, their surrounding the royal capital of Luang Prabang in 1969 without seizing it. There are a number of possible answers, all involving a good deal of speculation. Several rest upon the premise that to the North Vietnamese, just as to Americans, the war in South Vietnam is far more important than the war in Laos.

First, it may be that the communists have no specific policy as to a political settlement for Laos pending the outcome of the war in South Vietnam. Perhaps, either intentionally or not, they are carrying on a holding action in Laos as the United States is doing. They know that the course of fighting in Laos as it has been well into 1972 leaves their options open.

Second, they may once have feared that if they pressed on to the banks of the Mekong and seized Vientiane, they might remove a significant factor which for a long time had deterred American and South Vietnamese forces from invading the southern end of the Ho Chi Minh Trail in the Laotian panhandle. Keeping this route to South Vietnam open has always been more important to Hanoi than who governs in Vientiane.

A third reason why the communists have not marched to the Mekong may be their uncertainty about what the Americans and the Thais would do in that particular theater of the war. The communists may fear that such a marked shift in the military balance would lead to unforeseeable reprisals by American or Thai forces, including the possibility of a broad-scale invasion from Thailand into the Mekong Valley of Laos. Such a prospect would certainly concern North Vietnam's Soviet and Chinese mentors.

A fourth possibility is simply that the North Vietnamese in Laos lack the wherewithal to achieve a complete military victory there without overburdening resources needed elsewhere. Vang Pao's swift seizure of the Plaine des Jarres in September, 1969, revealed surprising weakness on the part of the communists at that time. Then their 1970–71 and 1971–72 offensives failed to accomplish their intended purpose of seizing Vang Pao's headquarters at Long Tieng.

Still a fifth possibility is a concern that, if the communists tried to seize Vientiane by conventional forces, they would look like aggressors or imperialists in the eyes of people whose support they want to keep. Such an attack would require a large North Vietnamese force. The Pathet Lao are too weak to do this by themselves. The Lao and the Vietnamese are ethnically distinct from each other and historically antipathetic toward each other. For a large North Vietnamese force to march into Vientiane would be ideologically and nationalistically incompatible with their announced policies.

Finally, it should be added that under the tripartite formula for governing Laos under the Geneva Accords, by which seats in the Laotian cabinet were distributed among the neutralists, the right-wing royalists, and the communists, the Pathet Lao could obtain effective control of the government without seizing Vientiane. This could be done by the Pathet Lao's obtaining through negotiation a greater share of those seats for themselves and for neutralist factions sympathetic to them than were accorded in 1962.

The American casualties in the war in Laos were still small by early 1972. The financial cost, however, was by then approaching the point which could no longer be considered insignificant in the light of the fairly limited American interests at stake in that war.

American interests in Laos are basically twofold. First, the United States wants to keep the communists away from the Thai border. Thailand, a SEATO ally, is considerably more important to this country than Laos. The Thais have been experiencing a communist insurgency in their northern and northeastern provinces. If communist forces were present in Laos all along the border with Thailand, the North Vietnamese and Chinese could greatly increase their aid to this insurgency, and even an invasion by infiltration or otherwise would not be out of the question. Such prospects would compound the defense problems for the Thais, and hence concern for the United States.

As one American policymaker has put it, if through "the nickels and dimes" effort we are making in Laos, we can put off the hard questions we would have to face in Thailand, the effort is well worth making. The only problem is that this effort is about at a level, as of this writing, where it can no longer be counted in nickels and dimes, although perhaps it may still be worthwhile.

The second American interest in the war in northern Laos rests on the fact that the continuation of a government in Vientiane that acquiesces in what the United States is doing against the communist traffic on the Ho Chi Minh Trail makes such efforts a bit easier. But this second interest must be kept in perspective. There is really very little Souvanna can do about events going on in that part of his country. One would doubt seriously that the United States would, or should, stop its interdiction efforts against the Trail even if a government opposed to such operations came to power in Vientiane. It is true, however, that the collapse of the Laotian forces in the panhandle would give the communists a little more elbow room for moving their forces and supplies through that corridor into South Vietnam and Cambodia.

In deciding upon American policy toward Laos, one should consider along with these two interests two other features of the war: the plight of the Laotian people and the relatively static nature of the battle line over the years. The Laotians have suffered greatly from this war, and most of them have very little to gain whichever side may prevail. The communists are politically authoritarian, oppressive, and sometimes brutal, although they are also usually honest, inspired, and socially egalitarian. The officials of the neutralist government are often lackadaisical, corrupt, and aristocratic in manner, although this is not always so. Furthermore, there is very little sense of national identity among the Laotians. They are much more village- and region-oriented. It is only a slight overstatement to say that in political development they stand today where the European states stood six hundred years ago. The other relevant feature is the course of the war since 1964. Throughout this period there has existed a serpentine battle line moving back and forth within fairly narrow limits down the center of the country.

In view of American interests, particularly the desire to keep the communists off the Mekong, the United States should welcome and encourage any settlement, de facto or otherwise, that recognizes the existing battle line as the peacetime demarcation line between communist and noncommunist forces in Laos. The front is a more definite concept in the Laotian war than in the rest of Indochina. Almost any peace is better for the Laotians than the existing conflict. Furthermore, the steadfastness of the present government in Vientiane, in the Byzantine circumstances of the Far East today, can never be assured. The ominous presence of thousands of Chinese troops in Laos today is another important impetus for peace. A cease-fire along any recent battle line would, therefore, probably maximize the chances that a noncommunist government will continue to function in the Mekong Valley.

Such a settlement could be made without regard to the war along the Ho Chi Minh Trail. The communists recently seemed inclined to make the same distinction. The war in southern Laos must await the resolution of the greater conflict of which it is a part. In this regard, President Nixon's calls in October, 1970, and January 25, 1972, for a cease-fire in place in all of Indochina are highly relevant. There is no need to await a solution to the wars in South Vietnam and Cambodia to suspend hostilities in the war in northern Laos.

In fact, President Nixon's proposal and American interests in Laos match rather closely with all but one part of the communist proposal of March, 1970, for settling the war in Laos. The communists proposed first a political settlement based upon the Geneva Accords of 1962. This country long claimed that to be its goal. Next the communists called for "free and democratic elections." Americans, of course, favor free and democratic elections, whatever that may mean in a country like Laos. Presumably the communists would control the electoral process in their area of the country and the noncommunists would control it in theirs.

The communists demanded the unification of the country based upon consultations among equals. This would seem to imply recognition of communist supremacy in the area they now hold and joining them at the conference table on that basis. This would not appear to jeopardize American interests. The communists also seek the evacuation of what they call "pro-American units" from areas they "illegally" hold. This probably means the removal of government forces behind the lines they held at the time of the Geneva Accords. There would no doubt be considerable dispute as to where that line actually was, but such matters could be relatively easily negotiated. Small deviations should be of no consequence to the United States.

Finally, as noted, the communists called for withdrawal of United States equipment, advisors, and bombing. A cessation of the bombing is, of course, part of President Nixon's proposal for a cease-fire in place. It is true that the original communist proposal called upon the United States to "stop completely the bombing of Lao territory without proposing any conditions," which would appear to apply to the Ho Chi Minh Trail as well as to northern Laos and hence would be unacceptable to this country without a resolution of the war in South Vietnam itself. However, the communists surely do not expect agreement to that any more than they expect to stop sending troops down the Trail under another provision of their proposal for Laos that would preclude that country "from allowing foreign countries . . . to introduce troops and military personnel into its territory." The communists seem more amenable to separate a settlement of the war in northern Laos from the situation along the Ho Chi Minh Trail, which is really more a part of the war in South Vietnam.

The negotiations could also lead to the withdrawal of American advisors so long as the country is at peace. All future American training could be performed outside Laos. President Nixon offered to negotiate a timetable for the withdrawal of all American forces from South Vietnam; the United States would surely be willing to do the same for its much smaller military presence in Laos.

The one point demanded by the communists that would seem

unacceptable is the insistence on an end to the American equipping of the noncommunist forces. Such a step would place those forces at the tender mercies of the communists and allow the communists to march unopposed to the Mekong. Regardless of the political settlement, through a reapportionment of the seats in the Laotian cabinet or otherwise, the noncommunist forces should continue to exist as effective fighting units.

But after eight years of fighting and more than six years of significant American involvement, the fighting is still about where it was when it began.

Although the Symington Subcommittee's hearings on Laos were held in October, 1969, the State Department was reluctant to approve the release of a reasonably complete transcript of those hearings until the pressure of public concern became so great five months later as to make an official declaration on Laos unavoidable. The reasons given by the State Department for so long refusing to draw public attention to American activities in Laos provide a revealing insight into the processes of foreign policy.

First, the State Department said the American government had agreed with Souvanna Phouma to keep such activities secret.

Second, they claimed that disclosure of a large American program in support of Souvanna Phouma would jeopardize his image as a neutral and thus hamper American efforts to reestablish the Geneva Accords under which his neutrality was guaranteed.

Third, they contended that if this country were to admit its violations of the Geneva Accords, the other side, never having admitted its own violations, would have a propaganda field day.

Fourth, such an official American acknowledgment, the State Department said, might require the Soviet Union to take more positive action in support of the adversaries of the United States in Laos than it had then done. This concern was based upon the proposition that the Soviet Union could ignore and generally had ignored unofficial press reports of American violations of the Geneva Accords, but could not do so when the admission was made by American officials.

Indeed, a high Soviet official had suggested as much to one of our diplomats.

The fifth reason for nondisclosure was the belief that so long as the operation remained clandestine, it would ·be relatively easy for the United States to wash its hands of the situation should its position in Laos ever become untenable.

There was a sixth reason present, although unexpressed, which stemmed from the inherent nature of operations conducted in the absence of outside review. This was a tendency, neither malicious nor particularly conscious but nevertheless real, to facilitate one's own mode of operation and to accommodate those people within one's line of vision. Thus it was tempting and convenient to agree with Souvanna Phouma when he asked that the operation be kept secret. He was the man with whom the American Ambassador would be dealing thereafter. Likewise it was easy to give undue weight to the comment of the Soviet official, a clearly visible member of the diplomatic community. The larger interests of coordination with the Congress and disclosure to the American people were vague and abstract; they had no advocate at the table or lobbyist in the anteroom.

The State Department did not seem to appreciate the full significance of the following factors which seemed to the subcommittee to outweigh those concerns.

—The American people were entitled to know the dimensions of so large an operation as that which the American participation in the Laotian war had become.
—The communists were fully aware of the extent of American involvement and could already make out of it whatever propaganda or political use they wanted.
—Souvanna Phouma himself had already publicly referred to a number of the more important aspects of the American involvement, such as the bombing raids.
—Failure to be forthcoming with information about Laos, in light of increasing press interest in the subject, would generate a

credibility gap for the Administration more costly than any hypothetical disadvantage that disclosure would create.

—The violations of the Geneva Accords on the part of the United
States were outweighed by the far greater violations on the other
side, a fact well known to all participants and easily appreciated
by any disinterested observer.

—The possible risk of overcommitment through publicity could be
minimized by a careful and moderate presentation of the actual
facts.

After months of bickering, the Symington Subcommittee's view
prevailed. For reasons similar to those advanced by the subcommittee, the President on March 6, 1970, disclosed a large measure of
what the United States was doing in Laos. It was not, however,
until August, 1971, that the Administration was willing to acknowledge the role of the CIA and the Thais in northern Laos.

Following release of the record of the subcommittee, none of the
parade of horrors which the State Department had imagined did in
fact occur. To the contrary, a step toward peace followed the President's disclosure, for which it may, in part, have been responsible.
By coincidence, on the same day that the President disclosed the
American role in Laos, the Pathet Lao announced their five-point
peace proposal. In contrast to Souvanna Phouma's replies to earlier
communist peace proposals, he responded more favorably to this
one. It is not unreasonable to assume that, as a result of the President's announcement, including his reference to sending no American combat troops to Laos, the Laotian Prime Minister was now less
certain of full American support and therefore more receptive to a
negotiated settlement.

Through release of the hearings on Laos, the basic principle of
maintaining a well-informed public with respect to major issues of
foreign policy was achieved without detriment to that policy.

VI

The Philippines

The American military role in the Philippines began with the Spanish-American War, passed through the colonial period, was tested by World War II, and continued in the postwar period in the form of an alliance with the newly independent and sovereign Republic of the Philippines. In 1947, shortly after Philippine independence, the United States entered into two agreements with the Philippines, a Military Bases Agreement, which gave the United States the right to occupy bases in the Philippines for ninety-nine years, and a Military Assistance Agreement to provide the Philippines with military equipment and training, which some Filipinos and Americans look upon as rent for the use of those bases. Then in 1951 the two countries entered into a Mutual Defense Treaty, and in 1954 they both joined the multilateral Southeast Asia Collective Defense Treaty (SEATO).

From time to time the Filipinos have sought to have their treaty relationship with the United States reformulated along the lines of the North Atlantic Treaty, believing that the terms of the NATO treaty call for more automatic response by its members in the event of an attack. One such attempt occurred in 1954. In order to induce the Philippines to sign the SEATO Treaty, Secretary of State Dulles, on the day before the signing, issued a declaration, at the request of the Philippines, that stated:

Under our Mutual Defense Treaty and related actions, there have resulted air and naval dispositions of the United States in the Philippines, such that an armed attack on the Philippines could not but be also an attack upon the military forces of the United States. As between our nations, it is no legal fiction to say that an attack on one is an attack on both. It is a reality that an attack on the Philippines is an attack on the United States.

This declaration was reconfirmed in a joint communiqué issued by President Eisenhower and President Garcia in 1958, which announced:

President Eisenhower made clear that, in accordance with these existing alliances and the deployments and dispositions thereunder, any armed attack against the Philippines would involve an attack against United States forces stationed there and against the United States and would be instantly repelled.

And in 1959 these declarations were embodied in a formal memorandum of agreement between the two countries signed by Ambassador Bohlen and Philippine Foreign Secretary Serrano.

These pronouncements by the Eisenhower administration were confirmed again in 1964 in a communiqué issued by President Johnson and President Macapagal in words virtually identical with those used in 1958, with one curious exception. The 1958 communiqué stated that an attack against the Philippines "would involve" an attack against United States forces, whereas the 1964 communiqué stated that such an attack "would be regarded as" an attack against such forces.

These declarations were reconfirmed again in 1966 in two declarations, one signed by President Johnson and President Marcos, and the other signed by Secretary Rusk and Philippine Foreign Secretary Ramos. There is no doubt that the government of the Philippines considers these statements of successive American administrations as adding a measure of security to that contained in the two basic treaties.

These statements by high officials have increased the degree of the American commitment to the Philippines beyond that which is stated in the bilateral treaty and SEATO. In 1954 it may have been little more than a statement of fact, based upon the disposition of U.S. forces and the source of danger at that time, to say that an attack upon the Philippines would necessarily involve the United States. Now, however, American forces are concentrated in a portion of the island of Luzon, and the Philippines could be attacked in any of its hundreds of other islands without there being an attack upon these forces. The changes from 1954 to 1964 in the formulation of the declaration show how a commitment such as this evolves from a factual statement to a legalistic assertion.

Beyond United States treaty commitments to the Philippines, as reinforced by the subsequent executive declarations, there is also probably an implicit commitment to defend the Philippines based upon the seventy-two years of close association between the two countries, including both the colonial period and the mutual sacrifices of World War II. This is the sort of "commitment" that rests on the line that borders current policy, as explained in the first chapter of this book.

In view of the advantages that the Philippines have enjoyed as a result of these written and historical commitments, Filipinos have become concerned from time to time during the course of the war in Vietnam that the United States might precipitately leave the Far East, thereby endangering the long-term security of the Philippines. Thus, President Nixon's new doctrine for Asia, first announced on Guam on July 26, 1969, received a rather mixed response in the Philippines. President Marcos and Foreign Secretary Romulo and other nationalist leaders declared confidently that the doctrine was consistent with their efforts toward lessening Philippine dependence on the United States. Other Filipinos, however, voiced fear that the doctrine might lead both to lessened security for the Filipinos and to the loss of the economic benefits which the Filipinos have derived over the years from the United States' military presence in the area. Filipinos were further unsettled when they heard President Nixon declare in Manila the day following his pronouncement on Guam: "I hope that we can initiate a new era in Philippine-American relations, not returning to the old special relationship."

In keeping with this uncertain sentiment as to the American role in the Far East, the Filipinos see both advantages and disadvantages in having American bases in their country. Some Filipinos feel, in line with the declarations of American leaders referred to above, that the bases assure United States involvement in the defense of the Philippines. They also recognize that the bases provide substantial economic benefits to the country. Some think, however, that the bases may well attract attack on the Philippines that would not otherwise occur. This concern has grown with the development of the communist Chinese nuclear capability.

Reflecting the growing sense of nationalism in the Philippines by 1959, the above-mentioned agreement between Ambassador Bohlen and Philippine Foreign Secretary Serrano required that "prior consultations" be held before direct use of the bases for military operations, such as the launching of bombing missions, except for operations conducted under one of the two treaties. The United States has never entered into any such consultations and does not consider this provision as giving the Filipinos a veto over American use of the bases, but even in the absence of such a provision, this country would be very reluctant to do anything from the territory of any country which its government specifically disapproved.

The United States has three major bases in the Philippines: Subic Bay Naval Station with its adjacent Naval Air Station at Cubi Point; Clark Air Base; and San Miguel Naval Communications Station. All these installations are on the island of Luzon. The operating costs for these facilities and the other American facilities in the Philippines in the fiscal year 1970 were $280 million, and the foreign exchange expenditures were $201 million. In 1971 the United States had about 18,000 military personnel in the Philippines and about the same number of dependents, having reduced its military presence by about 6,000 men in 1970, in keeping with the phase-down in Vietnam.

During the year 1968, at the height of United States ground action in the Vietnam war, there were 1,712 visits by United States naval ships to Subic Bay and 895 by merchant ships. On an average day that year 10,000 naval personnel stationed aboard ships of the Seventh Fleet were at Subic. By comparison, in 1965 there were 1,372 ship visits to Subic Bay.

Clark Air Base, which occupies 130,000 acres, is the headquarters for the 13th Air Force and serves as the base for a unit of F-4 fighter-bombers, four squadrons of C-130 tactical airlift aircraft, and two squadrons of F-102 air defense interceptors. The base serves as the air defense control center for the Philippines and also supports the First Mobile Communications unit and its 1,350 personnel and the Fifth Tactical Control Group and its 1,250 personnel. The first of these two units provides a highly mobile, rapidly deployable communications capability and the latter a similarly available aid to navigation and landing.

Besides the F-102 unit and the air control center at Clark, as part of its air defense responsibility in the Philippines, the United States operates a radar site, Wallace Air Station, at Poro Point. The Filipinos themselves fly F-5s and older air defense aircraft and operate three radar sites of their own as their contribution to air defense.

San Miguel is a large defense communications relay station and naval communications facility in support of the Seventh Fleet.

For some time, the United States had two other major facilities in the Philippines, Sangley Air Station and Mactan Air Base.

Sangley Air Station supported antisubmarine and ocean surveillance P-3 aircraft on a rotational basis. Since several of these airplanes were always detached to other bases in Southeast Asia, such as U Tapao in Thailand, and Cam Ranh Bay in South Vietnam, there were usually no more than twelve such aircraft at Sangley at any one time. Out of Sangley's 2,800 personnel (with 1,850 dependents), 748 naval personnel were directly assigned to these P-3 squadrons. This base was turned over to the Filipinos in September, 1971.

One result of the closing of Sangley was that the duties of the rear admiral stationed there as commander of United States Naval Forces in the Philippines were merged with those of the commander of the Naval Base at Subic Bay, thus removing a flag officer and the large expense attendant upon such a post.

The United States also operated another active base, Mactan Air Base, near the southern city of Cebu. This base was constructed in 1958 with American funds as a civil airport, a Philippine Air Force base, and a Strategic Air Command (SAC) recovery base. In 1965, because of overcrowded conditions at Clark, the United States obtained Philippine permission to station two C-130 airlift squadrons at Mactan. Before this, there had been no American personnel at Mactan; nevertheless, the base became operational as an American facility within one month after such permission was granted. Here is a demonstration of the feasibility of maintaining standby bases in some cases in lieu of much more expensive active bases.

The airlift squadrons at Mactan operated from there between 1965 and 1968, when they were redeployed to Clark. Mactan was deactivated as an American base in January, 1970.

All the major American military facilities in the Philippines support American military operations in the Vietnam theater. Among other functions, Subic Bay provides logistical support for the carrier task force on Yankee Station. San Miguel serves as a communications link between Vietnam and the United States. Clark Air Base provides rear echelon support for airlift and fighter squadrons in Vietnam. So, too, did Mactan, until its airlift squadrons were reassigned to Clark. The main function of Sangley's squadrons was the surveillance of the coastal waters of Southeast Asia.

These bases in the Philippines, however, have not been used for direct Vietnam combat operations, such as the launching of B-52s, even though the Bohlen-Serrano agreement, referred to above, permits the United States to use the bases without "prior consultations" for operations conducted in accordance with either the bilateral defense treaty or SEATO. The United States has chosen not to base B-52 bombers in the Philippines, although the cost of each B-52 sortie from Guam has been figured at $19,957 and an equivalent sortie from Clark or Mactan would have cost only $5,504 (in each case exclusive of munitions). To improve Clark Air Base so as to handle B-52s, according to some testimony provided to the Symington Subcommittee, would have cost about $20 million. To prepare Kadena Air Base on Okinawa for B-52s cost $16 million. To construct an entirely new base at U Tapao, Thailand, for B-52 operations cost $105 million. Even this last relatively large amount was amortized through operational savings in only eighteen months.

There is a substantial body of sentiment in the Philippines quite favorable to the United States. This is particularly prevalent in rural areas. Although there is evidence of an increase in anti-American agitation in the form of mass demonstrations and otherwise, a poll of 5,240 people taken by the Manila *Evening News* in 1968 showed that only seven percent were against retaining the bases and sixty-four percent were in favor.

There is little external threat, either conventional or nuclear, to the Philippines, because of the preponderance of American military strength in the region and the nuclear commitment reflected in our Mutual Defense treaties. As a result, the Philippine Republic is able to enjoy a very low defense budget, only about one and one-half percent of its GNP.

Among the less appealing features of the Philippines is the fact that the country, and both of its leading political parties, are run by an elite composed of 200 or so families, although a class of young technocrats is slowly developing. Because of the intransigence of the ruling class, progress in areas of social change, such as land reform, comes very slowly. Also, the Philippine Republic is generally suffering economically. Unemployment and underemployment at the end of 1969 stood at about twenty-five percent of the labor force. The per capita income that year was only $219. The United States military is the second largest employer in the Philippines.

Graft and corruption are widespread. The homicide rate is one of the highest in the world, running about thirty-five for every 100,000 people. In the categories of theft and robbery, however, the Philippine rate is less than that in the United States.

An area with a long history of social repression and economic difficulites is the Central Luzon Plain, where Clark Air Base is located and where 12,000 Huks carried on a large-scale insurgency during the 1950s. This region is an area of tenant farmers with good reason to be dissatisfied with their economic and social position, a situation well suited for supporting insurgent elements.

Most of the Huk forces today, however, are just bandits. The Huks' total strength is now about 400 regular armed men, about 500 armed support personnel, 3,000 to 4,000 unarmed supporting elements, and a mass base of perhaps 30,000 to 35,000 people, mostly in Central Luzon. The Huks' actual ties with communist China and the Soviet Union have so far been insignificant.

The Philippine counterinsurgency program is a combination of military, political, social, and economic measures. The nonmilitary measures have met with considerable difficulty because of inadequate funding, shortage of qualified or motivated personnel, and landlord opposition. The military measures have been more successful. However, they have not yet been able to stop the growth of the dissident forces in the area.

The small number of encounters and casualties reflects the rather limited nature of the Huk threat at present. From January, 1968, through August, 1969, there were eighteen armed encounters, resulting in eighteen soldiers killed and forty-six Huks killed, sixty-eight captured, and four surrendering.

In the past the American military assistance program in the

Philippines has not focused primarily on counterinsurgency measures. Nevertheless, the general military equipment, supplies, and training that the United States provides have been of some assistance in this program. In addition, from time to time, the American bases have provided Philippine forces engaged in counterinsurgency with items such as M-16 rifles, ammunition, helmets, aerial photography, C-rations and, on one occasion, a helicopter and its crew. Also, through the recurring unconventional warfare exercise known as Caribou Trail, the United States has helped to train Filipino special forces in counterinsurgency tactics. American military personnel on the bases, in the military assistance program and in such exercises, are not authorized to participate in actual military operations against the insurgents.

Whether the Philippines' economic difficulties and lack of social reform will bring incipient insurgency to revolutionary proportions is a subject on which American commentators differ. It is the Embassy's assessment that at this time there is little prospect of any coup or revolution.

The general climate of social unrest and the Huk movement in particular have had their effect upon the American bases, particularly Clark Air Base. The Huks control a large portion of the business interests in Angeles City, which adjoins Clark Air Base. This has allowed the insurgents to derive considerable profit from the economic activity generated by Clark, although it would not be correct to say that the Huks are dependent on the base for their economic survival. It has been estimated that the Huks obtain about $1 million a year from Clark.

In 1968 the amout of reported losses through theft and pilferage on the United States bases was $1.3 million, and in 1969 it was estimated to be $900,000. High American officials, including the base commander at Clark, could not give the Symington Subcommittee any estimate of the total amount so lost but never reported.*

---

* This was rather surprising, since any properly audited enterprise knows the periodic magnitude of its inventory shrinkage.

With respect to acts of violence and robbery, between August 1, 1968, and August 1, 1969, there was an average of one major and one minor incident involving a Filipino and an American every day. This situation was particularly serious at Clark Air Base as the following statistics reveal:

Major Incidents
August, 1968–August, 1969

Clark	271
Subic Bay	73
Sangley	11
San Miguel	3
Mactan	2
John Hay, Wallace, O'Donald	0
Total	360

The United States military assistance program to the Philippines in the fiscal year 1969 totaled $19 million plus $973,000 in excess equipment. As mentioned above, many Filipinos look upon such military assistance as rental for the bases.

Even though the military assistance program has allowed the Philippines to earmark one battalion combat team for fulfillment of its SEATO commitment, the Philippines did not choose to send that unit to Vietnam. Instead the Philippine government agreed to send a 2,200-man, noncombatant, civic-action-oriented military unit to Vietnam in the fall of 1966. This unit, known as the Philippines Civic Action Group, Vietnam, or PHILCAGV, performed road construction, bridge-building, forest-clearing, medical care, and other civic action functions there. It represented about three percent of the total armed forces of the Philippines, as compared with the Australian contribution of nine percent, the Thai contribution of seven and one-half percent, and the Korean contribution of seven percent of their respective armed forces, all of which included combat units. PHILCAGV casualties through September, 1969, were eight killed in action and seventeen wounded in action.

The United States agreed to provide the following to the Philippines, in part to make it feasible for the Philippine government to send the unit to Vietnam and in part to induce it to do so: the equipment for PHILCAGV; overseas allowances ·for its members; two swift craft; the equipment for three new engineer construction battalions; and M-14 rifles and M-60 machine guns for one Philippine combat team. President Marcos was very anxious not to have PHILCAGV characterized as a mercenary unit. Therefore, the American payment of overseas allowances was kept secret.

In September, 1966, when President Marcos met with President Johnson in Washington, there was a further public commitment by the United States to provide the equipment for two additional engineer construction battalions, and certain other assistance. Coming, as it did, just prior to the dispatch of PHILCAGV to Vietnam would tend to suggest that these further commitments were also related to the sending of that unit to Vietnam. However, the chief State Department witness before the Subcommittee on Commitments Abroad denied that these were part of the quid pro quo for PHILCAGV, and the General Accounting Office could find no clear evidence to the contrary.

The total cost to the United States to support PHILCAGV was $41 million. Most of this was expended to purchase, operate, and maintain PHILCAGV's heavy equipment, such as its bulldozers and trucks. The quid pro quo mentioned above, to induce the Philippines to send the unit to Vietnam, totaled $3.8 million. Per diem and overseas allowances cost the United States government $3.9 million.

In the Korean war, by comparison, the Philippines sent a combat force of about 1,500 men. The records are not clear whether the United States paid overseas allowances to those troops or not; but at that time the United States was providing direct assistance to the Philippines in the form of cash payments to finance the Philippine governmental budget.

In the fall of 1966, the time of PHILCAGV's dispatch to Vietnam and the Manila Conference on Vietnam, a poll in the Philippines showed seventy-one percent supporting PHILCAGV. After 1966, however, President Marcos was unable to obtain any further appropriation from the Philippine Congress for continuing PHILCAGV. The unit was accordingly reduced in the summer of 1968 to 1,500 men and funded thereafter from the general Philippine defense budget.

In June, 1969, the Philippine Congress called for the phased withdrawal of PHILCAGV. Many Filipinos believed that PHILCAGV was more needed for civic action projects in the Philippines and was inconsequential in Vietnam next to the 500,000 American troops there. Others believed that the United States was trying to pressure or purchase Philippine support for the war in Vietnam through PHILCAGV.

Shortly after the Symington Subcommittee released the information it had obtained on PHILCAGV and its financing, President Marcos withdrew the unit from Vietnam. Although the Marcos government objected to some sharp statements made by some of the members of the subcommittee with respect to PHILCAGV, it was apparent that the subcommittee's action provided a convenient excuse for President Marcos to remove an operation that had become politically awkward for him.

The United States has provided enormous benefits to the Philippine Republic, protecting it from external attack, providing a large part of its air defense, and furnishing military assistance for its internal security. This has meant, among other things, that the Philippines has been able to enjoy an extremely small defense budget. The American bases contribute greatly to the economy of the islands. The United States' fighting in Vietnam has decreased the prospects for a full-scale communist insurgency or nationwide bloodletting in the Philippines (once not so remote a possibility when one recalls Indonesia's experience). Furthermore, the United States has provided the Philippines with a tariff preference, an assured portion of the American sugar market, and support for the Philippine peso in the world market.

The Filipinos, in return, have provided the United States with bases in their country, but for a charge in the form of military assistance. They have also provided the United States a tariff preference, but not one as favorable as that which the United States provides them.

The Philippine contribution to the war in Vietnam reflects this unequal relationship. The United States did not seek the Filipinos' permission to use its bases in their country for combat operations in the war because of American awareness that the Philippine government would have been extremely reluctant to grant such approval. And the actual force which the Filipinos sent to Vietnam was an extremely small contribution. The South Koreans sent 50,000 combat troops to Vietnam. The Thais sent 12,000 and granted the United States the use of air bases for combat operations. The Australians sent 8,000 combat troops while maintaining 3,000 others in Malaysia. The nationalist Chinese were anxious to send troops, but this country declined to accept them lest the contribution serve as a precedent for communist Chinese intervention. The Cambodians entered the war against the North Vietnamese and Viet Cong. The Laotians continued their own war against the communists and allowed the United States freely to bomb the Ho Chi Minh Trail in their country. But the Filipinos could only send a 2,200-man noncombatant unit (shortly reduced to 1,500 men), this in spite of the fact that American military assistance had made it possible for the Philippines to earmark one battalion combat team for SEATO operations.

Failing to base B-52s in the Philippines for their bombing missions in Southeast Asia, which required such flights to be staged from more distant places in the Pacific, resulted in a financial loss to the United States of more than $400 million. Not only is the flying time much shorter from the Philippines to Vietnam, but also the requirement for aerial refueling would have been eliminated. The failure to use Clark for B-52s can be justified on the ground that that base was fully congested with other war-related traffic, but no such contention can be maintained with respect to Mactan Air Base. In 1969 Mactan was averaging about 160 operational flights a month as compared with about 20,000 a month at Clark. Indeed, Mactan had been built in the late 1950s as a SAC recovery base for the landing of heavy bombers. It was, thus, an essentially unused base, physically available, with some reasonable construction costs, for taking B-52 bombers. Furthermore, like the other B-52 bases, U Tapao (Thailand), Anderson (Guam), and Kadena (Okinawa), it had ready access to the sea for the delivery of fuel and munitions.

When one considers the financial advantages that the United States could have achieved by placing its B-52s in the Philippines instead of elsewhere in the Pacific for Southeast Asian operations, it is difficult to avoid the conclusion that this otherwise obvious step was never taken because American political relations with the Philippines over Vietnam would not have permitted it.

Units of the Sixth Fleet in the Mediterranean Sea, 1970. *Official U.S. Navy photograph*

U.S. Naval Station, Rota, Spain, 1970. *Official U.S. Navy photograph*

A U.S. Army sergeant advisor watches as a Laotian sergeant describes a jungle patrol training exercise, 1962. *U.S. Army photograph*

A C-130 unloads a Royal British military vehicle, Norway, 1970. *U.S. Army photograph*

Pontoon bridge on the Han River, Korea, 1969. *U.S. Army photograph*

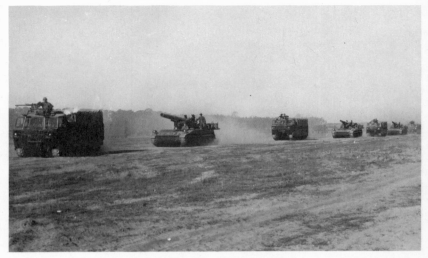

Men and equipment near Mannheim, Germany, 1971. *U.S. Army photograph*

U.S. Naval Station, Subic Bay, Republic of the Philippines, 1968. *Official U.S. Navy photograph*

U.S. and Spanish Air Force alert pilots break for their aircraft on the sound of the alert klaxon, Spain. *U.S. Air Force photograph*

Guided missile destroyer USS *Parsons,* attack aircraft carrier USS *Bon Homme Richard,* and amphibious task force ships en route from the Gulf of Tonkin to Yokosuka, Japan, 1970. *Official U.S. Navy photograph*

Destroyer tender USS *Cascade,* store ship, and escort ships in the harbor at Naples, Italy, 1971. *Official U.S. Navy photograph*

Aerial view of Bachelor Officers' Quarters, Chitose III, 12th U.S. ASA Field Station, Japan, 1967. *U.S. Army photograph*

VII

South Korea

American forces are in South Korea as a part of the United Nations Command sent there pursuant to the Security Council resolutions of June 27 and July 7, 1950. At the end of the Korean war, on July 27, 1953, the sixteen troop-contributing countries, including the United States, announced that, if there were another attack on South Korea, they would again unite promptly to resist it and warned that such hostilities probably could not be confined within the frontiers of Korea, a thinly veiled reference to communist China. Thus, this country waged a major war and continued to make commitments to Korea without a treaty or a declaration of war. Not until November 17, 1954, did the United States have a bilateral defense treaty with South Korea.

This treaty commitment has often been reconfirmed by presidential communiqué. In each year from 1965 through 1968, President Johnson confirmed in almost identical language "the readiness and determination of the United States to render prompt and effective assistance to defeat an armed attack against the Republic of Korea, in accordance with the Mutual Defense Treaty of 1954." Vice President Humphrey on February 23, 1966, could say: "As long as there is one American soldier on the line of the border, the demarcation line, the whole and entire power of the United States of America is committed to the security and defense of Korea."

In connection with South Korea's agreement to dispatch a second division to Vietnam, the American Ambassador formally reiterated several earlier statements of high American officials concerning the United States' commitment to the defense of Korea, along the lines of the foregoing communiqués.

A further reaffirmation of the commitment, though in somewhat different terms, was contained in a joint communiqué issued by President Nixon and President Park on August 22, 1969: ". . . the two Presidents reaffirmed the determination of their Governments to meet armed attack against the Republic of Korea in accordance with the Mutual Defense Treaty between the Republic of Korea and the United States."

This language in the Nixon communiqué contrasts sharply with that used in the joint communiqués issued during the Johnson administration. The former Administration time and again promised to render "prompt and effective assistance to defeat an armed attack." The more conservative language of the present Administration, "to meet armed attack . . . in accordance with the Mutual Defense Treaty," reflects the changing pattern of the United States' relationship with Far Eastern countries as a result of its experience in Vietnam. The Johnson administration, in effect, placed its own interpretation on the treaty, which the Nixon administration has wisely avoided doing. Not only did the earlier communiqués purport to commit the United States to assure the defeat of an attack but they also acknowledged that the American response would be as automatic as possible.

Besides the treaty and declarations of support, the United States has commitments to South Korea from the presence of its troops there and from the mutual sacrifices of the two countries in both the Korean war and the Vietnam war.

With respect to the continuation of American forces in Korea at existing levels, General Hamilton H. Howze, the commander of U.S. and U.N. forces in Korea, wrote to the South Korean Defense Minister on January 11, 1965: "I cannot provide you a formal guarantee for continued maintenance of the U.S. Forces in Korea at current level." With the dispatch of Korean troops to Vietnam, however, high U.S. officials reiterated that it was the American policy to maintain powerful forces in Korea and to provide sufficient support for Korean forces.

Until 1971, two divisions of the United States Army, totaling 24,000 men, stood guard along eighteen miles of the western sector of the 151-mile long demarcation line and demilitarized zone, or DMZ, between North and South Korea. The United States 2nd Division, which has been withdrawn, was deployed on the line and the 7th Division stood behind it in reserve. American forces have been in this sector of the line ever since the Korean war and were at the two-division level from 1955 to 1971. That American forces hold these positions is in part historical coincidence and in part because of the fact that this sector guards the route to Seoul. In recent years, about forty percent of the enlisted personnel in the two divisions have been draftees.

In mid-1970 the United States had about 54,000 military personnel and 3,000 dependents in South Korea. Then, on August 26, 1970, plans were announced to withdraw 20,000 men, including the 2nd Division, by June 30, 1971. This announcement was rather misleading, however. It was based upon a 63,000-man authorized strength in Korea, not the actual strength of 54,000. Thus, the actual withdrawal in terms which the American public could understand was closer to 11,000 men. United States operating costs in Korea in the fiscal year 1970 were $680 million and foreign exchange expenditures $360 million.

Besides the infantry forces on the DMZ, the U.S. Army has 4,500 personnel assigned to NIKE Hercules and HAWK air defense units. The South Koreans themselves maintain other NIKE Hercules and HAWK battalions, the first of which were given them in 1964. Another American unit is the Fourth U.S. Missile Command, stationed, ever since 1958, approximately twenty-five miles from the DMZ at Camp Page in the eastern sector of South Korea. Its mission is to support the First ROK Army with long-range artillery and missile support.

To back up the combat forces, major American support activities exist at points throughout Korea, from a port at Inchon/Ascon near Seoul back to Pusan. The American forces have their own communications network stretching the length of South Korea and a 255-mile petroleum pipeline from Pohang on the eastern coast to Osan and Seoul.

There is also a 678-man American military assistance advisory group with the Korean forces. And American military personnel operate the Voice of the United Nations Command, a broadcasting facility that transmits propaganda to North Korea and provides local broadcasts in the Seoul area. Since VUNC annually costs about $350,000, the Embassy has recommended its termination.

With over 100 aircraft and about 7,000 personnel in Korea, the United States Air Force has units at six air bases: Osan, Kunsan, Kwang-ju, Taegu, Suwon, and Kimpo. The Air Force also has seven bombing ranges in Korea. Unlike the North Koreans, who generally keep their Air Force well back of the DMZ, the United States has a frequently used bombing range only thirteen miles from the DMZ.

In March, 1969, the United States and South Korea conducted a large-scale airlift exercise, Focus Retina, involving 2,500 American troops based in the United States, to demonstrate the rapid reaction capability of American forces based in the United States. The South Korean attitude toward the exercise was, on the one hand, one of satisfaction in seeing visible evidence of American ability to deploy rapidly to defend Korea and, on the other hand, one of concern that the exercise might presage a reduction in American forces stationed in Korea.

Although American officials denied at the time and denied to the

Symington Subcommittee that the purpose of the exercise was to set the stage for a reduction in American forces stationed in Korea, such a reduction did in fact follow soon after.

The South Korean people, including their student population, have always been receptive to the reassuring American military presence in South Korea. To induce the United States to increase its forces in their country, the Koreans have made a standing offer of Cheju island, at the southern end of the peninsula, for use as an American military base, if needed as an alternative to Okinawa or otherwise. Also, one reason the Koreans sent 50,000 troops to South Vietnam was to induce the United States to continue the presence of American forces at existing levels in South Korea.

The announcement in August, 1970, of the intention to reduce American strength in Korea caused considerable discontent. To offset this somewhat, the United States promised to make extraordinary efforts to modernize the South Korean forces and also to relocate a wing of F-4 aircraft from Japan to Korea. This wing will initially be composed of two squadrons from Misawa Air Base.

Certain incidents led the United States to increase rapidly its military power in and around Korea. On January 21, 1968, the North Koreans attempted to infiltrate thirty-one agents into South Korea to assassinate President Park. The last one of these raiders was captured only a few yards from the presidential palace. Two days later North Korea seized the American intelligence-gathering ship *Pueblo* in the Sea of Japan and held its crew for eleven months. On April 15, 1969, the North Koreans shot down an American EC-121 reconnaissance aircraft over international waters and in August, 1970, shot down an American observation helicopter sixteen miles inside North Korea. The American command maintains that the helicopter was on a routine training mission and made an error in navigation.

Before the *Pueblo* incident there were only eleven American combat aircraft in Korea, and most of the alert aircraft were configured only for nuclear war. Following that incident the number of American combat aircraft in Korea was quickly increased to more than 100. A $100 million military construction program was also undertaken to strengthen Air Force and Army facilities, including the provision of hardened aircraft shelters. To build up South Korean forces following the *Pueblo* incident, the United States agreed to a supplemental $100 million military assistance package, including a squadron of 18 F-4s, all of which were delivered.* The United States also agreed to the establishment of a United States-Korean operational planning staff and annual meetings of the two Defense Ministers.

Deliveries of basic military assistance items to Korea totaled $165 million in the fiscal year 1968. With the supplemental program mentioned above and other assistance in connection with South Korea's participation in the Vietnam war, the United States' expenditures for Korean defense reached more than $350 million that year, over twice the amount of military expenditures made by the Koreans themselves. Total American military assistance to Korea in 1970 ran about $189 million; Korea's own defense expenditures, about $270 million.

Following the shoot-down of the EC-121, the United States began to protect similar aircraft flying near Korea with fighter escorts and also rapidly assembled a carrier task force and sent it into the waters just south of Korea. It was composed of three carriers and supporting vessels, originally totaling twenty-nine ships, but soon reduced to eight.

* Certain differences, as of 1970, between the F-4 aircraft and the F-5, the more common aircraft provided to military assistance recipients, are as follows:

	F-4	F-5
Initial cost/single plane	$2 million	$900,000
Operating cost/squadron	$3 million	$1 million
Range (low alt.)	450 n. miles	250 n. miles

The F-4 also has a bombing capability and a capacity for penetrating North Korean air defenses which the F-5 lacks.

After both crises the South Koreans were anxious to take reprisals against the North and were concerned over the reluctance of this country to do so. It was made clear to the South Koreans, however, that this country would not support any aggressive military action on their part against North Korea undertaken without American consent.

South Korea has experienced two coups d'état, one in 1960 and another in 1961, the latter bringing its current President, General Park, to power. American forces were not involved in either incident. In the coup d'état of 1961, the Koreans temporarily removed their forces from the United Nations Command. Under an agreement entered into shortly thereafter between the Command and the South Korean government, Korean forces may be withdrawn at any time of urgent need upon the request of the South Korean Defense Minister. Thus, the operational command of these forces by an American general has proved of small consequence as far as barring independent action on their part is concerned. This experience undercuts one of the arguments of the Pentagon for keeping large numbers of American forces in South Korea. The military argued to the Symington Subcommittee that the United States needed to keep an American general in command of the South Korean forces so that they would not act on their own against our wishes, and the best way to maintain this chain of command was to have lots of American soldiers present to justify the role of an American as commander-in-chief. This was the pitch made to the subcommittee in its hearings in February; not once did the witnesses imply that within the following six months the withdrawal of one of the two American combat divisions would be announced.

South Korea has made impressive gains since the ravages of the Korean war. In spite of a dearth of natural resources, a million wartime casualties, almost a million refugees, and a tradition of xenophobia, South Korea has achieved considerable prosperity, an impressive growth rate, democratic institutions, and a position in international affairs.

The South Korean rate of growth has been about thirteen percent annually in recent years. Because of advantages in natural resources and existing heavy industry, North Korea's per capita income, $235, is still larger than South Korea's at $212. However, North Korea's rate of growth has been about four percent, and an excessive amount of its resources, twenty percent of GNP, is devoted to military expenditures.

South Korea has a much larger population and larger ground forces than North Korea. The South Korean population is 32,-000,000; the North Korean, 13,500,000. The ROK Army totals almost 600,000; the North Korean Army about 350,000. Both forces can be supplemented proportionately by active reserves.

The North Korean defense budget, however, exceeds that of the South, and North Korea has a larger air force. The North Korean defense budget is about $700 million; the South Korean about $288 million. The North Koreans have over 500 combat aircraft, MIG-15s, 17s, 19s and 21s. However, during the Korean war the MIG-15 suffered losses to the F-86 at the rate of ten to one. In up-to-date aircraft, including F-4s, F-5s, F-102s, and F-106s for the South Korean and American forces in Korea, and the MIG-19s and MIG-21s for the North Koreans, the numerical advantage is with the South.

Both the Soviet Union and communist China have defense treaties with North Korea, which state: "Should either of the contracting parties suffer armed attack by any state or coalition of states, and thus find itself in a state of war, the other contracting party shall immediately extend military and other assistance with all the means at its disposal."

The North Koreans have made numerous efforts to infiltrate agents into the South through the DMZ and by sea. The most dramatic instance was the attempted assassination of President Park on January 21, 1968. Another large-scale effort was made in October, 1968, when 120 North Korean infiltrators landed on the east coast of South Korea. To meet this force the South Koreans sent out 40,000 men. Even so, it took several months to round up all 120. In almost every case of infiltration, however, the agents have been detected and have been killed or captured; almost always the South Korean people have cooperated fully in resisting such infiltrators.

These North Korean tactics increased markedly in the years 1967–68, and tapered off thereafter. The reason for the increase was not clear. Possibly it was a result of a change in command in Pyonyang; possibly it was a result of the war in Vietnam; possibly it was to discourage investor confidence in South Korea, which was beginning to show substantial strength at that time. The reduction in effort thereafter was partly the result of tighter anti-infiltration techniques both along the DMZ and elsewhere in South Korea.

The preponderance of reported infiltration and skirmishes in the past has been in the American sector, perhaps because Americans present a special political and propaganda target. However, North Korean agents have not made any concerted efforts to attack United States military installations behind the lines, and the U.N. commander believes that such attacks in significant proportions are only a remote possibility. Another possible reason for the concentration of North Korean probes in the American sector is that it is the main route to Seoul. Another reason for these statistics may be that Americans are more conscientious in reporting incidents than are South Korean troops. American losses in 1967–68 as a result of skirmishes along the DMZ and infiltration by North Korean agents totaled twenty-eight men killed and 119 wounded. In 1969 the American losses fell to five killed and six wounded, and in 1970 there were no American casualties.

Besides resisting infiltration in the American sector of the DMZ, small numbers of American personnel have gone along as observers on ROK anti-infiltration operations. Also, U.S. Air Force and Army aircraft have flown air patrols to assist the South Koreans in locating infiltrators.

The contrast between the response of the American government and public to the attacks upon the *Pueblo* and the EC-121, on the one hand, and the reaction over the killings and woundings of American soldiers along the DMZ, on the other hand, is striking. In the case of the *Pueblo* and the EC-121 the government took great strides costing hundreds of millions of dollars to bolster the commitment to Korea. Some Americans called for an even clearer answer to these challenges to national pride. This shows how under the right circumstances a commitment can grow out of the presence of even a small unit of American forces. By contrast, the killings along the DMZ were hardly noticed in the public media. The reason for this distinction seems to lie in people's expectations. A series of minor incidents between two opposing forces is not startling. Attacks on or over international waters, where attacks have not been the pattern in the past, call into play all the psychological factors of national pride and dignity that tend to compel some form of vindication.

The dispatch of South Korean troops to South Vietnam received a good deal of public attention, some favorable, some less so. Early in 1965 the South Koreans sent noncombat engineering, transportation, and medical units to South Vietnam. In May, 1965, President Johnson and President Park discussed the possibility of Korea's sending a combat unit, and this was agreed to in June of that year. The first ROK division to go to Vietnam, the Tiger Division, arrived there in October, 1965. A second ROK division, the White Horse Division, arrived in July–September, 1966.

The South Koreans sent these forces to Vietnam for several reasons: (1) to induce the United States to maintain its existing level of forces in Korea; (2) to show Korean willingness to act as a responsible ally and to repay the United States for what it had done for Korea in the Korean war; (3) to obtain foreign exchange and material benefits for their own armed forces as a quid pro quo for sending these units; (4) to train their forces in actual combat; and (5) to gain the satisfaction and prestige of participating abroad in a significant way.

South Korean forces in Vietnam reached a peak of about 48,000 men. They had suffered casualties as of February 7, 1970, of 3,094 killed in action, 6,051 wounded in action, and four missing in action. Reported enemy casualties in their area of responsibility were 30,070 killed in action.

In connection with the sending of the first Korean combat division, the United States agreed to several important points: that there would be no reductions in the American or the Korean forces in Korea without prior consultation; military assistance for the fiscal year 1966 would be increased by $7 million; the United States would continue to purchase commercial consumables, such as clothing and automotive gasoline, as part of its 1966 military assistance program and to make such purchases in Korea; Korean forces in Korea would be modernized; and the United States would provide all equipment and all necessary support for the Korean forces fighting in Vietnam.

In connection with the dispatch of the second Korean combat division, the United States, in a letter from Ambassador Winthrop Brown to Foreign Minister Tong Won Lee of March 4, 1966, agreed that: the United States would provide substantial items for modernizing the ROK forces in Korea; provide all equipment and all additional war costs for the forces going to Vietnam; equip, train, and finance replacement forces for those going to Vietnam; improve the ROK anti-infiltration capability; improve the ROK arsenal for ammunition production; improve the living quarters for ROK forces in Korea; pay overseas allowances and death and disability gratuities to the forces going to Vietnam; continue to procure commercial consumables in Korea for the military assistance program so long as two Korean divisions were in Vietnam; make special efforts to procure goods and services in Korea in support of the Vietnam war; and provide more economic assistance loans to Korea.

All these payments and benefits to Korea have totaled about $1 billion. Even so, it costs the United States about $5,000 a year to support a single Korean soldier in Vietnam, as compared with $13,000 to support a single American soldier.

Modernization of the ROK forces has been delayed under this arrangement as a result of the use of military assistance funds for the purchase of commercial consumables instead of new items of equipment. This allocation of funds to commercial consumables in 1970 ran about $50 million per year. In some instances, the ROK government could have obtained some of these consumables at a lower price than could the American government.

The recent opening of direct negotiations between North and South Korea with a view toward improving relations, following on the heels of President Nixon's dramatic trip to communist China, may augur a new era for the Korean people. If a lesson is to be drawn from the recent course of events in Korea, particularly the remarkable change in North Korea's attitude from one of increasing antagonism and belligerence to one of peaceful negotiation, it may be this. In a place where visible American strength can deter attack without appearing unduly threatening to the other side, it has a reasonable prospect of changing the adversary's posture to one of live-and-let-live, *détente* or even peaceful cooperation. It should not go unsaid in this regard that this unfolding with respect to North Korea would appear to be, at least in part, a sequel to a similar pattern of events in Sino-American relations on a broader scale.

VIII

Thailand

The American commitment to Thailand is composed of many parts: the SEATO Treaty; executive agreements and unilateral declarations; an implicit commitment based upon the presence there of American forces; moral obligations growing out of the Vietnam war; and, to some extent in the past, joint planning.

The basic commitment rests on the multilateral SEATO Treaty, which both countries signed in 1954. The commitment in the treaty has been reinforced by the statements of high executive branch officials. For instance, in 1960 President Eisenhower reaffirmed to the Thais "the unwavering determination of the United States fully to honor its treaty commitments undertaken in the cause of collective security." President Kennedy provided a similar assurance. President Johnson assured the Prime Minister of Thailand in 1966 and 1968 that "America keeps its commitments."

In March, 1962, Secretary of State Rusk and Foreign Minister Thanat issued a joint communiqué in which the Secretary of State reaffirmed that

. . . the United States regards the preservation of the independence and integrity of Thailand as vital to the national interest of the United States and to world peace.

105

In that communiqué the two governments also affirmed that the obligation of each party under SEATO did not require the consent of all the other treaty members, since such obligations were individual as well as collective. Australia and the Philippines have publicly stated their agreement with this position and officials of New Zealand and the United Kingdom have orally expressed their concurrence. The Secretary of State also said in this communiqué:

. . . the United States regards its commitments to Thailand under the Southeast Asia Collective Defence Treaty and under its bilateral economic and military assistance agreements with Thailand as providing an important basis for United States actions to help Thailand meet indirect aggression.

In interpreting the significance of the 1962 Rusk-Thanat communiqué, Foreign Minister Thanat said on May 21, 1969, that there were two points in the document:

According to the present charter, all decisions must be taken by unanimity. That joint communiqué says that even if the decision is not endorsed by all, any individual country or countries may agree to take action even though there is no consensus. . . . This is one point.

The second point is that the charter of the SEATO talks about open aggression by conventional means, though we know for a fact that the other side, our opponents, have been resorting and will think of resorting to . . . a composite warfare system or what the Communists themselves call revolutionary wars or wars of national liberation, and the understanding put forward by the joint communiqué was that if aggression would take the form of that composite warfare both sides would consider action under SEATO.

On his trip to the Far East in 1969, President Nixon pledged to keep all American treaty commitments "as with Thailand." In Bangkok he also said, "The United States will stand proudly with Thailand against those who might threaten it from abroad or from within." These statements were, however, qualified by the doctrine announced on Guam a few days before, which implied that the

United States would only provide equipment and training unless a nuclear power were the aggressor. Also, in private conversations with Thai officials it was made clear that, in the case of an internal insurgency, the United States expected only to provide equipment and training. The Thais expressed some concern over the Nixon Doctrine, fearing that the transition to greater responsibility for the countries of Asia might occur at too rapid a pace.

In July, 1971, the United States had 32,000 military personnel in Thailand, stationed at seven air bases, a large port facility, a large depot, several Special Forces training camps, a Loran-C navigational aid facility, and the Military Assistance Command, Thailand (MACTHAI), which for the most part was an ordinary military assistance mission with its headquarters in Bangkok. The seven air bases were located at Don Muong (Bangkok's international airport), Udorn, Ubon, U Tapao, Korat, Takhli, and Nakhon Phanom. From all of these bases except Don Muong, the United States launched combat aircraft against targets in Laos, South Vietnam, and North Vietnam. Some of these bases also supported helicopter flights into Laos, mainly for search and rescue and the transportation of refugees, and Udorn provided intelligence information about hostile forces. The American air unit at Don Muong had only an air defense responsibility. To place these bases on standby, the Air Force believes that it would still need 200 to 800 American personnel at each one to keep equipment such as lighting, generators, and communications functioning. The American military operating costs in Thailand in the fiscal year 1970 were $455 million and the foreign exchange costs were $247 million.

In 1970 there were seven American generals in Thailand, including the commander of MACTHAI, his deputy, the commander of 7/13th Air Force at Udorn, the wing commander at U Tapao, the commander of the U.S. Army Support Command, another Air Force brigadier general at Nakhon Phanom, and the chief of the Military Planning Office at SEATO headquarters in Bangkok.

The American military presence in Thailand grew slowly in the eleven years between the signing of the SEATO Treaty in 1954 and the sending of American combat units to Vietnam in 1965; after that it grew enormously. The earlier buildup was in response more to the military situation in Laos than in Vietnam. American military construction in Thailand between 1954 and 1962 totaled only $97 million. This included the provision of minimal facilities at seven Thai air force bases and the construction of the 450-mile-long Friendship Highway from Bangkok to the Laotian border north of Vientiane.

The American commitment to the air defense of Thailand in the form of interceptor aircraft stationed at Don Muong began in April, 1961. Also in that year and in each of the next two years, the United States deployed American ground forces to Thailand for limited periods as evidence of its commitment to the defense of Thailand. In 1961 a Marine battalion landing team was sent. In 1962, as the military situation in Laos worsened, about 10,000 United States ground and air personnel were deployed to Thailand, some of them in connection with an already scheduled SEATO military exercise. Also at that time the United States established the Military Assistance Command for Thailand and assigned its command to the American general in Saigon. With the assurance evidenced by this deployment and the Rusk-Thanat communiqué, the Thai government was willing to join in the Geneva Accords for Laos signed in July, 1962. As a result of the temporary degree of stability achieved in Laos through these accords, the American troops were able to withdraw from Thailand by the end of the year.

In June, 1963, SEATO ground forces totaling 24,000, including 16,000 Thais and 7,000 Americans, participated in an exercise in Thailand, again intended to demonstrate readiness to defend that country. Also in that year, the United States entered into the SLAT agreement (Special Logistics Action for Thailand), under which it agreed to provide the Thais with certain railroad cars, upgrade the air base at Nakhon Phanom, and place some heavy equipment and other materiel at Korat. Several other SEATO nations made minor contributions to Thailand's defense at that time.

In 1964, as the situation in Laos again worsened, the United States increased its air power in Thailand. By March, six F-100s were stationed at Takhli, and in August, following the Gulf of Tonkin incident, the squadron was increased to eighteen aircraft. Also, a squadron of F-105s was deployed to Korat. In November, an F-105 squadron replaced the F-100s at Takhli. By the end of the year, about 3,000 Air Force personnel were in Thailand supporting approximately seventy-five aircraft, including search and rescue helicopters. By the end of 1964 the U.S. Army had increased its personnel in Thailand to about 3,300, represented mainly by the 9th Logistics Command, which was growing at a rate proportionate to the Air Force buildup.

By June, 1964, it was apparent that serious hostilities were to continue in Laos. In response to Thai concerns over this situation, this country agreed to engage in bilateral contingency planning with the Thais. This step was taken as an alternative to the actual deployment of American troops to Thailand, the American response in each of the three preceding years. The contingency plan was completed in 1966 and signed by Lieutenant General Richard Stillwell as commander of MACTHAI and by the Thai Defense Minister, Field Marshal Thanom Kittikachorn, who was also Prime Minister at the time. The plan stated that subsequent agreement by the two governments was needed before it could be implemented.

In March, 1965, following the Viet Cong raids on Pleiku in South Vietnam, the United States began bombing North Vietnam from Thailand, as well as from naval carriers in the Gulf of Tonkin, and more strike aircraft were deployed to Thailand. By the end of 1965 there were over 9,000 U.S. Air Force personnel and about 200 aircraft in the country. Army personnel increased by approximately 1,400. Most of this Army force was composed of construction personnel arriving in August to build a road from Kabinburi to Korat, to assist in the development of the port at Sattahip, and to construct petroleum facilities at various points.

Although the Thais agreed to the use of their country for staging bombing raids against North Vietnam in 1965, they did not publicly acknowledge this until March, 1967, for fear of reprisals and, ironically, because of the presence of a North Vietnamese negotiating team in Bangkok in 1965 to discuss the possibility of repatriating 40,000 North Vietnamese refugees living in northeast Thailand.

Also in 1965 the United States appointed a new commander, to be stationed in Bangkok, to head MACTHAI, separating it from the command in Saigon. This was done to assuage Thai sensitivities at having so many Americans in their country under the command of a general outside of Thailand and to give greater credibility to the bilateral planning that was going on at that time.

American economic assistance to Thailand, which had been declining in 1963–64, increased substantially in 1965. Military assistance, which also had been decreasing, went up from 1966 onward, reaching $76.5 million in 1968. One reason for these increases was to counter the growing insurgency in Thailand itself, which had been stimulated to some extent by the growing American presence in the country.

The year 1966 saw the greatest Air Force expansion in Thailand. Additional squadrons of F-4s and F-105s were deployed, together with tanker aircraft and other support aircraft. By December, 1966, the Air Force numbered about 25,000 personnel and its aircraft about 400. Also that year the 606th Air Commando Squadron was dispatched to train the Royal Thai Air Force in counterinsurgency and to provide helicopter support to the Thai counterinsurgency program between August, 1966, and January, 1967. At the end of this period the Thais acquired a capability of their own, and direct American helicopter support was ended. The U.S. Army's forces in

Thailand, except those engaged in training Thai personnel, were reorganized and placed under a new command, the U.S. Army Support Command, Thailand. Also that year a Special Forces company was sent to Thailand and put under the operational command of MACTHAI. At the end of 1966, U.S. Army strength stood at about 8,000.

In 1967, the United States began to station B-52s at U Tapao for striking targets in South Vietnam and Laos. This saved a considerable amount in operating costs. A typical B-52 sortie from U Tapao cost $3,440, compared with $19,937 for a sortie from Guam, in both cases exclusive of munitions. By the end of 1967 there were approximately 33,300 Air Force personnel, approximately 10,300 Army personnel, and 527 aircraft in Thailand.

Air Force personnel remained fairly constant in 1968, growing only to 33,500. Army personnel reached 11,494, and the aircraft total reached 589. With the suspension of bombing over North Vietnam in October, fighter-bomber sorties from Thailand were directed more heavily toward Laos.

Maximum American military strength in Thailand reached 48,000 personnel by 1969. In keeping with the phase-down of the American ground forces in Vietnam undertaken by the Nixon administration, on September 30, 1969, the United States and Thailand announced the withdrawal by June 30, 1970, of 6,000 American military personnel. In August, 1970, the United States announced another reduction of 9,800 personnel to be accomplished by June 30, 1971. But in the spring of 1972 the number of American military personnel in Thailand was increased again to approximately 40,000. The added personnel were mainly airmen sent during the North Vietnamese all-out offensive then going on in South Vietnam.

In 1970 the United States increased the number of B-52s at U Tapao, relocating a few of the aircraft that were formerly striking targets in Vietnam from distant points in the Pacific.

The total cost of American military construction in Thailand from 1954 to 1969 was $702.2 million in annual increments as shown in the following table:

	Total
1954–62	$ 97.5
1963	42.9
1964	4.3
1965	29.7
1966	200.0
1967	135.8
1968	24.3
1969	167.7
Total	$702.2

This construction to support American bases—including roads, a harbor, a reservoir, railroad mileage, and various depots—provided considerable economic and social benefits to Thailand, particularly the economically depressed northeastern region. For instance, the roads made it easier for the farmers of this region to market their produce, thus tying this area more closely to the central region around Bangkok.

The construction program also had secondary consequences of a more military nature. Although all of the construction was justified on the basis of existing and planned operations for the war in Vietnam, some of it also facilitated contingent operations which so far have not occurred. One example is Route 223, which leads from Sakon Nakhom to That Phanom on the Laotian border, passing twenty-five to thirty miles south of the American base at Nakhom Phanom. One of the purposes in building this road seems to have been to facilitate the rapid deployment of troops to the Laotian border in case defensive or offensive operations were needed there. Another such effort was the development of the port at Sattahip, which was certainly needed for the movement of supplies and munitions to American air bases, but which also provided a new deep-water port to support future military and naval operations in the area. The United States also constructed for the Thais an Air

Force flying school at Kaemphaeng Saen at a total cost of $19 million, in order to move their cadets away from the busy base at Korat.

Some waste inevitably occurred. The Pentagon started to construct another air base in 1966 at Nam Phong, only to realize, after spending $14.5 million, that it was not needed. However, the base did become activated in 1972, when American air power in Thailand was augmented to counter the large North Vietnamese spring offensive of that year. To transport munitions and other supplies to its bases throughout Thailand, the United States entered into an exclusive contract with the government-owned Express Transport Organization (ETO), at Thai request. The initial contract provided the company with a thirty to forty percent profit. Following General Accounting Office objections, a new contract was negotiated in 1968 reducing the profit to the fifteen percent range.

Both Thailand and the United States expressed their view that after the present hostilities it would take "compelling reasons" for American forces to remain in Thailand. Nevertheless, there is little doubt that some of the American presence in the form of bases will remain after the Vietnam war.

The existence of so large an American military presence in an Asian country such as Thailand was bound to have an impact on that country's traditional society. To keep this effect to a minimum, the Embassy and the Thai government placed arbitrary ceilings on the number of American military personnel in Thailand, which could not be exceeded except for urgent military reasons. Neither the war in Vietnam nor the large American presence was an issue in the 1969 parliamentary election in Thailand, which by all reports was a reasonably honest one. Only a small handful of the 1,200 candidates criticized American policy in Southeast Asia or the American presence, and none of these candidates was elected.

Smaller than the Korean contingent, but still substantial by Thai standards, was the Thai combat force sent to Vietnam. In September, 1964, Thailand sent a small airlift unit to serve there, subsequently totaling forty-five men. In December, 1966, they sent a small naval patrol unit, which now numbers about 200 personnel. Then in 1967 they sent a ground combat unit of 2,207 men. Following the visit of Clark Clifford and Maxwell Taylor to Thailand in July, 1967, the Thais agreed to increase this combat force to about 11,000 men. After an extensive training program, these men arrived in Vietnam in January, 1969. Including the number of personnel in training for rotation to Vietnam, this contribution to the war in Vietnam comprised about fourteen percent of the Thai Army's total strength. The commitment of so large a portion of the Thai forces lessens the number available for counterinsurgency operations within Thailand; but the combat experience in Vietnam may be valuable training for future use in Thailand. The Thais withdrew their last forces in Vietnam in February, 1972.

To support these Thai forces in South Vietnam, the United States has spent about $200 million since 1966, the greatest portion of which was expended to equip, supply, and sustain them in Vietnam. Other American expenses within this total included the payment of overseas allowances, a $15 million increase in military assistance to Thailand for each of two years, and the provision of a Hawk antiaircraft battery.

Ambassador Martin informed the Subcommittee on Commitments Abroad that the main reason the Thais sent their men to Vietnam was to satisfy the strong desire of the United States that they do so.

Thailand has been plagued for many years with an organized communist presence within its borders. It was not until 1965, however, that overt insurgency first broke out in the northeastern region, prompted, as mentioned above, by the growing American base presence there. The occurrence of the insurgency at that time may have been fortunate for the Thai government. The communists were not yet adequately prepared for this type of action; and, in part because of American urging, the Thai government was able to pursue a relatively energetic and successful counterinsurgency program in that area. The insurgency began to recede by the latter part of 1967. The communists since then have been retrenching and rebuilding their organization in that region, but they have not been participating in substantial violence. The number of insurgents in the northeast in 1970 was estimated at 1,200 to 1,500 men, down from a high of 2,000 in 1967. They were probably supported by ten times that number of followers.

In late 1967 the insurgency moved into the northern region. While the insurgency in the northeast is mainly among ethnic Thais, that in the north is carried on predominantly by Meo tribesmen. These insurgents number between 1,300 and 1,600. The Thais perhaps face their toughest challenge here, where the sturdy Meos are well entrenched in the mountains. The Thai soldiers do not like to operate in this area. The roads are poor, the weather bad, and the insurgents have free access to the communist-controlled area of Laos. One ranking American military advisor remarked, in what might have been overstatement, that the insurgents could not be rooted out of that area by an entire American Army.

There is an insurgent element in the south as well. In 1970 the communists had about 300 to 400 armed men in the center of Thailand's southern panhandle, and in the border region between Thailand and Malaysia they had 1,200 to 1,400 well-trained troops. The effort of this latter force, however, seemed more directed toward Malaysia than Thailand.

In contrast with South Vietnam, Thailand has a number of favorable factors which keep it from being quite so vulnerable to an insurgency. These include a long history of independence, strong feelings of nationalism, loyalty to the King, a common religion, and growing prosperity. Nevertheless, among the ethnic minorities, including Meos of the north and the 40,000 North Vietnamese in the northeast (out of a total population of 11,000,000 in that region), there does exist a source for insurgency. The Thais have now resumed the negotiations with North Vietnam for the repatriation of these North Vietnamese expatriates, broken off during the earlier phase of the Vietnam war.

By January, 1971, the communists had made only three raids on American bases in Thailand; one in July, 1968, at Udorn, killing two and wounding five personnel and damaging two aircraft and a helicopter; one in July, 1969, at Ubon, where they wounded a sentry and damaged two C-47 aircraft; and one in January, 1970, at Ubon, slightly wounding a guard.

Both the Thai government and United States officials have re-iterated that counterinsurgency is a Thai responsibility, not an American one. As American policy, this view is based upon the double assumption that the Thais are better equipped to handle insurgency in their own country than foreigners and that, in recog-nizing this, the United States will avoid the risk of overinvolve-ment experienced in Vietnam.

To oversee the American contribution to the Thai counterinsur-gency effort and to see that the principle of Thai responsibility is observed, the Ambassador appointed a special assistant whose time is devoted solely to these matters. The American role in counter-insurgency-related economic and military assistance is carried out under his coordination.

The most important Thai social program that the United States supports is the Accelerated Rural Development Program, begun in 1964, by which in a variety of ways the income of the rural popu-lation is increased, their ties to the national government are im-proved, and their local government is strengthened. This effort includes road-building, well-digging, small village projects, technical training, and the development of farmer cooperatives. Another, similar, American-supported program is the Mobile Development Unit, also started in 1964. This provides civic action, educational help and other programs to the villages. USIS helps by advising the Thai government on its information programs to reach the rural population.

On the military side, regular military assistance is provided in the form of training, equipment, and advice through the 800-man MACTHAI mission. This assistance totaled $65.8 million in the fiscal year 1970 (not including excess equipment). In addition, special training is provided to the Thai armed forces and police through several American units, including the Special Forces. So far there have been no casualties among the American counterinsurgency advisors. All such training is guided by the concept of preparing Thai instructors, who in turn train the Thai personnel who will conduct the actual counterinsurgency operations. Also, the Advanced Research Projects Agency (ARPA) with an office in Bangkok supports the Thai counterinsurgency program with technical and scientific studies.

Since 1962 Americans have been conducting Special Forces counterinsurgency field training exercises with the Thais. These exercises have involved approximately 1,000 Thai troops and a small number of U.S. Special Forces. Then in 1966, as mentioned above, a Special Forces company was stationed in Thailand, which has varied in size since but totaled 301 men as of September 30, 1969. Of this number, 163 were at the Special Forces center at Lopburi, which provides the command and control element over the other personnel at the fifteen (formerly twenty-two) Special Forces facilities elsewhere in Thailand. The facility at Lopburi is replete with extensive communications and order-of-battle maps for this purpose. Thus, their primary function is for training, but they are also available for combat operations if required.

One Special Forces unit is located in the Phu Phan Mountains in northeast Thailand. The outskirts of the facility are only six miles from an area of insurgent activity, but so far there have been no reported encounters.

The American military has also engaged in a number of civic action projects in Thailand, but these have now been restricted to an area within a few miles of each of the American bases. This limitation was imposed on the theory that if Americans kept doing this work, the Thais would never learn it, and the United States would remain exposed to overinvolvement.

To implement the principles guiding the various American contributions to the counterinsurgency program in Thailand, the Embassy has insisted upon certain very specific rules. American military advisors are forbidden to go below the battalion level of the Thai armed forces in doing their work. Americans are not allowed to go on any counterinsurgency operations nor are they allowed to go into any areas where there is actual fighting or where any danger of fighting is imminent. American advisors are not supposed to participate in the planning process, but they are allowed to give general advice. Furthermore, American advisors are allowed to carry only shotguns, on the theory that these weapons are less lethal than rifles. American personnel do go on field exercises with their students, but areas of insurgency are avoided.

An exception to this rigorous rule of noninvolvement occurred in 1966, on the recommendation of the Ambassador, when twenty-five American helicopters and eighteen airplanes were specifically assigned to provide airlift to staging areas for major Thai counterinsurgency operations. This assistance was authorized for a specified time and on the understanding that the Thais would develop during that period a similar airlift capability of their own. The American operation commenced in March, 1966, and was terminated on schedule on January 31, 1967. This operation was approved so that the Thais would have such a capability during that year's dry season. Otherwise they would have had to wait another year for similar favorable weather conditions. The helicopter crews were instructed not to engage in combat, not even to shoot back when fired upon. There was some reluctance among Thai and American officials to terminate the operation when the time for its cessation arrived because they liked having the logistics capability represented by the helicopters and airplanes involved.

The ways in which the United States has dealt with the insurgency in Thailand and the conflict in Laos are in marked contrast to its enormous involvement in Vietnam. In Thailand there is a reasonably effective counterinsurgency program without any American involvement in operations, although it is true that this program has not had to face challenges like those in the other two countries. In Laos for eight years the United States has sustained a noncommunist government, whose prospects for survival each year were considered to be poor. This has been done without any American ground combat units.

Even as American policies in Thailand and Laos are in marked distinction from those in Vietnam, they are likewise very different from each other. In Thailand the rules against involvement are rigid. In Laos Americans are very much involved, both in the air and on the ground, in operations, support, and planning. It is difficult to reconcile the concepts underlying the two quite different policies in these adjoining countries. In practice this has not yet been necessary because the insurgency in Thailand is so small, and the communist forces in Laos are so large.

One possible distinction between the two countries is the fact that at present the problem in Thailand is truly an insurgency; whereas in Laos it is the presence of large numbers of conventional North Vietnamese troops that accounts for the difficulty. As we have found in Vietnam, insurgency is not as controllable by conventional military tactics as is an invasion by outside forces. The insurgent's strength lies in his ability to harass and disappear, to hit and run, to terrorize and avoid engagement. A quick knockout blow by conventional armed forces is not as suitable a defense as a more pervasive presence of local forces continually patrolling, visibly available to reassure the local population over a very long period of time. One should recall that it took the Philippines eight years to control its insurgency and Malaya twelve years.

Basic to the philosophy of American counterinsurgency experts in Thailand is the belief that involvement leads on to greater involvement. They fear that at each higher stage of participation, American inclination would be to make still another marginal investment in the program rather than to see earlier expenditures and efforts come to naught. Indeed this phenomenon is occurring in Laos, to judge by the increasing American sortie rate and military assistance over the years.

On the other hand, there are programs, such as the helicopter support provided to the Thais in 1966, which did not follow this pattern. The contribution was made and withdrawn, and replaced by a similar indigenous effort. Also, there are thresholds in this process. A large identification of American prestige with the Laotian war has not yet occurred. The air action could stop tomorrow and the CIA agents on the ground could disappear.

Perhaps, up to a certain point, as important as the scale of American participation is the manner in which it is made and the degree to which it is controlled, in scope and time, by a single rigorous authority, conscious of the risks of open-ended commitment.

Thailand is a country where the American commitment is truly multi-layered. Most basic, of course, is the SEATO Treaty, but this document is ambiguous in a number of ways. In fact, the Thais were so concerned over one ambiguity in the treaty that they induced this country in 1962 to make a clarifying declaration in the Rusk-Thanat communiqué. As in that communiqué, each Administration since 1954 has reaffirmed the commitment.

On top of the somewhat ambiguous commitments in SEATO and the declarations of American officials, there are numerous commitment-making elements arising from the large American presence in Thailand. Ground combat forces were sent to Thailand in 1961, 1962, and 1963. Had an attack come during any of those deployments, Americans would have been engaged in combat. Beyond this risk of actual engagement at the time was the implicit commitment that the United States would dispatch such forces to

Thailand again in the event of crisis.* Similarly, the continuous stationing of an air defense unit in Bangkok ever since 1961 assures that this country will become engaged if Thailand should ever be attacked from the air.

The establishment of bases in Thailand does somewhat the same thing. If they are attacked the United States will probably want to defend them. Besides the commitments made in these ways, some believe an American moral obligation to the Thais is being generated by their letting the United States use their country for all these bases, so important for prosecuting the war in Vietnam.

Still another commitment-making element was joint American-Thai planning. By engaging in such planning in 1964, when the Thais were anxious for reassurance of the American defense commitment, this country was implying that it would come to their defense if they were seriously threatened. Had the circumstances contemplated in the plan actually occurred before the period of American de-escalation in Southeast Asia, it would have been awkward to avoid implementing the plan. This planning contained the dynamics of a moral obligation and also elements of what might be called a bureaucratic commitment. When any extensive operation, such as a large-scale planning program, is created, it builds up involvements and relationships of its own, sometimes in very inscrutable ways.

Prime Minister Thanom, who had signed the plan on behalf of Thailand in 1966, summed up his understanding of the plan in a press conference in 1969. He described it as

putting in practice cooperation between Thailand and the United States to help prevent Communist aggression. . . . The United States asserts

---

* Most Americans remember President Kennedy's dispatch of 10,000 American troops to Thailand in 1962, but few recall that he sent 7,000 in 1963. The reason for the difference in public attention may have been the overwhelming importance we were attaching to Vietnam by 1963. This difference in public interest in the two deployments is relevant in measuring the degree of implicit commitment each conveyed.

it will not desert us, that it will help prevent Communist aggression. . . . It gives us the certainty and confidence that the United States will not desert us and let us fight against the Communists on our own.

All this is not to say that joint planning must always be avoided. It is often a part of good generalship, but it must be carefully pre-scribed and developed so as to preserve necessary political flexibility.

Concerning the enormous construction program undertaken in Thailand in 1965-69, the two American Ambassadors during the period and the commanding general of MACTHAI during part of this period testified to the Subcommittee on Commitments Abroad that the decisions to undertake these projects were reached solely on the basis of their contribution to the war in Vietnam, but they also spoke about the future implications of this program. Ambassador Unger testified:

While the timing and magnitude of this program for U.S. forces was dictated by the buildup of combat operations in Vietnam, these facilities also enhanced Thailand's ability to defend itself. They also constitute an infrastructure which would be available, if needed, for any possible future SEATO operations . . . [This] referred to the kind of emer-gencies that might develop, . . . the possibility of, let's say, an invasion through Laos or something of that nature. In other words, the develop-ment of military emergency and attack on Thailand of the sort that could conceivably call SEATO into action.

He went on to say:

the specific reason for the construction of the base at Sattahip was to provide port facilities to relieve overcrowding at Bangkok because of the air operations out of Thailand. . . . That was the purpose. . . . Certainly if at some time in the future a decision should be made that an American or regional naval base should be looked for, Sattahip could provide the beginning of that kind of facility, if the Thais were willing.

Of course, it lacks a tremendous amount of the kinds of outfitting that would be required for any kind of a base remotely resembling any-thing like Singapore. But this would be a possibility.

Ambassador Martin, who was ambassador when much of the construction work was carried on, told the subcommittee with respect to the possibility of Sattahip's serving as a future naval base like Singapore:

. . . it sounds very much like my own thinking at that time.

I myself would reiterate that, to my very great chagrin and disappointment, these considerations were never allowed to be put into the equation by the Department of Defense.

General Stillwell added: ". . . having constructed those facilities for those specific [Vietnam-related] purposes, they are then extant facilities for whatever future eventuality may develop." A similar comment could also apply to the Special Forces unit sent to Thailand in 1966. It is in Thailand primarily to train Thai forces in counterinsurgency techniques; but it is also available in case it is needed for another purpose.

The same may even be said of the commanding general of MACTHAI. His main responsibility may have been to give the appearance of command within Thailand itself for the large American military presence there, but he is also available, with authority parallel to that of the commander of MACV in Saigon, to take charge of the American military effort in defense of Thailand should that become necessary. In this regard, it is curious that the first Thailand-based commander of MACTHAI was an Army general, who remained in the post from August, 1965, to July, 1967, even though throughout this period there were two to three times as many Air Force personnel as Army personnel in Thailand. The deputy commander of MACTHAI today is an Army general.

Beyond the specific dynamics of each of the commitments mentioned above is the more general identification with Thailand which the totality of these various efforts creates. As in some other areas of human endeavor, the whole is greater than the sum of its parts. In many ways Americans are common partners with Thailand in the defense of a "free" Southeast Asia—through the bases, some of which will remain after the Vietnam war is over, through the Thais' going to Vietnam, through the American role in the Thai counterinsurgency program, through the creation of MACTHAI, through the presence of the Special Forces in Thailand, the joint planning, the Thai contribution to the war in Laos, the Rusk-Thanat communiqué, and through the construction of a vast network of physical facilities in Thailand that has important social and military implications beyond the war in Vietnam. All these tied together create a political relationship between Thais and Americans that is not easily dissolved.

There is yet another dimension of the American commitment to Thailand to be mentioned: the war in Vietnam itself, irrespective of the Thais' participation in it. If the United States is able to prevent a communist-controlled government from coming to power in Saigon, that in itself will tend to tie this country more closely to the defense of Thailand just as it will to the future defense of Vietnam itself. The American relationship with Thailand has historically been more fundamental than that with Vietnam. Thailand is a full SEATO member; South Vietnam only a protocol state. Thailand has always been an independent country with direct diplomatic relations with the United States, whereas all the Indochinese states were once French colonies. Thailand is one of the more prominent "dominoes" in American policy toward Vietnam. To save Vietnam and lose Thailand could make success in Vietnam rather hollow.

One further comment prompted by the large construction program in Thailand. The Symington Subcommittee discovered a number of situations in Southeast Asia where this country was carrying on operations or pursuing policies under one justification, or guise, that actually served another purpose as well, or instead. The construction of roads, railroad mileage, a port, and a reservoir in Thailand was one example. Another, less defensible, instance was the placing of the Defense Department's request for Congressional authorization for military assistance for Thailand in the general Defense Department appropriations on the pretext of its relationship to the war in Vietnam, instead of leaving it in the Foreign Assistance budget, where it could be scrutinized more closely by the Congress.

The subcommittee discovered similar dubious justifications for projects undertaken in Laos and Cambodia as well as in Thailand. In northern Laos the United States is carrying on a full-scale air war under a claim of supporting the war in South Vietnam, whereas the two conflicts are only tenuously connected. The main American purpose in northern Laos is to save the noncommunist government of Souvanna Phouma. This is discussed more fully in Chapter V. Another instance was in Cambodia. The raids against the communist sanctuaries there in May–June, 1970, were certainly done to support the American effort in South Vietnam; but at the same time they also served to support the Lon Nol regime in Cambodia itself.

In one respect, this is a good way to provide help of a military nature to other countries. By providing assistance as a collateral effort to some other project, much less American prestige is at stake if the assistance should fail. However, there are certain requirements for congressional consultation and public disclosure that must not be overlooked in the process, principles that were violated in some of the instances mentioned above.

The communist Chinese have definitely viewed Thailand as a country for which their espousal of wars of national liberation is relevant. However, so far, Peking's support for the communist insurgency in Thailand has not reached the point of immediate danger to the Thai government. It has mainly been in the form of ideological and strategic guidance, cadre training, and limited financial and material support. In 1971 the Chinese had more than 14,000 troops in Laos and probably some in Burma, and they were continuing to construct a road in northern Laos toward the Thai border.

The large American presence in Thailand on the periphery of communist China raises the fundamental question of how American policy toward China's neighbors interacts with that country's policies. Inherent American interest in a country such as Thailand is not very great. The fact that Thailand is not in the adversary's camp makes somewhat more secure the American position in the region occupied by Indonesia, Malaysia, Singapore, and the Philippines, which is probably more important to the United States than Thailand is, because of factors such as population, resources, geography and, in the case of the Philippines, history. Thailand also provides the United States with some military facilities.

Beyond these factors, however, the interest of Americans in the continued independence of Thailand lies mainly in the fact that the United States has a commitment to Thailand both in American eyes and in the eyes of the rest of the world. Thus, the United States is in a logical circle. It is committed to Thailand because of its interest in Thailand, and its interest in Thailand rests mainly on the fact that it is committed to that country. As one foreign policy analyst, Morton Halperin, has put it: "Our main interest in Thailand is in not losing it the wrong way."

Foreign policy experts are very wary of making predictions about Chinese communist behavior. This uncertainty is compounded by the fact that, with President Nixon's visit to China, the United States is entering a new and unpredictable stage in its relations with that country. However, there appear to be three broad possibilities, respecting China, if the American presence in Thailand should be phased down after the conclusion of the role of the United States in the current Indochinese hostilities. Taking the most favorable possibility first, the Chinese may become less belligerent, more *détente*-oriented, as a result of feeling less threatened by an American military presence on their threshold. Turning to the most pessimistic view, the Chinese may see in an American withdrawal a weakening of resolve; they may conclude that they can march their army into Southeast Asia with little opposition, and may be tempted to do so. The middle, and perhaps the most likely, position will be that the communist Chinese will continue pretty much as they have in the past, seeking to expand their influence through insurgency and political maneuvering, but avoiding conventional warfare, since the latter would be inconsistent with their ideology, pose very difficult problems in logistics and morale, and raise substantial risks in terms of American and perhaps Soviet reaction.

With these considerations in mind, it would seem that a *judicious,* gradual, step-by-step, downward turn in the multi-layered commitment in Thailand would be in order. The United States could thereby (1) try for better relations with communist China, (2) retain flexibility for determining response in ambiguous situations, and (3) perhaps achieve a modest reduction in the military budget. Nevertheless, the continuation of some American military presence in the region for the foreseeable future would seem to be in order to provide that type of manifest but nonthreatening strength which has led from crisis and tension to stability and *détente* in Europe, in Korea, in our strategic relationship with the Soviet Union and in our relations with communist China.

Toward this end it is helpful that the Thais reiterate that it is their strong wish not to have foreign forces directly involved in their counterinsurgency program. American officials have wisely repeated this Thai policy at every opportunity. The crucial test of this noble sentiment will come only if and when the Thais can no longer handle the situation themselves. As espoused by Thai officials, it is possible but doubtful that the policy may help the United States to remain on the sidelines.

IX

North Atlantic Treaty Organization

THE NATO COMMITMENT

The American military presence in Western Europe, except for Spain and Berlin, rests upon the North Atlantic Treaty, which was signed on April 4, 1949. The existence of the 3,400-man American garrison in Berlin stems not from the North Atlantic Treaty but from the Four Power Agreements on Berlin at the end of World War II. The American position in Spain rests upon the 1953 base rights agreement with that country, which was renewed in 1963 and superseded by a new agreement in 1970.

The United States commitment to defend Western Europe is the strongest that it has, with the possible exception of the commitment to the other countries of the Western Hemisphere. This commitment to Europe is clearly in the interests of the United States and would be almost as strong even in the absence of a formal treaty alliance. The loss to the United States would be enormous if it were to be denied the industrial, commercial, technological, military, and demographic strength and strategic space which a friendly Western Europe represents for it.

Besides these more or less tangible and quantifiable factors are the conceptual and psychological factors that stem from the close American cultural and political ties with Europe. If the democratic countries of Western Europe were to come under the hand of a power antagonistic to the United States, this country would face severe consequences in terms of morale, self-image, and freedom from fear and anxiety. One need only recall the effect in this country of the fall of France in 1940 to sense this dimension. Furthermore, the loss of this area, considered so important in the hierarchy of American interests, would have immense effect upon the ability of the United States to maintain its influence and resist challenge elsewhere in the world.

In representing the American commitment to Europe, NATO has been enormously successful. It has provided the shield which has allowed a weak and dispirited Western Europe to regain its confidence, repair its economy, and grow strong again. NATO has maintained the peace in Europe for more than twenty years without the loss of a single foot of territory. Relations with the Soviet Union and the rest of Eastern Europe have become more peaceful and stable, thanks in no small degree to the effectiveness of the NATO deterrent. The military cooperation achieved through NATO's integrated military structure represents a greater total strength than would be possible with each member operating separately. Finally, the alliance has played an important part in restoring West Germany to the status of an equal, respected, and self-respecting member of the European community and able to endure the division of the German nation.

AMERICAN FORCES

Well over half of all American military personnel stationed abroad, exclusive of Vietnam, and well over half of major American military facilities abroad, again excluding Vietnam, are in Europe. The approximate numbers of American servicemen, American civilian employees of the United States armed forces, and their dependents in Europe in 1970 were as follows:

	Servicemen	Employees	Dependents
Total	309,000	13,800	242,000
NATO area (including Berlin and Sixth Fleet)	300,600	13,100	227,400
Germany (including Berlin)	213,000	9,500	155,000
Spain	8,400	700	14,600

Of the 373 major American military facilities abroad outside of Vietnam in 1970, 209 were in Germany alone. There were thirty other major American installations in the rest of NATO-Europe. Most of the facilities in Germany were barracks, kasernes, and depots to support the Seventh Army, plus ten air bases and air fields. There were six more air bases in the United Kingdom, two in Italy, and one in the Netherlands.

The operating costs of maintaining this American military power in Europe, excluding the annual investment in major equipment and construction, was estimated in 1970 to be about $2.9 billion a year. According to Defense Department figures, the total annual cost borne by the United States for the conventional American forces allocated to a NATO contingency, both those based in Europe and in the United States, including operating costs and annual investment, was $14 billion in 1970. However, the Defense Department has used this figure for this purpose ever since 1964. The Brookings Institution, by assuming several other military units to be properly allocable to a NATO contingency and taking into account certain inflationary factors, priced the American commitment to NATO for the year 1970 at about $19 billion (excluding strategic nuclear weapons). Because of inflation and military pay increases, the figure today is unquestionably higher. The Brookings allocation included eight active Army divisions, of which four and one-third were (and still are) stationed in Germany, seven fully equipped reserve divisions, sixteen Air Force tactical air wings, of which seven were (and still are) stationed in Europe, the two carrier task forces in the Mediterranean and one Marine Corps air wing, as well as certain antisubmarine, amphibious, airlift, and sealift units.

The strategic nuclear forces of the United States annually cost about $18 billion (both in 1970 and today). These include the Polaris submarines, Minuteman missiles, and nuclear-armed B-52s, which account for a large part of the nuclear deterrent that serves NATO as well as the continental United States and its allies in the Far East. In addition to these forces, the United States keeps about 7,000 tactical nuclear warheads in Europe for delivery by aircraft and artillery.

THE MILITARY BALANCE

As for the communist forces facing NATO, if one includes the Soviet forces in the western part of the Soviet Union, the Warsaw Pact has a predominance over NATO *in numbers* of men, aircraft, and tanks in place in Europe north of the Alps. According to the highly respected Institute for Strategic Studies, the statistics in 1970 were as follows: *

	NATO	French †	Total Warsaw Pact	Soviet Forces Only
Manpower	600,000	100,000	925,000	600,000
Divisions	24	5	65	39
Tactical aircraft	2,050	1,000	3,795	2,145
Tanks	5,250 ‡	(not available)	12,500	8,000

† Not included in NATO totals.
‡ Includes only tanks for which crews were actually assigned.

These NATO deficiencies in numbers are offset to some extent by several factors. The reliability of some communist satellite units for offensive operations is open to question. Other Warsaw Pact

* ISS. *The Military Balance, 1969–1970,* pp. 62–63.

units may well be needed to maintain internal security in Eastern Europe. Also, NATO's defensive posture would provide it the advantage of operating from protected positions, although the element of surprise would favor the offense.

The events in Czechoslovakia in 1968 probably have done little to change the overall balance. The Soviet Union now has more divisions deployed forward than before, but this is offset by the demonstrated unreliability of Czechoslovakia as a satellite and by the somewhat greater devotion of the NATO members to their own defense as a result of the crisis.

The NATO air forces have qualitative advantages over their Warsaw Pact rivals in range, loiter time, payload, training, and maintenance. Most of the aircraft of the Warsaw Pact countries, including the MIG-21, are primarily designed as air defense interceptors, not as fighter-bombers. Furthermore, worldwide the NATO countries have a far greater inventory of aircraft than do the Warsaw Pact members. This superiority could be brought to bear rather promptly in the event of actual combat.

NATO tanks have greater accuracy at long range and NATO forces have fifty percent more antitank weapons. Furthermore, Warsaw Pact interceptors have a relatively poor capacity for defending against low-flying NATO fighter-bombers, which could be used as tank-killers. NATO also has certain advantages in the fields of conventional artillery, armored personnel carriers, and other vehicles.

The Warsaw Pact probably has a superior capability for reinforcement of its ground forces in the first weeks of mobilization, which might or might not precede the outbreak of hostilities. Even during the early stages of a mobilization, however, NATO would have certain offsetting advantages that are not often mentioned. The state of readiness of many American reserve units is higher than that of equivalent Soviet units. Also, as stated above, United States-based tactical air units could be deployed to Europe during this period. And today more Soviet units are deployed in distant parts of Siberia facing the Chinese border than was so in the past. There has also recently been an improvement in reserve techniques among the NATO members, making more men available promptly in the event of hostilities.

After this initial period, the greater capacity of the NATO countries in manpower and production would be likely to have its effect. The NATO countries have a larger population and greater wealth, spend more on defense and have more men of military age, larger ground forces, larger total armed forces, and more military aircraft than do the Warsaw Pact countries. The approximate figures in 1970 were as follows:

	NATO Countries	French *	Warsaw Pact Countries †
Population (millions)	479.0	50.3	341.9
GNP (billions)	$1,599.2	$115.0	$596.0
Defense exp. (billions)	$ 71.8 ‡	$ 5.6	$ 64.0
Men—military age (millions) §	89.5	11.3	67.4
Ground forces (millions)	3.38	.33	2.83
Armed forces (millions)	5.51	.57	4.8
Military aircraft (thousands)	11.0	1.0	8.0

* Not included in NATO totals.

† Includes: USSR, plus Bulgaria, Czechoslovakia, E. Germany, Hungary, Poland and Rumania.

‡ Excludes U.S. defense expenditures in Southeast Asia.

§ Physically fit (ages 15–49).

THE THREAT

When we speak of the "threat to NATO," we are actually referring to four different types of danger: (1) the possibility of a massive surprise attack (e.g., a full-scale thrust across the northern German plain); (2) the chance of hostilities breaking out between NATO and Warsaw Pact forces as a result of an insurgency or the like in Eastern Europe (e.g., a revolt in East Germany); (3) the risk that the Warsaw Pact countries might attempt a limited probe into NATO territory (e.g., a seizure of West Berlin); and (4) the possibility of a political incursion into Western Europe (e.g., a communist political victory in Italy).

None of these risks is very great today. For the Warsaw Pact countries to launch a sudden all-out conventional attack against the West would require complete cooperation among the members of the pact, total surprise, almost perfect preparations, an entire lack of credibility in the NATO nuclear deterrent, and a high degree of faith in the Warsaw Pact's ability to overcome NATO's long-term advantages in conventional warfare at an acceptable cost to the pact members.

The experience with respect to insurgency in Eastern Europe over the last twenty years suggests that the second risk, the possibility of such events leading to East-West hostilities, is also rather remote. We have witnessed an uprising in East Germany in 1953, widespread discontent in Poland in 1956, revolution in Hungary the same year, the building of the Berlin Wall in 1961, and an invasion of Czechoslovakia in 1968. None has resulted in hostilities with NATO. Since the brutal and swift putting down of the Czechoslovakian deviation, a repetition of dissent on such a scale in Eastern Europe now appears remote. After Tito's death, it is possible that Yugoslavia may emerge as a new area of contention in Eastern Europe, as centrifugal nationalistic forces reassert themselves. In any event, should a wide-scale insurgency occur again, it will almost surely present NATO with considerable time for preparation before any serious risk develops for the NATO countries themselves.

The third type of risk is most often exemplified in the form of pressure on Berlin, although there are other relatively exposed points on the NATO frontier that could conceivably be subject to such tactics. Any actual hostilities, however, for the purpose of snipping off a small piece of NATO territory are today exceedingly unlikely because the communists would be running enormous risks for little gain. Such action would also reflect a willingness to negate all the steps taken in the last nine years or so toward a more peaceful and stable Europe.

The fourth risk, a political incursion, being more amorphous is more difficult to evaluate, but also seems remote. One form this political threat might take lies in the possibility that, fearful of overwhelming Soviet strength, one or more Western European nations would enter into some form of political surrender to the Soviet Union. This might be brought on, for instance, by Soviet tactics at pressure points such as Berlin. But the European mood today is in exactly the opposite direction. There is prevalent throughout Western Europe a faith, wisely held or not, that the Cold War may be nearing its end. Added to this are an optimism and a sense of independence founded upon an ever-rising standard of living. Today's European believes he is reasonably secure from Soviet domination, so long as there is some American presence in Western Europe. He is not likely to feel there is any need to give up his birthright for a greater measure of security.

Another form that the political risk might take is of a more internal nature. France experienced in May-June, 1968, an alarming general strike with large-scale communist and radical participation. Italy has recently had great difficulty in forming stable governments. For the present, however, difficulties such as these have not led to any lasting communist success in Western Europe. Following *"les événements de mai"* the French people returned the Gaullist party to office with an even greater majority than they had given it before. The Italians do not appear to be turning to the communists to relieve them of their political difficulties.

The prosperity and freedom that Western Europe has enjoyed since the early postwar years and for which their ties with the United States have been in no small measure responsible, as well as the very strong social, cultural, economic, military, and political bonds that continue to unite this country with Western Europe are rather good insurance against a political collapse in Europe from internal or external forces. Furthermore, the memory of the

Soviet invasion of Czechoslovakia can only reinforce the aversion which much of Western Europe feels for the Soviet system.

TROOP REDUCTION

Through the years there have been numerous calls for reductions in the level of American forces in Europe. One of the best-known statements was made by General Eisenhower in 1963:

Though for eight years in the White House I believed and announced to my associates that a reduction of American strength in Europe should be initiated as soon as European economies were restored, the matter was then considered too delicate a political question to raise. I believe the time has now come when we should start withdrawing some of those troops. . . . One American division in Europe can "show the flag" as definitely as can several.

Nevertheless, nine years later, the American troop level in Europe is hardly lower than it was when Eisenhower was President. It was substantially increased during the Kennedy administration in connection with the Berlin crisis of 1961 and only gradually reduced from that high level thereafter.

Measures have also been introduced in the Senate in recent years calling for reductions in our troop strength in view of the continuing financial difficulties of this country. In 1967 Senators Mansfield and Javits introduced separate resolutions to this effect. In 1968 Senator Symington introduced an amendment to the defense procurement bill to accomplish this. In 1969 Senator Mansfield reintroduced his resolution. It received the endorsement of a majority of the members. This resolution states:

. . . with changes and improvements in the techniques of modern warfare and because of the vast increase in capacity of the United States to wage war and to move military forces and equipment by air, a substantial reduction of United States forces permanently stationed in Europe can be made without adversely affecting either our resolve or ability to meet our commitment under the North Atlantic Treaty; . . .

In the phasedown following the Berlin crisis, over the last six years, more than 100,000 American servicemen and dependents have in fact been withdrawn from Europe. In 1966–67 the United States was able to return home 18,000 military personnel and 21,000 dependents in connection with the redeployment of American troops from France. This resulted in an annual savings in foreign exchange of more than $100 million. As part of that move also, the U.S. Army was able to bring together its formerly separate European headquarters and Seventh Army headquarters, thereby reducing American and local personnel by 1,276 and saving $9 million.

In 1968 under the program known as Reforger, two-thirds of the 24th Infantry Division and its support units were returned home and have been held in a high state of readiness for rapid redeployment to Europe. Under the contemporaneous Air Force program, Crested Cap, five of the nine tactical fighter squadrons of the 17th Air Force based in Germany were redeployed to the United States, also to be kept available for rapid return to Europe under a concept known as "dual-basing." Subsequently, by converting four air defense squadrons stationed in Germany to F-4 aircraft, the Air Force was again able to have nine squadrons of F-4s stationed in Germany.

Reforger and Crested Cap resulted in a return to the United States of about 35,000 servicemen and 25,000 dependents. The balance of payments savings was approximately $76 million. Secretary of Defense Robert McNamara informed the Combined Subcommittee on U.S. Forces in Europe in 1967 that he believed that twice as many servicemen could have been withdrawn from Europe at that time but for the fact that the Joint Chiefs of Staff would not agree. Secretary Rusk informed the same subcommittee that the announcement of these redeployments had been relatively well accepted by the Germans, the ally most concerned.

Under another program known as REDCOSTE, which originally envisaged reductions on the order of 30,000–60,000 men, about 6,000 more support personnel were withdrawn from Europe.

Apparently, the Nixon administration has decided not to make any further significant cuts in American forces in Europe. On November 30, 1970, Secretary Laird said that the United States would make no "force capability reduction until at least July 1972." Then, on December 2 of that year, the NATO defense ministers reaffirmed the need for the present level of American forces in Europe and, in order to induce the United States to maintain that level, announced a five-year, $1 billion program financed entirely by the European members to improve bases, forces, and weapons in Europe. Finally, the next day, December 3, President Nixon said that the United States would "not reduce [U.S. forces] unless there is reciprocal action from our adversaries."

Ever since 1968 NATO has been proposing mutual troop reductions with the Warsaw Pact countries. In March, 1971, the Soviets expressed greater interest than ever before in the possibility of such reductions. Since then, however, discussions toward this end have been desultory. One of the reasons for this has been the recent quiescence in the Senate with respect to unilateral reduction in American forces in Europe. When the State Department and the Pentagon expected that Congress might compel them to make unilateral cuts, they voiced greater enthusiasm for the prospect of mutual reductions. But when the alternative appears to be the existing force strength, they seem to prefer that to mutual reductions because it appears unlikely that the Soviets would agree to any equation for reductions greater than one Soviet unit for one American unit; and a withdrawal of Soviet forces in East Germany to the Soviet Union, along with the removal of American forces across the Atlantic, would work to the disadvantage of NATO's military posture.

Nevertheless, some reductions to streamline American forces in Europe should and perhaps will be made. There are various steps that could be taken to reduce American expenditures in Europe without reducing the most visible symbols of the United States commitment, its combat divisions. The European allies could be asked to make direct budgetary contributions for the support of American troops in Europe. Items which such contributions could cover might appropriately include the salaries of local employees hired by American forces, items procured locally, and local services. The annual costs of these things in Germany alone were as follows in 1970:

	Millions
Local employees	$260
Local procurement	55
Local services	160
Total	$475

Discussions toward this end were pursued in 1970, but stimulated little enthusiasm on the part of the Europeans. Instead, they opted for a five-year, $1 billion (i.e., $250 million a year) program to improve their own forces and facilities. Very little of this amount will go to relieve existing American expenditures.

Instead of contributing to direct American budgetary costs, or in addition to the contribution of some such costs, a second step may be for the Europeans to assume some of the operations now carried on by American military personnel. One good example of this may be the assumption of the air defense role in Germany now performed by American units. If the Nike-Hercules and Hawk units, as well as the related air defense radar facilities, were turned over to the Germans, about 11,000 American military personnel could come home and be demobilized. Some of the Hawk units are so integrated into the tactical operations of the American divisions that a turnover of such units may not be appropriate, but this is not true for the bulk of the air defense responsibilities now borne by American personnel. By way of comparison, the Japanese are entirely responsible for the air defense of their own country. The Germans have air defense units in other parts of Germany comparable to the American units. Also, the assumption of further air defense responsibilities by the Germans would not represent any increase in their combat capability that would be likely to concern any other European countries.

Other functions that could appropriately be turned over to the Germans to operate and finance are the transportation, depot, and other logistics functions now performed by Americans. However, simply to turn over such functions to the Germans but to have the United States continue to bear their cost would result in greater foreign exchange expenditures for this country. Although a GI is paid more than a German truck driver, all of the German worker's salary would be foreign exchange. A large part of the GI's salary, on the other hand, goes back to the United States through PX purchases, allotments, and other channels. Another arrangement that could significantly reduce foreign exchange expenditures would be the extending of PX and commissary privileges to local employees of American armed forces abroad.

Whether any of the foregoing steps are taken or not, substantial savings can be achieved through the streamlining of a number of the American headquarters and other support units in Europe, which have become overstaffed. Reductions in this area would produce both foreign exchange and budgetary savings. The removal of a single senior staff officer would result in a financial saving about four times greater than the withdrawal of a combat soldier. Estimates of potential reductions that could be accomplished in this category run as high as 54,000 American military and civilian personnel, representing budgetary savings of as much as $400 million and foreign exchange savings in the range of $200 million.

Reductions could be made, for instance, at the headquarters at Wiesbaden and London. The complex of Air Force facilities at Wiesbaden could be deactivated, and those of its functions that must stay in Europe could be assumed by the nearby headquarters at Ramstein, with relatively minor construction there. This would permit the withdrawal of as many as 10,000 American personnel. If the Army, with 180,000 men in Germany, can get along with its European command and its Seventh Army command colocated, then the Air Force with only 80,000 men should be able to function adequately with its European command, currently at Wiesbaden, colocated with its 17th Air Force command, already at Ramstein. The naval headquarters at London should likewise be deactivated, and whatever functions it now performs that must remain in Europe could be assumed by the naval headquarters at Naples. This step would provide facilities in London to which the Air Force could relocate its U.K. headquarters now at South Ruislip.

Further savings could be accomplished by bringing to one location, the overall European command, which is now at Stuttgart, and the Seventh Army command at Heidelberg. The commander of the Seventh Army could take over the functions now assigned to the commanding general at Stuttgart. There is generally an overabundance of American commands in Europe. In addition to the fifteen or so NATO headquarters in Europe, the United States has an overall American command at Stuttgart (USEUCOM); the U.S. Army has a command at Heidelberg (USAREUR and Seventh Army) and eight subordinate commands; the Navy has its European headquarters at London (USNAVEUR), its Sixth Fleet command afloat and another command at Naples; and the Air Force has its European headquarters at Wiesbaden (USAFE), its 17th Air Force headquarters nearby at Ramstein, its Third Air Force headquarters at South Ruislip in England, its 16th Air Force headquarters at Torrejón in Spain, and another headquarters at Ankara, Turkey. The United States has 128 generals and admirals in Europe to command 300,000 men. In Vietnam it has had only ninety generals to command, in actual combat, as many as 550,000 men. Even as some other American units have been deployed to the United States in a state of readiness for rapid redeployment to Europe, some headquarters units could also perhaps be placed in this status.

There are now seven American fighter wings in Europe. Large foreign exchange savings could be realized if most of the squadrons in these wings were returned to the United States under the "dual-basing" concept. These units can be rapidly returned to Europe in the event of crisis, and this capability can be exercised periodically, as is done with the four tactical fighter squadrons presently stationed in the United States under dual-basing. It also happens that the C-130 airlift squadrons now assigned to Europe operate under a similar concept: they are deployed on a rotational pattern, with their crews and their dependents based in the United States.

The American squadrons remaining in Europe could be located on a few active bases. The other bases could then be turned over to the host countries or placed on standby with not more than about 200 personnel present, most of whom could be local nationals. This could apply to bases in the U.K., Spain, Italy, Greece, Turkey, and the Azores as well as those in Germany. It is similar to the arrangement originally envisaged, but never accomplished, under the Crested Cap program.

The Army's missile and support units in northern Italy could also be substantially reduced. If the threat to NATO in its center region is small, it is even less in Italy.

Beyond some of the foregoing efficiency reductions, however, it would seem inappropriate at the present to reduce American forces in Europe. The arguments often heard in favor of such reductions are inadequate, inaccurate, or exaggerated. The degree to which the present enormous balance of payments problem could be relieved by any feasible cuts in American forces in Europe would be minor. The belief that by bringing troops home from Europe the United States could effect a substantial reduction in its overall defense budget is simply wrong. The argument that it should cut its forces in Europe because the Europeans have not carried their fair share of the defense burden is exaggerated. On the other hand, the arguments made by those who favor maintaining the present level of forces in Europe because the military or political threat to Western Europe would be seriously aggravated by a reduction in American forces are also exaggerated.

The United States balance of payments figures are persistently poor. The deficit for the calendar year 1971 was worse than ever: $29.6 billion by the official reserve transactions measure and $22.2 billion on the net liquidity balance. Military-related expenditures in Europe that bore upon this balance of payments situation totaled about $1.7 billion. If U.S. troops there were reduced by one-half, the savings would probably be in the $600–800 million a year range. Alain Enthoven, the former Assistant Secretary of Defense for Systems Analysis, calculated with fiscal year 1968 figures that the reduction of one and one-third divisions and three air wings would result in an annual balance of payments savings of about $250 million. The historic trend in these costs has been upward and is likely to continue so. If military pay increases and price rises in Europe occur at the same rate as in the past, U.S. military expenditures in Europe in the next ten years will go up by about fifty percent.

American expenditures in Germany account for $1.1 billion of the total $1.7 billion spent in Europe for military-related expenditures. In the face of growing demands in this country for the return of a substantial portion of the troops in Europe, the Germans have entered into a series of formal offset arrangements to minimize the impact on the balance of payments situation caused by United States military spending in their country. Under the agreement in force in 1971, the Germans provided the United States with foreign exchange in the amount of $1.52 billion over the two-year period 1970–71. This amount comprised the following:

	Millions
Military procurement in the U.S.	$ 800
Civil procurement in the U.S.	125
Loan to the U.S. (repayable in ten years)	250
Other financial measures	345
Total	$1,520

The loan and certain of the other financial measures bore the exceptionally low interest rate of three and one-half percent.

This arrangement, however, has not proved to be a completely satisfactory solution to this country's military-related balance of payments problem. Several members of the Nixon administration, including the former Secretary of the Treasury, the former chairman of the Federal Reserve System, and the former director of the Bureau of the Budget, have so acknowledged. Of the hardware-purchases portion of the arrangement, which represents sixty-one percent of the total, a substantial part, one-half being perhaps a conservative estimate, would have been purchased by the Germans in the United States in any event. The other portion of the plan, the financial arrangement, representing thirty-nine percent of the total, can be said to constitute only a deferral of the existing foreign exchange problem. To the extent that it relieves foreign exchange expenditures during the war in Vietnam, which may be considered a time of excessive overseas costs, the arrangement is commendable. On the other hand, there can be no certainty that the balance of payments situation will be better in the future, when the various loans provided under the agreement come due; and these loans do bear interest, although at a concessional rate. It is relevant to observe that since 1970, as Vietnam-related expenditures dropped, the balance of payments deficit has risen to unprecedented levels.

Another German effort to ameliorate the burden placed on the American balance of payments by military spending in Germany has been the Germans' assurance that they will not convert their dollar holdings into gold. This assurance was contained in a letter from Karl Blessing, the president of the Deutsche Bundesbank (the German Central Bank) to William McChesney Martin, the chairman of the Board of Governors of the Federal Reserve System, on March 30, 1967, confirmed by a letter the same day from Chancellor Kiesinger. Mr. Blessing's letter stated:

By refraining from dollar conversions into gold from the United States Treasury the Bundesbank has intended to contribute to international monetary cooperation and to avoid any disturbing effects on the foreign exchange and gold markets. You may be assured that also in the future the Bundesbank intends to continue this policy and to play its full part in contributing to international monetary cooperation.

However, by this letter the Germans did not promise to refrain from using the dollars they hold to settle international transactions. Also, it should be noted that subsequent to this declaration the Germans did convert $500 million of nonliquid "Roosa bonds" into liquid dollars for use in such transactions.

Since balance of payments difficulties have continued to mount in spite of such financial arrangements, the hard question becomes whether to undertake the major surgery of cutting the forces in Europe by about one-half or whether there is a better way to deal with the problem. Any larger cut than one-half could generate the military, and more likely the political, difficulties that the State Department fears. But the savings derived from cutting troops abroad by one-half would be rather inconsequential in face of the enormous American balance of payments deficit. It may well be that monetary steps such as those associated with the new Economic Stabilization Program, the first phase of which was announced by President Nixon on August 15, 1971, are a more appropriate way of dealing with the American balance of payments difficulties than any amelioration which troop reductions could provide. It is worth noting that, even in the presence of worsening balance of payments difficulties, the Administration has proposed a significant new program that will heighten the balance of payments deficit. This is the Navy's proposal for home-porting more of its ships abroad, particularly in Japan and Greece. This would imply that the Administration is not particularly concerned at the present time about the linkage between military forces stationed abroad and balance of payments.

As to the prospect of reducing the defense budget by returning troops from Europe, it should be noted that to return forces to the United States but to keep them in being here will not reduce budgetary expenditures. It costs the American taxpayer just about the same whether troops are kept in Europe or in the United States.

To answer the question whether it is appropriate to withdraw *and demobilize* American combat units now in Europe in order to achieve reductions in the overall American defense budget requires a consideration of the entire United States worldwide defense posture and the relationship of United States units in Europe to that posture. The Administration is reducing the total number of active Army divisions to thirteen. With the three Marine Corps divisions continuing, this would leave a total of sixteen active ground combat divisions still in being. Such a posture may require a greater reliance on reserve units, rapid mobilization and deployment methods, and the availability of single units to cover contingencies that were the responsibility of several units in the past. In this relatively quiescent time at most places along the East-West frontier, such a reduction in active forces seems appropriate.

For present purposes, however, the important point is that even at the present level of American forces—sixteen active ground combat divisions, or even the lower levels that have been suggested by some, about thirteen divisions—there would still be a substantial margin above the number necessary to meet the NATO peacetime commitment of eight active divisions, four and one-third in Europe and three and two-thirds in the United States, which are now earmarked for NATO. A similar observation holds true with respect to the Air Force's tactical air wings. That is to say, whatever number the total forces are likely to be reduced to, it can still include well over the number of units necessary to keep the present level of American forces in Europe.

As for this country's sharing the burden of defense with its European allies, the following statistics show that, as a percentage of gross national product, by per capita spending, and as a fraction of population serving in the country's armed forces, the United States in 1969 was devoting more to defense than its leading NATO allies:

	Defense Expenditures as % of GNP	Per Capita Defense Expenditures	Servicemen Per Thousand of Population
France	5.1	$121	11
Germany	4.7 *	107 *	8
Italy	3.1	43	9
United Kingdom	6.0	100	8
United States including Vietnam increase	8.7	389	17
excluding Vietnam increase	6.3	376	13

* Including Berlin expenditures.

From the foregoing statistics it might seem obvious that the United States is carrying too great a defense burden in comparison with its allies. Indeed, thoughtful commentators have so stated. For instance, Alain Enthoven and K. Wayne Smith wrote in the October, 1969, issue of *Foreign Affairs:*

The facts about NATO's burden-sharing are quite straightforward. The Europeans are spending a much smaller fraction of their GNP on defense than is the United States and this fraction continues to grow smaller.

However, the problem is not as simple as it may appear on its face, and in fact there is a respectable argument for the proposition that the Europeans are bearing just about their proper share of the defense burden of the NATO alliance. As in certain other cases, this "financial" question is as much a political one as it is an economic one. First, when the increase for Vietnam is excluded, we see that the American GNP percentage devoted to defense, 6.3 percent, is not much more than that of one of the leading allies, the United Kingdom, which devotes six percent of its GNP to defense. The second point, one often overlooked, is that the United States is a global power and its European allies are only regional powers. This country benefits from its preeminence. Probably the chief benefit is the right to have its finger on the nuclear trigger to the practical exclusion of its allies.

In slightly different terms, the United States, like the Soviet Union, but not like its European allies, has two (or more) frontiers to defend. The European allies have essentially only one frontier to guard. Thus, in terms of percentages of GNP, it may not be unreasonable for the United States to have to devote to defense twice as much as its European allies. It is not appropriate to count against the other members of the NATO alliance the cost of the American defense burden in the Pacific.

Next, let us calculate the percentages of American and European GNPs allocated to the defense of Europe. Taking the Brookings Institution figure of about $19 billion as the United States contribution toward general purpose forces devoted to this mission, let us add to that the portion of the American strategic budget of $18 billion which is properly allocable to Europe. It would not be fair to say that more than half of this $18 billion would be so allocable. Surely the United States pays this price of $18 billion more for the defense of the continental United States than for the defense of Europe. If we take $9 billion, or one-half of the strategic budget, as the amount of that budget allocable to Europe, this would produce a total of $28 billion as the American contribution to the defense of Europe. Actually, it is safe to say that much more than half of the cost to the U.S.A. of its strategic weapons is properly attributable to the direct defense of the American homeland.

If $28 billion is taken as the amount of the American contribution to the defense of Europe, that gives us a figure of 2.8 percent as the percentage of the trillion-dollar American GNP so allocated. When we compare this figure with the percentages of GNP devoted to defense by most of the leading European allies of the United States, we see that their contribution is one and one-half to two times greater. This is as it should be. A free Germany, for instance, is important to the United States—and therefore this country helps to maintain it—but it is worth more to the Germans themselves.

A further factor in the burden-sharing picture is that the United States has a much larger per capita income than its allies, so that it is a lot easier for Americans to bear a given percentage of GNP for defense. Six percent of this country's income devoted to defense is not as great a burden on its citizens as is the same percentage of the smaller incomes of its allies.

Thus, in the absence of any clear-cut reason for reducing American troops in Europe, the present level of forces might as well continue in order to preserve the military and political advantages which such a level provides. To place the issue in proper perspective, however, the next few pages attempt to show that these advantages are in fact only marginal.

If the present forces, now 300,000 men strong, were cut in half, with the remaining 150,000 distributed: 100,000 in Germany, 25,000 in the Sixth Fleet, and 25,000 elsewhere in Europe, and if a large portion of the forces withdrawn from Europe were kept in the United States in ready reserve, the threat to Western Europe in its four forms would not be noticeably different from what it is today.

This would be true even though the other NATO allies might well be unwilling to make up the difference in NATO forces in Europe created by such an American reduction. One hundred thousand American troops in Germany and 50,000 elsewhere in Europe would constitute a very substantial American military presence in Europe, giving clear and tangible evidence of the United States' continued commitment to the defense of Western Europe, in its own interest. Furthermore, NATO would still have a credible conventional defense, more than a "trip-wire," in view of the true nature of the threat.

To expect the Soviet Union to gamble on the success of a sudden all-out attack against NATO in the face of the West's nuclear deterrent and conventional reinforcement capability simply because the locus of American forces was shifted more to the United States would be nonsense. To believe that serious disorders in Eastern Europe might occur that could lead to uncontrollable fighting across the East-West frontier, without significantly degrading the Warsaw Pact's capacity for offensive tactics through the sector where the disorders occurred, and without providing sufficient political warning for adequate reinforcement of NATO forces, is to compound unlikelihood upon unlikelihood.

The Soviet Union would be no less deterred from attempting a limited probe than it is now. The imbalance for it between risk and gain would still be enormous. Not only would it be risking World War III for limited gain, but such tactics would lead NATO to increase its forces, as it did during the Berlin crisis of 1961. Such a threat, by definition, is of the type that would allow NATO a sufficient area for reinforcement. Furthermore, the most likely points for such Soviet tactics—Berlin one hundred miles behind the Soviet lines, northern Norway, the Thracian region of Greece and Turkey, and eastern Turkey—are not the sectors of the NATO front that are at present guarded by large numbers of American troops.

With respect to the risk of a political incursion, one must distinguish those forms of accommodation that are detrimental to American security interests from those other *détente*-oriented accommodations that have been endorsed by governments on both sides of the Atlantic. Examples of the latter are the German *Ostpolitik,* the SALT talks, the Berlin negotiations, and President Nixon's "Age of Negotiation" in general. A reduction in American forces, which most European leaders recently expected, would only tend to confirm their own assumption that the threat from the East is low; thus it is unlikely that, out of fear of the Soviet Union, they would appease the communists in any detrimental fashion.

As to any other form of political collapse in Western Europe, none appears likely today, but in some form it could, conceivably, occur over the course of time as a result of an unforeseeable chain of enormous social, political, military, and economic events. In that case, a reduction in American forces in the current time-frame would hardly be consequential. The assurance of American protection, based upon the NATO treaty, the many bonds of a social, cultural, commercial, and political nature, the still extremely large and important military relationship, and the evident interest of the United States in European security will yet remain a bulwark against an apocalyptic deterioration in the political fabric of Europe.

Moreover, for Italy, the country in NATO most susceptible to a communist political incursion, the level of American forces in Germany is not of prime importance. To the extent that marginal shifts in military power may affect the course of political events in Italy, it is the reassuring presence of the Sixth Fleet that is important.

In short, above a certain minimum level of American forces in Europe—and 150,000 distributed as suggested above is well above that level—a greater number of American forces there in this quiescent period contributes very little in added deterrence. Before a difference between 300,000 and 150,000 American troops becomes significant in deterring military attack or political incursion in Western Europe, the situation there must be subjected to marked and unexpected change for the worse, and a limited and orderly reduction of American military personnel itself will not bring about this change. As former presidential advisor McGeorge Bundy told the Senate Foreign Relations Committee in 1966 with respect to the American military presence in Europe: "The precise numbers are unimportant and the use of some of them as a strategic reserve when the European scene is quiet is simple good sense."

Two other risks sometimes mentioned in regard to reducing American troop levels in Europe are (1) that the countries of Western Europe may thereby be prompted to acquire new or greater nuclear forces of their own, or (2) the Germans may under circumstances of great stress seek to reunite their country by force. As to the first of these risks, 150,000 Americans are as credible evidence of a nuclear guarantee as are 300,000. Moreover, the economics of acquiring large-scale nuclear forces continue to be a great impediment. And if Germany were to acquire an independent nuclear force it would incur tremendous political disfavor among all its neighbors and in the United States.

As for the second risk, a unilateral German attempt at reunification by force, the European scene would have to change radically for this to become a possibility. In any event, a difference between 300,000 and 150,000 American troops would hardly increase German aspirations in this regard. On the contrary, to the extent that it might increase German uncertainty of American support, it would tend to discourage such a gamble.

A related concern lies in the unease with which some of Germany's neighbors, both in the West and in the East, might regard an American reduction in strength in Europe as making the present German military forces loom correspondingly larger. Already, however, the Germans have a ground force of twelve divisions and total forces of 460,000 men, compared to the United States' ground forces of four and one-third divisions and total forces in Germany of only 200,000 men. Moreover, although there would be some discomfort for Germany's neighbors from a relatively increased role for the *Bundeswehr,* it seems unlikely that this sentiment would prompt either Germany or the other countries of Europe to act contrary to Western defense interests.

That actual hostilities would break out on a large scale across the East-West frontier without any radical change in the political climate of Europe from what it is today and without any significant changes in the deployment of forces on both sides of the Iron Curtain is quite remote. Looking at that unlikely hypothesis, nevertheless, one can still conclude that NATO's capacity to fight a successful conventional war against the Warsaw Pact is not as inadequate as may have once been the case. The crucial factor would be the reinforcement capability on both sides.

Even to anticipate a surprise attack—an extremely unlikely event —NATO need only be sure to maintain the capacity for rapid reinforcement. The German reserve system, which the Federal Republic is now improving, should be able to provide promptly front-line forces in numbers that would measurably offset any reduction in the present level of American combat troops in Germany. The Germans have more than 750,000 ready reservists. Also, American airpower stationed in the United States could be available rapidly in a quantity equal to or greater than the number of aircraft and Air Force personnel to be redeployed to the United States. And the time for redeployment of American troops would be significantly cut by the operation of the C-5A transport, together with arrangements for pre-positioning certain equipment.

A Warsaw Pact attack would not push NATO forces off the continent. Even in the remote eventuality that the forces of East and West were tested in combat in a political climate little changed from that of the present, NATO's greater manpower pool, superior industrial might, and technological advantages could probably be brought to bear to defeat the attack without resort to ultimate weapons.

Whatever negative political consequences there might be from a reduction in American forces in Europe, they could be minimized by full and frank consultation with the other NATO members before any reductions were made. For example, such reductions could be proposed only as alternatives to other arrangements such as those mentioned above; reductions could be phased over a period of several years; and responsible American and European leaders could publicly make clear the actual significance—that is, the insignificance—of the American reductions. It could be shown that a reduction in the American military presence in Europe would in no way be intended as a lessening of the American willingness to come to Europe's defense, and the United States should be entitled to expect European political leaders to point out this fact to their constituents.

There are several further propositions to be considered in weighing the question of troop reduction. Counterbalancing the political disadvantages of somewhat disconcerting the allies of the United States are some positive political consequences in the direction of *détente*. Reducing American forces in Europe would be a clear signal to the Soviet Union that this country has no intention of challenging their control over Eastern Europe. This might well induce similar *détente*-oriented steps by them, either through troop reductions or through other East-West negotiations. If it did, the step would be well worth making, since it would not endanger Western security. It would also be consistent with the multitude of East-West negotiations now in progress directed toward improved relations.

The political gains to be derived from such a move are too conjectural at this point to serve as a basis alone for such a reduction, although their possibility counts for something in the total balance. Both Secretary Rusk and Secretary McNamara gave their approval to the reductions made in 1967 not only because of the financial savings but also in the hope that such a step might lessen East-West tensions through the process known as mutual example.

The present period is as appropriate as any likely one for making cuts in American troop strength. The shock of the French withdrawal in 1966 is well behind us, and the present French government is not as vocally antipathetic to the United States as was its predecessor. The Germans have signed the Non-Proliferation Treaty, so the divisive nature of that negotiation is past. Now in the White House is a President interested in Europe. The British have joined the Common Market. The German *Ostpolitik* has now been launched and is well under way with the signing of treaties with the Soviet Union and Poland. Furthermore, the Soviet Union is experiencing problems with communist China and with its own economy. Now in the Kremlin are relatively conservative bureaucrats, whose tenure is never certain. United States ground action in the Vietnam War has phased down. The crisis of the Czechoslovakian invasion has passed. As a result of that invasion, the countries of Eastern Europe are not likely to repeat Czechoslovakia's attempt towards freedom but, at the same time, they are not especially reliable from the Soviet point of view; witness the Polish riots of December, 1970.

There is also some historical evidence to support the conclusion that the deterrence represented by the American commitment to Europe can operate effectively without the presence of as many troops on the ground as the United States has today in Germany. In the late 1950s and early 1960s NATO's forces were significantly weaker vis-à-vis the Warsaw Pact than they are today. In 1961 NATO had only the equivalent of sixteen fully ready divisions in the center region, and in 1962 only twenty such divisions, instead of its present twenty-four in that region (including the two French divisions in Germany). Those lesser forces were adequate to deter the Soviet Union, and the communists were much more belligerent then than they appear to be now. To argue that this experience is irrelevant to the present question because the Soviet Union was in an inferior position to the United States in terms of nuclear weapons is to ignore the dynamics of nuclear deterrence, inasmuch as both superpowers had assured second-strike capabilities at that time.

Also, looking elsewhere than at the center region of NATO, one sees that the United States has been able to deter a Soviet attack against Greece and Turkey in the NATO area, Iran in the CENTO area, and Israel in the Middle East without the presence of large numbers of American combat forces stationed on the territory of those countries. And it is no answer to say that the heartland of Europe is a greater prize than these countries. The Turkish straits have been a prize sought by Russia for centuries. We similarly have faith in the capacity of the American deterrent to operate effectively against other communist would-be aggressors without the presence of large American ground combat forces, in Thailand, for instance, and now apparently even in Korea.

The recent experience in Turkey is particularly relevant. In that forward flank of NATO in recent years the number of American military personnel has been reduced by about seventy percent without damaging the deterrent.

The effect of the French withdrawal from NATO is likewise informative as to the quality of the deterrence provided by the alliance. This withdrawal from the alliance's military structure did not entice the Soviet Union to attempt even a limited assault upon NATO, nor was there a political collapse on the part of the other members of the alliance. Therefore, it would seem even less likely that an attack or a collapse would occur as a result of what is in fact a more modest change in the alliance's organization of force. The deterrence represented by the NATO alliance is much more durable than some believe.

The experience of the neutral countries in Europe is also of some relevance to the prospects for continued deterrence based upon the presence of 100,000 American servicemen in Germany and 50,000 elsewhere in Europe. Sweden and Austria have survived without the necessity of any basic accommodation to the Soviet Union detrimental to American interests in those countries. If those countries can stand firm without any American troops within their borders, it would seem that the members of NATO, with the continued presence of 150,000 American servicemen, can do at least as well.

Even West Germany, the NATO ally most eager to have the United States retain its present troop level in Europe, has indicated by its actions that it regards any actual threat as minimal. As an economy measure the West German government has been blocking the expenditure of a portion of its defense budget ever since 1967. For the 1970 budget the amount blocked was $300 million or 5.3 percent of that budget. The Germans have also indicated an intention to cut their conscription period from eighteen months to fifteen months (the period for U.S. draftees has been twenty-four months ever since 1951). And, of course, West Germany has launched upon a broad-gauged diplomatic effort toward normalizing relations with Eastern Europe, the *Ostpolitik,* including simultaneous negotiations with the Soviet Union, East Germany, and Poland.

There is no denying the fact that a rapid return to Europe of an American force of 150,000 in a time of tension would tend to increase those tensions. Offsetting this, however, are several points. First, before the present American units in Europe could become a first-class fighting force, there would have to be a deployment to Europe of thousands of American support personnel anyway. Second, a crisis would be more likely to develop gradually, with each side's reinforcements coming at a rate that in itself need not add significantly to the other factors increasing the tension. Third, the tension-building effect of a rapid return could be dissipated somewhat by recurring redeployments for exercise and other purposes, i.e., a continual floating, random deployment. Somewhat similar exercises are being carried on now with the troops sent home under the Reforger program. Fourth, there are some situations in which a controlled show of force is a good thing. The buildup of United States forces in Europe during the Berlin crisis of 1961 may have been such an instance. If the forces in question are in the United States, they are available to be moved to Europe as a demonstration of American determination. If they are in Europe, this step is not available, and other less convenient or more dangerous forms of demonstration might have to be taken.

Finally, there is at least one indication that the Defense Department itself believes the threat to Europe today is rather remote: the fact that it allows 227,000 dependents to be with American forces in Europe. The American military leaders thus acknowledge their faith that there would be sufficient warning to evacuate these people before any crisis came to a head.

To sum up, the debate over American troops in Europe has been out of focus on both sides. The tentative conclusion, however, would be this: since there seems to be no compelling financial reason at present for troop reductions, the existing level of American forces in Europe should be continued, at least in the absence of mutual East-West troop reductions, in order to avoid the marginal military and political disadvantages which could occur by disturbing the status quo.

TACTICAL NUCLEAR WEAPONS

An excessively large, and for that reason troubling, dimension of the American military presence in Europe today is the more than 7,000 nuclear warheads the American forces have there. This is far more than the number of such weapons that could conceivably be needed for either deterrence or actual defense. Such weapons were introduced into NATO defenses in the 1950s. The stockpile in Europe was greatly increased following the decision of the heads of government of the NATO countries in December, 1957, to reorient NATO's strategy around these weapons. This decision was explained in the official NATO publication *NATO Facts and Figures* as follows:

A new strategic concept was evolved, based largely on the assumption that it would be necessary to use nuclear weapons at the outset in response to any aggression that was not of a minor character. SACEUR * was requested by the North Atlantic Council to base his forward planning on the assumption that a large variety of nuclear weapons would gradually be introduced into the forces both of the NATO countries and of the Soviet bloc, and to take account of a levelling off of the defence expenditures in member countries.

All of these assumptions are now outmoded. NATO's strategy does not contemplate the immediate use of nuclear weapons at the outset of an attack. Instead, under the flexible-response doctrine, conventional arms would probably be used first. The Warsaw Pact has not introduced a large variety of tactical nuclear weapons into its forces. Instead the communists have opted only for weapons with relatively high yields. Furthermore, these weapons have not been deployed in great numbers in the satellite countries. Finally,

* Supreme Allied Commander, Europe.

the defense expenditures of the NATO members, particularly those of the United States, have not stayed at or near their 1957 levels.

The change in thinking since 1957 with respect to nuclear warfare in Europe was summed up by Secretary McNamara in 1967. "In the 1950s," he said, "our people were placing greater reliance on nuclear response than our political and military leaders were, and it is exactly the same thing that is happening in Western Europe today." It is not hard to discover the reasons for the declining enthusiasm among European leaders for this type of defense. The casualties and destruction likely to ensue from the firing of a small number of the 7,000 American warheads plus those which the other side would almost surely use are very high. On the assumption that the battlefield in Europe would be a front 155 miles long with a depth of thirty to sixty miles, the firing of only 100 tactical nuclear weapons with an average yield of 100 kilotons each could devastate about one-tenth of the area; 400 weapons of this type would inflict physical damage equal to six times that caused by all the bombing in World War II. The firing of 500 to 1,000 such weapons would devastate more than one-third of the area and leave the rest severely damaged. If these 500 to 1,000 weapons were all exploded in the air above the ground, 1,500,000 people would be exposed to lethal doses of radiation, 5,000,000 other people would be subjected to considerable but nonlethal doses, and the homes of 3,500,000 people would be destroyed. If such weapons were ground-burst, half the people of the area would be fatally or seriously injured and 5,000,000 people would lose their homes.* With the use of even more tactical nuclear weapons, some estimates of the probable fatalities run as high as 100,000,000.

The inherently improbable prospect that a tactical nuclear exchange could occur with only a modest level of casualties is rendered

* These statistics on probable casualties are from a United Nations study reported in *U.S. Naval Institute Proceedings,* October, 1969, p. 48; and a Western European Union Assembly study reported in George W. Herald, "New Challenges to NATO," *The New Leader,* November 4, 1968, p. 13.

even less likely by the fact that the Soviet Union, as mentioned above, has not designed its tactical nuclear weapons system for pinpoint, discreet targeting. It has instead chosen the higher yields, which are more suitable for blanketing barrages and striking at interdiction targets such as airfields and ports. That the United States does not need to keep 7,000 warheads in Europe is reinforced by the fact that the Soviets do not keep anywhere near that number in the satellite countries.

Of course, the extremely grave risks of escalation to intercontinental weapons, proliferation of nuclear weapons to other countries, and the "legitimization" of the use of nuclear weapons after the initial exchange should be self-evident.

Moreover, it is not clear that a war somehow limited to tactical nuclear weapons would favor the West. It would need airfields and ports as entries for reinforcements—tempting targets for Soviet strikes. The Soviet Union does not need such entry points to reinforce its ground forces. There is considerable doubt, also, whether tactical nuclear weapons could offset an existing imbalance in manpower, or whether they would particularly favor the defense over the offense. Such warfare would be so different from all hostilities that have ever before been fought that assumptions based upon conventional hostilities, such as the massing of troops for attack, would not apply. Command and control arrangements might well collapse. The battlefield would be totally chaotic, and the need to reestablish the decimated fronts of the opposing forces would tend to favor the side with the greater available reserve of manpower.

The continued presence of some tactical nuclear weapons in Europe is an important addition to the credibility of the Western deterrent, but the large number of such weapons there today creates risks and costs far out of proportion to their utility. The direct costs of the manning, maintenance, movement, storage, and manufacture of these weapons and their delivery systems amount annually to many hundreds of millions of dollars. The indirect costs—including the R & D attempts to design standard equipment to survive in a radioactive environment and the commitment to this function of resources such as aircraft and pilots that could be utilized better in other ways—increase the actual cost significantly.

There is also ever present the risk that some of these weapons could fall into the wrong hands. Whether ordinary military units or other factions could arm these weapons is not known, but American policymakers would nevertheless have to face some agonizing questions if any of these weapons were seized. A recollection of the Palomares incident is a convincing reminder of the enormous psychological consequences that would follow.

Another risk from the abundance of these weapons in forward positions lies in the effect they could have on the decision-making process itself during a period of crisis. For instance, their vulnerability to a preemptive strike might prompt a decision for their use before such would otherwise be absolutely necessary. Certainly SACEUR would want to get his nuclear-armed aircraft airborne as soon as possible to avoid their loss on the ground.

There is also a more intangible risk. The fact that these weapons are so numerous fosters an attitude of plausibility as to their use. The very size of the American tactical nuclear system in Europe today lends respectability to a belief that such weapons should be used in the event of general hostilities in Europe.

It could be added that a substantial reduction in the number of tactical nuclear warheads in Europe might improve the setting for other efforts at East-West arms limitations. Any gain in this direction accomplished by withdrawing half of these weapons now in Europe would outweigh any possible gain from their continued presence. So many nuclear weapons poised and pointed at the Soviet Union and its allies must be considered by them to be ominous and threatening. The installation of Soviet missiles in Cuba in 1962 was so viewed by the United States.

It should also be added that the presence of these weapons creates political difficulties in our relations with the countries in which they are located as a result of the secrecy and other restrictions attendant upon their location and movement.

There is no doubt that some high American military officers believe that it would be a "rational" choice in some situations for the United States to be the first to use these weapons. To the extent that such an attitude convinces the Soviet Union that this country may actually use such weapons, it has some value as a deterrent; but on the other hand it may confuse our own judgment, and to this extent, it is exceedingly dangerous.

X

Greece and Turkey

GREECE

The United States began to provide protection for Greece in the postwar era through the Truman Doctrine of 1947. The relationship deepened into full alliance when Greece joined NATO in 1952. Today the external threat to Greece is small. What danger there is from abroad comes mainly not from a communist country but from Greece's NATO ally Turkey, as a result of persistent differences over Cyprus. Even the situation on that troubled island is relatively quiescent. The two sides are conducting quiet negotiations, but so far with little progress. Both sides are eager, however, for the talks to continue.

To support NATO and American defense objectives in the eastern Mediterranean, the United States operates a number of military installations in Greece, including (1) a logistics facility at the Athens Airport, (2) the Sixth Fleet communications facility at Nea Makri near Athens, (3) the air station at Iraklion on Crete, (4) five outlying communications stations, (5) the NATO naval installation at Souda Bay, Crete, and (6) the NATO missile firing facility at Namfi, also on Crete. There are about 3,000 military personnel and about 4,000 dependents in Greece, including a seventy-two-man military advisory mission. The American military operating expenses and foreign exchange expenditures in the fiscal year 1970 were both $29 million. On February 5, 1972, the U.S. government announced plans to home-port a carrier task force of the Sixth Fleet at Piraeus, the port that serves Athens. This will mean an increase of about 10,000 Americans in Greece.

A Pentagon study several years ago recommended a ninety-five percent reduction in the American personnel level at the Athens Airport in order to save overseas costs. However, so far, only a relatively small cut has been made there.

Besides military installations, the United States also has three Voice of America facilities in Greece, one on the Island of Rhodes, which broadcasts to the Middle East in Arabic, one at Thessalonika, and one under construction at Kavalla. The latter two are for broadcasting to Eastern Europe.

In April, 1967, during a period of pre-election turmoil in Greece, some relatively low-ranking army officers, colonels, led by George Papadopoulos, overthrew the existing civilian authorities. The following December the King of Greece attempted his own counter-coup, but failed and now lives in exile in Italy. The colonels' coup apparently took the American diplomatic and military community by surprise. Before the coup the commanding general of the American military advisory group had hardly known these colonels because they had held positions well below the level at which he normally dealt. Some of the younger American officers knew them, however, as they had been classmates together at command and staff college in the United States in earlier years.

With the coming to power of a military junta in Greece, the relative effectiveness between American military officers, on the one hand, and American diplomats, on the other, in dealing with the Greek government shifted markedly in favor of the military. The Greek Foreign Office, the normal channel for diplomatic communication with the Greek government, declined in esteem and effect under the new order. Also, the junta was leery of American Embassy officials, who urged it to reform; whereas American military officers seemed to "understand" the military men of the junta. The rapport between these American officers and members of the Greek junta may well have gone to the point where it interfered with the efforts of American diplomats to improve political conditions in Greece.

The solution to a problem such as this, however, does not lie in eliminating all contact between American military officers and Greek officers. To end these contacts abruptly would remove this country's best channel of communication with military regimes such as that in Greece. Instead, the answer lies in careful guidance and direction of these American generals and admirals, necessarily turned diplomats, so that they foster overall American policy in such places.

The military regime that has existed in Greece since April, 1967, is not popular there, but it is accepted as the prevailing authority by a large portion of the Greek population. There are differing estimates as to how well the members of the regime would do if they ran for office in a general election. The greater the freedom allowed to opposition candidates to organize and campaign, of course, the less likely it would be that the colonels could win such an election.

At present there are about 350 to 400 political prisoners held in Greece. These are prisoners other than those who are incarcerated for acts of violence for which they would be imprisoned upon conviction under the American judicial system. At least during the early days of the regime, some prisoners were subjected to a degree of torture excessive even by the standards of what was customary in that part of the world.

The regime has, however, announced some steps toward the restoration of constitutional government, in part because of the quiet efforts of the American Embassy. On April 10, 1970, the requirement for warrants before arrests and certain other safeguards against arbitrary judicial process was reinstated. Then in June, 1970, the right of appeal from sentences imposed by courts-martial was re-established. Of even more significance, on August 10, 1970, the regime released about 500 of the political prisoners it was holding, and on December 19, 1970, the government announced the immediate release of 300 more prisoners. This latter announcement was reported in the *New York Times* under a headline that read "Greek Premier Sees No Democratic Rule in 1971." Since the August, 1970, release the number of political prisoners has been no greater than the number incarcerated during the Karamanlis government of 1956–58. Furthermore, the present number of prisoners is less than the number in prison for an extended period under the liberal government of George Papandreau. When Papandreau came to office, there were 959 political prisoners. The Papandreau government did not increase this number, but it did not immediately release most of those whom it found incarcerated when it came to office. Instead, it gradually reduced the number to seventeen over the four years in which Papandreau was Prime Minister. Also in August, 1970, the Papadopoulos regime allowed many who formerly had been active politicians to travel abroad once again.

Some indication of the level of tolerance toward the press in Greece is the fact that the published transcript of the Symington Subcommittee hearings on Greece was carried in its entirety in at least one Greek newspaper.

Many of the laws needed to implement the Greek constitution have now been enacted. This does not mean, however, that general elections will ensue. The regime shows no inclination to call such elections in the near future. Perhaps the following statement by the former foreign minister Averoff rather accurately describes the situation in Greece today:

The reality in Greece is that the situation has been improved, that we live under a dictatorship that is more lenient but that individual liberties have not been reestablished, that human dignity is trampled upon and that the conditions for a return to democracy have not been created.

On the contrary, it appears that conditions are being created for a very long prolongation of the dictatorship under the comic masks of democracy.*

A large number of Greeks believe that the United States supports the present government. The basis for this assumption rests in factors such as the continuation of American military assistance to the regime, frequent visits to Greece by high American military officers (more than 100 in the first three years following the coup), a visit by Vice President Spiro T. Agnew, the presence of American military facilities, and our continued diplomatic relations.

At the time of the coup the American military assistance program for Greece stood at $70.4 million. Shortly after the coup, to indicate American disapproval, a selective suspension was imposed on such assistance, restricting delivery of the larger types of equipment. The United States continued to provide small arms, ammunition, communications equipment, and trucks to Greece. Following the Soviet invasion of Czechoslovakia in August, 1968, even this partial suspension was relieved, in part to allow for the delivery of $28 million of major items, including F-102 aircraft and self-propelled artillery. On September 22, 1970, however, the entire suspension was lifted by the United States in the belief that its usefulness had been exhausted. The $56 million of suspended items are being delivered to Greece over a two-year period.

For the first three years following the coup, the level of deliveries of American military assistance, including excess equipment and in spite of the suspension, were as follows:

Fiscal Year	Millions
1968	$47.5
1969	$81.8
1970	$46.5

* Staff report of the Senate Committee on Foreign Relations, 92nd Cong., 1st sess., *Greece: February, 1971* (1971), p. 15.

Besides the aircraft and artillery mentioned above, these deliveries included F-104, F-5, and training aircraft as well as helicopters, sidewinder missiles, minesweepers, trailers and trucks. In short, the American embargo on military assistance was always only partial, and even the portion suspended was partially relieved in 1968. During the suspension a large part of the American public had the mistaken impression that military assistance to Greece had been virtually terminated. To many of the Greek people, on the other hand, it appeared that most of the aid was continuing. However, to those Greeks who were aware of the aid suspension, both within the regime and among the opposition, the embargo was not popular. Even those opposed to the regime did not wish to see Greece's defenses against the Soviet bloc impaired.

The amount of American military assistance programmed for Greece in each of those years, excluding any excess equipment, was as follows:

Fiscal Year	Millions
1968	$39.1
1969	$37.5
1970	$24.5

The amount programmed in a particular year is not the same as the amount delivered that year because of factors such as delivery time and the suspension.

No NATO country besides the United States has provided grant military assistance to Greece since the coup. Before the coup, West Germany had provided sizeable military assistance. Also, lesser military assistance had been provided by Canada, Belgium, Italy, Luxembourg, and the United Kingdom. However, some NATO countries, including West Germany and France, are selling military equipment to the new regime in Greece.

There are at least four competing considerations for the United States in dealing with the regime in Greece. First is the important cultural, sentimental, historical, and ethnic attachment to Greece, which makes the presence of an undemocratic and repressive regime there repugnant to many Americans. (Qualifying this consideration somewhat, however, is the little-publicized fact that a majority of the Greek-Americans are probably not unsympathetic to the present regime in Greece.)

Second, American identification with such a regime through military assistance and cooperation has negative consequences for this country's reputation elsewhere in the world, as well as for the image we hold of ourselves.

A third consideration, on the other hand, is that Greece provides this country with some military facilities which contribute to the overall American military position in the Mediterranean. These facilities do have some value for the United States, but there are alternatives available for each of them. The Nea Makri communications station, for instance, was built entirely of mobile units in order that it could be rapidly and economically moved elsewhere if necessary. In fact, the expenditures for military assistance to Greece since the coup would probably have paid for relocating most of the necessary facilities.

The fourth consideration is that Greece occupies a geographic position that is important both in checking communist entry into the Mediterranean basin and for staging operations into the Middle East. There is little likelihood, however, that the authorities in Greece will seek to withdraw from NATO no matter what steps the United States is likely to take toward that country, and so long as the United States commitment to Greece represented by NATO continues, the Soviet bloc is not likely to try to seize that country. To justify full American military assistance and cooperation for the Greek regime by saying, "NATO needs Greece," is to oversimplify the matter and to fail to consider precisely what Greece's contribution to NATO is.

As for staging operations into the Middle East, however, Greece can be expected to be more cooperative than any other country in the area in time of crisis. This consideration is perhaps the most significant one favoring good relations between the United States and the Greek government.

Another mistaken assumption concerning Greek-American relations is that the United States can do little toward restoring legality in Greece. The continued good will of the most powerful country in the world must certainly be important to a country in as exposed a position as Greece. There are few places other than the United States to which the colonels can turn for military protection. They cannot obtain this help from the communist bloc. Although they may be able to purchase military equipment from countries such as France, large amounts of grant assistance can come only from this country. Although the Greeks on the peninsula and home islands are reasonably secure from attack—in its own interest the United States would not with to withdraw its NATO commitment—the security of the Greek Cypriots is another matter. Their protection lies, as in the past, in a willingness on the part of the United States to take strong measures on their behalf. Furthermore, an assumption of helplessness on the part of the United States to ameliorate the political situation in Greece ignores the improvements already made there, for which American insistence has been in part responsible.

The steps yet to be taken toward political freedom in Greece include greater freedom of the press, the release of the remaining political prisoners, the reestablishment of political parties, and the holding of elections. Whether such steps will be taken in the foreseeable future is problematical.

TURKEY

In 1960 certain military officers in Turkey seized power in that country but returned governmental control to civilian authorities one year thereafter. For the better part of the next ten years, the country held regular elections, enjoyed a free and active press, and generally observed the other provisions of its constitution. Then in March, 1971, Turkish military officers interceded once again to depose the existing government and establish a new one more to their liking.

The United States defense relationship with Turkey, like that with Greece, was conceived in the Truman Doctrine of 1947 and grew into full alliance in 1952, when Turkey also joined NATO. Both major political parties in Turkey support the alliance. Only the procommunist Labor Party, which received a mere two and one-half percent of the vote in the last general election, is opposed to Turkish membership in NATO.

The United States has military facilities at over twenty locations in Turkey. Since 1957 it has had a tactical fighter unit at Incerlik near Adana, and until recently another one at Cigli near Izmir. At Ankara and Izmir are large American headquarters and logistics support elements known as the United States Logistics Group (Turkey), or TUSLOG. Twenty-four TUSLOG activities function in about ten buildings in downtown Ankara, and further units are located in the Ankara suburb of Balgat. In Izmir are twenty TUSLOG facilities, including warehouses, motor pools, personnel support offices, schools, and medical facilities. Among their other responsibilities, these facilities support the NATO headquarters known as LANDSOUTHEAST and the 6th Allied Tactical Air Force, both located in the Izmir area. There are about 800 American military personnel and 1,400 dependents in the Izmir area, including more than 500 officers and men at these headquarters units. In addition, the United States has an air station at Karamursel on the Sea of Marmara and some communications and other facilities elsewhere in Turkey.

In 1967–68, there were about 24,000 American military personnel and dependents in Turkey. By the fiscal year 1970 this number had been reduced to about 18,000, and in the fiscal year 1971 it was reduced further to approximately 16,000. In fiscal 1972 it was reduced again to 7,000. The operating costs for American military facilities in Turkey in the fiscal year 1970 were $90 million, and the foreign exchange expenditures were $45 million. These installations are, of course, available for NATO operations against the Soviet Union. It is doubtful, however, whether they could be used to support other military operations in the area except for limited humanitarian relief.

The significant number of American military activities in the heart of two of Turkey's leading cities, Ankara and Izmir, as well as a few in Istanbul, have been a source of friction for Turkish-American relations. One striking example was the motion-picture theater located in a congested neighborhood in downtown Ankara and reserved exclusively for the entertainment of American military personnel and their families. Although this theater was identified as a problem for American-Turkish relations as early as 1959, it was not until 1970 that it was moved to another location. Not only was the theater a cause of traffic congestion, it was also a symbol of American privilege, reminding Turks of the old rights of extraterritoriality formerly enjoyed by the European powers. Another instance of American-Turkish difficulties was the strike in 1969 by the Turkish employees of the Air Force's maintenance contractor, the Tumpane Company.

The leaders of Turkey's opposition parties have from time to time accused the government of being too lenient in allowing the American armed forces to operate in Turkey with little restriction. To counter this charge, the government of Prime Minister Demirel insisted upon a new base-rights agreement with the United States, which was signed on July 3, 1969. Although the Turks sought to make the American defense commitment more specific in this agreement, no such language was ultimately adopted. The agreement is basically a codification of the numerous existing agreements that have been entered into over the twenty years or so of American military presence in Turkey. The agreement permits the United States unilaterally to reduce its personnel and to withdraw from any base.

The cause of the greatest controversy in Turkey's relations with this country, however, has been the Cyprus issue. The United

States first involved itself with Cyprus in support of the London and Zurich Accords of 1959, under which the independent status of the island was guaranteed. Under this multinational agreement the United States authorized both Turkey and Greece to transfer to Cyprus certain specified items of military equipment provided to them under the American military assistance program.

The crisis in American-Turkish relations over Cyprus came in June, 1964, when Turkey was on the verge of launching military operations on the island to protect the Turkish Cypriots. To stave off open hostilities between two members of the NATO Alliance, President Johnson informed the Turkish Prime Minister Inonu that such action on the part of his military forces would jeopardize the American guarantee to defend Turkey in the event of Soviet intervention. In the face of this direct assertion by the United States, the Turks desisted, literally at the eleventh hour. The bluntness of this statement by the American President has left a scar on our relations with Turkey ever since, but warfare was averted. Another Cyprus crisis developed in 1967, and this time the United States was able to prevent hostilities by inducing the Greeks to step down.*

Further friction between the United States and Turkey has arisen from ship visits by the Sixth Fleet to Turkish ports. On the visit of a carrier and five destroyers to Istanbul in July, 1968, ten or twelve American sailors had to leap into the water to avoid an angry crowd. In connection with another visit by an American carrier and three destroyers to Istanbul in February, 1969, three Turks were killed by other Turks in a scuffle arising from a demonstration over the visit. Then in December, 1969, when an American cruiser and four other vessels were visiting Izmir, several of the Americans stationed in that city were harassed. Since then, to avoid such inci-

---

* The 1964 letter to the Turkish Prime Minister from President Johnson reflects a little appreciated fact about American relations with its allies and clients. That is that the United States does have considerable (albeit not unlimited) power to influence these other countries along lines it thinks appropriate. This point is discussed further in Chapter XIII.

dents, fewer ships participate in any particular visit, and such visits are made to smaller ports more often than in the past.

The United States provides Turkey with both economic and military assistance. In the fiscal year 1970, economic assistance was $43 million (plus $54 million of foodstuffs), and military assistance was $100 million. Besides providing equipment for a NATO ally, this military assistance gives the United States some degree of influence with the important Turkish general staff. American policymakers hope to end grant economic assistance to Turkey by the mid-1970s and to convert military assistance to forms other than grant aid by that time.

A final consideration is Turkey's position at the entrance to the Black Sea. Under the Montreux Convention, which regulates the passage of warships through the Turkish straits, Soviet naval vessels must pass in daylight and identify themselves. This is important to the United States in keeping up with the number and location of Soviet vessels in the Mediterranean Sea. Under the same restrictions, destroyers from the American fleet have regularly passed through these straits into the Black Sea ever since 1959 to demonstrate that it is an international body of water. In the last several years, the Soviet Union has not expressed any particular concern over these Black Sea movements.

XI

Spain and Portugal

SPAIN

The United States has more than 8,000 military personnel and more than 13,000 dependents in Spain, most of whom are stationed on four bases: Rota, Torrejón near Madrid, Zaragoza, and Morón. Rota's primary missions are to support a squadron of Polaris submarines, to serve as a base for naval reconnaissance aircraft, and to provide a point for long-haul and naval communications. Torrejón is the home base for a wing of F-4 aircraft, detachments of which are deployed forward to Italy and Turkey. Following the recent closing of Wheelus Air Base in Libya, Zaragoza was reactivated, and 600 men stationed there, to support a nearby bombing range for the use of American Air Force units stationed elsewhere in Europe. Since 1970 Morón Air Base has been officially on a standby status but, even so, it had 521 American military personnel assigned in 1970, only fifty fewer than in 1969, when it was on active status. The United States also has a military assistance advisory group in Spain of fifty-five personnel. The operating costs for these facilities in the fiscal year 1970 were $90 million and the foreign exchange costs were $50 million.

In addition to the bases themselves, a significant factor to be considered in the defense relationship with Spain is the right of the United States to overfly Spanish territory to reach the Mediterranean. However, freedom to exercise this right and to use the bases in some Mediterranean area contingencies is somewhat problematical.

The presence of American bases and military personnel in Spain for seventeen years has been important in attracting American investment and tourism to Spain and in building prestige for the Spanish government both at home and abroad. This presence has probably also contributed somewhat to the liberalization of Spanish society.

The United States first established bases in Spain in 1953, in the wake of the Korean war, for the short-legged SAC B-47 bombers. This initial presence was authorized by a base-rights agreement on September 26, 1953, which merely allowed the establishment of American bases in return for military equipment. Eager to establish a Polaris base near the Mediterranean ten years later, the United States renewed the agreement and, at the request of Spain, made the following declaration:

> The two governments recognize that the security and integrity of both the United States and Spain are necessary for the common security. A threat to either country, and to the joint facilities that each provides for the common defense, would be a matter of common concern to both countries, and each country would take such action as it may consider appropriate within the framework of its constitutional processes.

The United States also agreed at that time to prior consultation with the Spanish before making any major changes in the equipment on or the use of the bases. It is not clear whether this "consultation" is tantamount to a requirement for their consent, as in Japan, or not, as in the Philippines. In any event, as elsewhere, this country would be very reluctant to use its bases for a purpose expressly disapproved by the host country.

The State Department argued before the Senate Foreign Relations Committee that the declaration quoted above did not constitute a defense commitment but only acknowledgment of the inherent right of our armed forces to defend themselves. However, if the declaration did mean as little as this, it is curious that the Spanish were so anxious to have it stated. It is an equally acceptable interpretation of this language that the United States was acknowledging that a threat to Spain would indeed constitute a threat to the bases and hence necessitate action on the part of this country. Under this interpretation, the bases constituted the device by which the United States attempted to satisfy Spain's insistence upon something in the way of a defense commitment.

In the course of the hearings in 1970 on the new agreement with Spain, Under Secretary Johnson practically conceded that the language in the 1963 agreement was a defense commitment, although subsequently he was to take a different position. He informed the Foreign Relations Committee on July 24, 1970:

. . . let me say during our discussions with the Spanish [over the new agreement] in their efforts to get language which I would interpret as a commitment they pushed very, very strongly for getting this language that was in the Joint Declaration of 1963. I have said that we could not do that without entering into a mutual defense treaty, and this was a road that we did not want to go.

Following the expiration of this agreement in 1968, the two countries entered into a two-year extension of the agreement to September 26, 1970, after extensive negotiations over the quid pro quo to be paid by the United States. The Spanish initially requested a very large amount of military assistance for five years. Following military-to-military discussions and after strong objections from the Senate Foreign Relations Committee, however, the agreement was to reduce the price tag to $50 million for a two-year period. During the course of the negotiations General Wheeler informed the

Spanish: "By the presence of United States forces in Spain the United States gives Spain a far more visible and credible guarantee than any written document."

These negotiations in 1968 added yet another step in the ever-closer defense relationship with Spain. These talks involved high-ranking American military officers' joining with their Spanish counterparts to arrive at a common assessment of the threat to Spain and a joint determination as to respective missions for the two armed forces. Although the United States may have adopted this procedure in the hope of reducing the Spanish price for continuation of its bases, it comes as no surprise that the Spanish readily accepted it as drawing them closer to the mutual defense relationship they have always sought.

The public impression created by the press accounts of these joint military discussions somewhat missed the point, however. Skeptical news correspondents gave the impression that American generals were secretly agreeing directly with the Spanish that the United States would come to the defense of Spain in the event of hostilities of various types. The actual risk was of a much more indirect nature. It arose from the almost imperceptible dynamics of ongoing defense programs. Generals Wheeler and Burchinal, the main military participants in this affair, acting basically at the request and direction of the State Department, did not contractually commit the United States to defend Spain, but their dealings with the Spanish in threat assessment and mission allocation added still another bond between Spain and the U.S. government. Since these talks were rather carefully controlled and reviewed, however, it seems in hindsight that they probably added little risk of overinvolvement. If they saved a few million dollars in quid pro quo, as they probably did, the benefit they achieved probably outweighed any risk they may have added.

In many instances in foreign policy such as this one, positive and negative values must be weighed against each other. Too often, public commentators fail to present this balance. Reporting may be incomplete and may suggest stupidity or even malevolence on the part of government officials, while in fact they are trying diligently and quietly to resolve the hard question of competing considerations.

On August 6, 1970, the United States and Spain signed a new five-year agreement which in some ways reshaped and broadened the relationship. The Spanish sought an agreement this time that would cover such subjects as education, science, and agriculture, instead of military matters alone. The Spanish did this in order to establish a closer relationship with the United States in numerous fields, also to deemphasize the military terms in the agreement, and perhaps to extricate themselves gracefully from the awkward position of having sought without success in the previous negotiations an incredible amount of military equipment.

The language of the new agreement no longer ties American defense support for Spain to the defense of the bases, as was explicitly done in the 1963 joint declaration. Both sides promise to "make compatible their respective defense policies . . . and . . . grant each other reciprocal defense support." It goes on to say that each "will support the defense system of the other and make such contributions as are deemed necessary and appropriate to achieve the greatest possible effectiveness of those systems to meet possible contingencies. . . ."

It also commits the United States to an attempt to establish a Spanish liaison presence at certain NATO headquarters and to create a joint Spanish-American defense committee similar to the one the United States has with Japan, on which will sit the American Ambassador and, as his military advisor, CINCEUR,* who happens also to be the commander of NATO forces in Europe. The agreement also obligates this joint committee to "prepare and present . . . an annual plan to facilitate making compatible . . . respective defense policies in areas of mutual interest."

* Commander-in-Chief, United States Forces in Europe.

Under this agreement also the American air defense role in Spain will be coordinated more closely with Spanish forces, increased in capability, and more fully integrated into the overall European air defense network.

The quid pro quo under this agreement includes F-4 aircraft, equipment for the Spanish army, machine tools, several naval vessels, and the turnover of the existing American military pipeline in Spain. This military equipment will be provided to Spain through the utilization of Export-Import loans (which bear commercial interest rates and must be repaid), excess equipment, and grant assistance. The total of such assistance requiring current expenditures by the United States averages about $14 million per year, for each of the five years of the agreement, which is less than the amount for Greece, slightly more than the amount for Ethiopia, and about fourteen times the amount provided to Portugal or Morocco.

The Administration claimed that the present agreement, like its predecessors, represented no defense commitment to Spain. To reinforce this proposition, the Senate adopted on December 11, 1970, a resolution introduced by Senator Church, stating it to be the sense of the Senate that nothing contained in the present agreement "be construed as a national commitment by the United States to the defense of Spain."

Whether this new agreement is tantamount to a defense commitment or something less, what it provides, as outlined above, is still so important that it should have been submitted as a treaty. Senator Javits was the leading exponent of this position on the Foreign Relations Committee. The State Department suggested that to submit the agreement to the Senate for ratification might have implied a defense commitment that was never intended. To avoid this result, it would seem that a senatorial understanding expressed in the legislative history or appended to the ratification itself making clear that no such defense commitment was intended would have sufficed. The language could have been very similar to that of the Church resolution.

Both the Symington Subcommittee and the full Committee on Foreign Relations time and again inquired as to the actual need for the American bases in Spain. In most instances they were given only a conclusion: that the bases should be kept (because of growing Soviet naval strength in the Mediterranean); or they were given elaborate and, it seemed to the committee, unrealistic argumentation about the enormous expense involved if the United States should cease to have those bases.

With respect to the Polaris base at Rota, the committee was told that to lose it would require this country to expend enormous sums to procure more Polaris submarines if it was to keep the same number of boats on station at all times. For instance, on April 22, 1970, Deputy Secretary of Defense Packard said to the Foreign Relations Committee:

If we could base the submarines in the United States, it would require [deleted] more submarines to have the same ready force in target distances from the Soviet Union. Simply because of the transit time, it would cost more and that particular thing is a strictly economic calculation to figure out what the costs are whichever way we went.

There are two important facts to the contrary, however. First, a Polaris base is essentially only a highly mobile submarine tender that could be stationed elsewhere, such as at Holy Loch or in the Azores. Second, and more basic, is the fact that in light of the survivability of these submarines wherever they may be at sea, having them on station as much as we do may be desirable but is not absolutely necessary. The Soviets have never achieved such a high degree of readiness in number of submarine-launched missiles.

Turning to the F-4 wing at Torrejón, the Foreign Relations Committee was told by the Deputy Commander of American Forces in Europe that these aircraft have no mission in Spain itself besides defending themselves. They are there solely as a rear echelon for forward positions in Italy and Turkey. This forward deployment could also be achieved through a rotation pattern from other bases in NATO-Europe or from the United States.

With respect to the few maritime patrol aircraft stationed at Rota, the senators were told that, to remove them, the United States would have to purchase an entire additional unit of such aircraft at very substantial cost. The senators were not informed, but it is reasonable to believe, that if American forces were actually required to leave Spain, this mission would probably be covered by similar aircraft based in Sicily, Sardinia, or the Azores without additional aircraft.

As to the need for a bombing range in Spain, the committee was told that the alternative would be to do similar training in the United States at an additional cost of many millions of dollars. The more plausible alternative, not mentioned, would be a tightening of the training schedule at available ranges elsewhere in Europe, including Sardinia and Turkey.

In 1969 the Defense Department assured the Symington Subcommittee that the Naval Communications Station at Rota "is a key communications link in the unilateral control of U.S. Naval forces in the Eastern Atlantic and Mediterranean . . . a necessary link in the Sixth Fleet command and control system." Nevertheless, a year later this station went off the air.

Deputy Secretary of Defense Packard also argued to the Foreign Relations Committee that the right to overfly Spain to get into the Mediterranean was as important as base rights in that country. However, flights from the United States itself could almost as easily pass over the Straits of Gibraltar, and flights from Western Europe could probably pass over France as readily as Spain.

In short, the American military presence in Spain obviously adds something to this country's overall military strength, but to portray it as virtually irreplaceable is misleading.

There is no serious external or internal threat to Spain today. Therefore, the risk of American involvement in actual hostilities in Spain is minimal. Although Spain has a disagreement with Morocco over the future of Spanish Sahara, and over the Spanish enclaves in North Africa, Ceuta, and Melilla, as well, this is not likely to result in open hostilities.

The recent dispute with Great Britain over the status of Gibraltar has also quieted down somewhat. Had hostilities broken out between Spain and Great Britain over this matter, the United States could have found itself in a very awkward position, with American bases in Spain and military assistance to that country, including antiaircraft missiles facing Gibraltar and, on the other hand, the American NATO commitment to Great Britain. Presumably, as in the earlier confrontations between Greece and Turkey, American diplomatic steps would have been sufficient to avert actual hostilities.

Even with Franco's passing, it is not likely that Spain will be plunged into serious internal disorder. (It is worth noting that no such trouble occurred when the Salazar regime ended in Portugal.) Therefore, American policy toward Spain should not be based on an assumption that internal strife is likely to occur.

Since September, 1965, the United States has conducted various types of joint exercises with Spanish forces, including an unconventional warfare exercise known as Pathfinder Express. In this instance American forces joined Spanish forces in a scenario which envisaged the quelling of an internal revolt. Following discovery of this exercise by the Symington Subcommittee, the activity was discontinued.

Some publicists concluded that this exercise might have led the United States into defending the Franco regime against its internal foes. However, renewal of any widespread insurgency in Spain is exceedingly remote; and even if insurgency were to break out, it is hard to see how the exercise in question would involve the United States in an internal struggle. The fault of the exercise was rather that it implied that it was American policy to favor the Franco government against whatever internal foes it might have.

PORTUGAL

The United States has one major base on Portuguese territory, Lajes Air Base in the Azores, with 1,600 American military personnel and 2,800 dependents there. Operating costs in the fiscal year 1970 were $19 million and foreign exchange costs were $4 million. For most of the last ten years American rights at Lajes stemmed only from the NATO Treaty itself and an ad hoc understanding with Portugal following the expiration in 1962 of a formal base rights agreement. Recently, however, the United States and Portugal finally entered into a new base rights agreement, to which the Senate Foreign Relations Committee has objected on the grounds that the agreement should have been submitted to it as a treaty. American military assistance to Portugal has been about $1 million per year, and has avoided items that could be of use in Portugal's colonial wars in Africa.

Lajes serves as a transit point for military airlift aircraft flying between the United States and Europe, as well as a base for a few antisubmarine warfare aircraft, search and rescue operations, and communications. All major airlift aircraft, including the C-130 and the C-141, can now make the transatlantic hop without landing in the Azores.

XII

Ethiopia and Morocco

ETHIOPIA

The United States has no mutual defense treaty with Ethiopia. From time to time there have been American expressions of support for the security and territorial integrity of Ethiopia. It is one of the four countries in the world where the United States has a major military facility without a defense treaty, the others being Spain, Morocco, and Cuba.

The United States' installation in Ethiopia, Kagnew Station at Asmara, dates from World War II. Its status was made formal under a base agreement signed May 22, 1953, which allows this country to retain the facility until 1978. On the same day in 1953 that the base agreement was signed, a military assistance agreement was also executed. Although this latter agreement makes no reference to the base, it is generally acknowledged that a substantial portion of the military assistance provided to Ethiopia constitutes a quid pro quo for Kagnew Station.

At Kagnew there are about 1,800 military personnel and about 1,300 dependents. Its functions include a communications relay as part of the worldwide defense communications system, an earth terminal for the defense satellite communications system, ship-to-shore communications for naval vessels in the area, and high-frequency transmission for diplomatic telecommunications. Because of its remote location in the American defense communications system, Kagnew serves some of the least-used trunks in the system, such as the long leap from Africa across the Indian Ocean. Its naval communications usually support only about six American naval vessels in the Indian Ocean and Persian Gulf area. Operating costs at Kagnew are $16 million a year and foreign exchange costs run $9 million.

At present there is no strong opposition within Ethiopia to the continuation of the base. On his tour of Africa in February, 1970, Secretary Rogers reaffirmed that it was American policy worldwide not to attempt to continue to maintain a facility such as Kagnew if the government involved wanted it closed.

Under the 1953 military assistance agreement, the United States has now provided Ethiopia with military equipment and training worth over $159 million. This amount represents almost one-half of all the military assistance provided by the United States to African countries. In the fiscal year 1970 Ethiopia was provided with military assistance worth $12 million, which constituted two-thirds of all United States military assistance to Africa that year.

For the sake of comparison, the other African recipients of American military assistance in the fiscal year 1970 were as follows:

	Millions		Millions
Tunisia	$3.0	Libya	$.2
Congo	1.8	Nigeria	.1
Morocco	.8	Ghana	.1
Liberia	.5		

The amount of grant military assistance to Morocco, $800,000, is of particular significance since the United States has a facility there, Kenitra, the functions of which are similar to those of Kagnew. Nevertheless, the exceptionally large amount of military assistance provided to Ethiopia, in comparison to other African countries, is due to the presence of Kagnew.

In 1960 the former Italian and British colonies of Somaliland on Ethiopia's southern and southeastern borders united to form the independent Somali Republic. It immediately called for the union, under its sovereignty, of all ethnic Somalis, including those living in the Ogaden province of Ethiopia. In response to this potential threat Emperor Haile Selassie anxiously sought to strengthen Ethiopia's defenses through assistance from abroad. On August 29, 1960, the United States agreed to provide the equipment and training for expanding the Ethiopian armed forces to 40,000 men, subject to congressional authorization and appropriation of the necessary funds. This was done to forestall a similar offer by the Soviet Union and to preserve the American position at Kagnew.

This commitment also expressed United States support for the security and territorial integrity of Ethiopia. This government meant, by this expression, support in the form of military equipment and training and the use of American political support at the United Nations and elsewhere in the event of hostilities. Some writers have tried to make more out of this document than it deserves.

When the Somali Republic also sought military assistance here, the United States was reluctant to provide it because of the relationship with Ethiopia. The Somalis turned to the Soviets and received $35 million in military assistance in 1963, leading ultimately to the stationing of about 200 Soviet advisors in Somalia. The Ethiopians then sought and obtained from this country more military assistance including F-5 fighter planes.

Nevertheless, Somalia, with a population of 12,500,000 and an army of 13,500, would be little match for the Ethiopians. More difficult for the Ethiopians to control are the nomadic Somali tribesmen who roam across the border at will. Since 1967 there has been a sort of *détente* in Somali-Ethiopian relations, and that *détente* has survived the coup in Somalia that occurred in 1969.

Since 1953 the United States has had a Military Assistance Advisory group (MAAG) in Ethiopia. At present it consists of 104 personnel led by a brigadier general. In 1966 a special team of 164 Army personnel was sent to Ethiopia in an effort to increase the professionalism of the Ethiopian Army. This team stayed in Ethiopia for two and one-half years, extending its originally scheduled stay by some eighteen months. Since 1964 other small American Special Forces units, known as Mobile Training Teams, have been sent to Ethiopia for brief periods to provide instruction in civic action work. According to Administration witnesses, this has included projects such as road-building, medical care, and well-digging. For instance, a fifty-five-man unit was sent in 1964. Another unit, of twelve men, was sent for a twenty-six-week period in 1968. All American military personnel, both those permanently stationed in Ethiopia and those sent on special assignment there, are instructed not to go on operational missions. They are allowed to go to the smaller unit headquarters of the Ethiopian forces, such as company headquarters, but they are not regularly assigned to that level.

Ethiopia is a country of 24,000,000 inhabitants, composed of forty ethnic groups, of whom the dominant two are the Amharas and the Tigres. The country is ninety-five percent illiterate and extremely poor. Most of its people live outside of the money economy, and its per capita income, based mostly on estimates, is only $64 a year, one of the lowest in Africa. The extent of the country's actual resources is yet unknown. Despite its being a very traditional society under the impact of modern scientific and technological innovation, Ethiopia achieved in the 1970s the respectable growth rate of five percent per annum. The country's rate of investment is 12.6 percent of GNP.

Emperor Haile Selassie, born in 1891, has ruled Ethiopia in a highly personal fashion for fifty-six years. His death is not expected to affect Kagnew Station.

Ethiopia now has armed forces of 38,000 men, of whom 35,000

are in the army. These forces do not constitute a large portion of the Ethiopian population in comparison with the size of other armed forces in Africa. In light of the potential threat to Ethiopia, however (Somalia's armed forces are about 15,000 men, the Sudan's about 25,000 and the insurgents in Eritrea 2,000), and in competition with the demands of economic development for the limited available resources of Ethiopia, its armed forces are probably too large.

The Ethiopian government devotes more than thirty percent of its budget to security expenditures (i.e., armed forces and police). This is a high proportion in comparison with the other large African countries.

Besides its difficulties with Somalia, Ethiopia also has security problems in its northeastern province, Eritrea, where Kagnew Station is located, particularly among elements of the Moslem population there. After World War II the United Nations placed the former Italian colony of Eritrea in a special status under Ethiopian custody. In 1962, however, Ethiopia peremptorily integrated it into the Ethiopian Empire, making it a province no different from any other.

Ever since 1962 there has been an incipient insurgency in Eritrea fomented by the largely Moslem Eritrean Liberation Front, or ELF, numbering about 2,000 active insurgents, and supported by some of the radical Arab countries such as Syria, Iraq, and South Yemen. Although the ELF's activities have increased somewhat in the last few years, so far it still only represents a harassment for the Ethiopian government. The Ethiopian forces kill about 100 insurgents each year; the insurgents inflict far fewer casualties on the government forces. The ELF has not yet bothered Kagnew Station.

The United States has provided some general military equipment and training to the Ethiopian forces which they have used in dealing with the ELF. Israel, on its own initiative, has provided more direct support for Ethiopia's counterinsurgency program against this Arab-sponsored threat.

Another threat to the Ethiopian government lies in the numerous dissatisfied groups elsewhere within the country. The Emperor has already experienced a significant but unsuccessful coup attempt in 1960 and lesser ones in 1964 and 1969. The country is controlled by a conservative elite whose views on numerous issues are not in keeping with the aspirations of various other elements within the country.

The United States is not likely to become directly involved in any local war in Ethiopia as a result of its occasional training missions or MAAG presence there. Even if some American servicemen should be killed in such a capacity, these losses would not contain the dynamics of greater United States involvement. These units are few in number, ancillary to Ethiopian forces in their mission, and limited as purveyors of American prestige. If these units began to suffer casualties, the American attitude would probably lean toward retrenchment, not toward expansion.

Even if the base at Kagnew came into danger as a result of local hostilities in the area, the most likely prospect would be that the United States would withdraw from the base, as it did from Wheelus Air Base in Libya. If, however, the base were attacked in such a way as to present a direct challenge to the United States, no one can say with certainty that this would not lead to some form of American reprisal and greater military involvement.

The connection between Kagnew Station and American military assistance to Ethiopia, and the further connection between that assistance and Soviet support for Somalia, present a classic example of how a great power-client relationship can develop. Now each superpower has its client in that part of Africa, each facing the other with more arms than before.

Whether the United States has followed the right policy is problematical. Kagnew does provide certain functions of some value. However, alternative locations are available. These would necessitate some additional construction cost, but they are certainly not out of the question. Thus the loss of Kagnew would not endanger the security of the United States. Moreover, the savings in military assistance achieved by withdrawing Kagnew could offset the relocation costs in a few years.

One of the reasons that this lesser need for Kagnew is not as fully recognized as it should be rests in the deference paid by the State Department to the military in defining strategic requirements. The Assistant Secretary of State for African Affairs informed the Symington Subcommittee:

I think the State Department, of necessity, must be prepared to take on faith the assessment of DOD [Department of Defense], the agency that is most directly involved technically in the operation of this station.

Furthermore, the Ethiopian government needs the favor of the United States. There can be little doubt that the conservative leaders of Ethiopia would feel very uncomfortable in any close embrace with the Soviet Union, especially since the Soviet Union has now committed itself to Somalia. With Ethiopia's economic base what it is, there are no other likely alternatives to the United States as a provider of military assistance. Beyond this is the general political support by the United States, which is worth more than is often assumed.

In 1968 the American Embassy called for more assistance to Ethiopia than was ultimately provided. None of the dire consequences that the Embassy predicted ever came to pass.

In military assistance to Ethiopia the United States is probably paying out several million dollars each year unnecessarily. But, compared to American worldwide military assistance of more than $400 million each year, excluding Vietnam and excess equipment, this problem is minor.

Whether the arms race in the Horn of Africa has heightened the risk of bloodshed there is not clear. The Ethiopians may be tempted, with their newly acquired military strength, to undertake punitive missions against their foes. On the other hand, there has been a *détente* with Somalia for the last few years. A similar question arises with respect to the use of American military assistance in putting down the Eritrean rebels. Would more people die, or fewer, if this country were not providing such equipment and training? The United States refused to get involved in the Nigerian civil war, and more than 1,000,000 people died. It did aid the Congo government in 1964, and the insurgency there collapsed. The question is a hard one, and initial assumptions are not always well founded.

Excessive American military assistance for Ethiopia may have interfered with its economic development in two ways. First, to the extent that the United States has provided military assistance instead of economic aid, Ethiopia has failed to receive funds which it otherwise could have obtained for needed development. Second, any augmentation in a country's military forces as a result of military assistance requires that country to devote some of its own assets, human resources if no others, in order to support such an expanded force. These resources could otherwise have been devoted to economic development.

MOROCCO

In 1950, when Morocco was still a French protectorate, the United States received permission from the French to construct four SAC bases and a naval station there. Following Moroccan independence in 1956, the presence of these bases appeared to be inconsistent with the country's neutralist foreign policy, and President Eisenhower and King Mohammed V agreed in 1959 that the United States would evacuate all the bases by the end of 1963. The SAC bases were evacuated on schedule, but by an informal agreement in 1963 American forces were allowed to stay at the naval station, Kenitra. At that time it was not expected that they would be allowed to stay there long. Therefore, a duplicate communications facility was built in southern Spain at Rota.

But contrary to this expectation the United States was never asked to leave Kenitra, and it still operates the station there. The station provides the Moroccans training in various aspects of aviation and provides the United States an additional communications capability in the Mediterranean and eastern Atlantic. This base has 1,700 military personnel, operating expenses of about $9 million a year, and foreign exchange costs of $5.6 million. Besides the training provided to the Moroccans at Kenitra, they currently receive $1.8 million a year in military assistance grants and are allowed $9.5 million in military credit sales each year. There is a 33-man American military advisory mission in Morocco.

The Russians and Czechs have provided the Moroccans with some military and economic assistance. However, there are no Soviet military advisors in Morocco. A few Czech advisors are there. The French have provided the Moroccans about half as much military and economic assistance as the United States has since independence.

In 1963 this country agreed to train Moroccans at Kenitra to preserve its communications capability for the United States. With the establishment of an alternative installation in Spain the need for the communications site in Morocco has decreased, but the value of the training presence has increased, since this training provides the United States a convenient (although certainly not necessary) liaison with this politically moderate Arab state. If the Americans at the base became endangered, it is likely the United States would withdraw from the facility, as it did from Wheelus Air Base in Libya.

XIII

Some General Observations and Conclusions

The investigation by the Symington Subcommittee brought several matters into the open that deserve comment but are not connected with a particular country. These topics are: the respective roles of the State Department and the Defense Department in foreign policy; the relationship between individual American commitments abroad and the size of the defense budget; the influence the United States holds over its various allies and clients; and the electronic intelligence-gathering program.

CONTRASTING ROLES OF STATE AND DEFENSE

There is no doubt that there has been an intrusion by the military into the traditional role of the diplomat in formulating American foreign policy—in many ways perhaps unintentional, but nonetheless real. There have been numerous attempts to explain and correct the declining influence of the State Department in American foreign affairs. One recent instance was the State Department's own 600-page analysis entitled "Diplomacy for the 70's," issued on

194

November 20, 1970. What follows are those features of the problem that came to attention in the subcommittee investigations and in the writer's earlier experience in the office of the Secretary of Defense.

Some of State's difficulties with Defense have to do with the resources available to the two departments. The sheer size of the military establishment overall and locally in many individual countries gives American military leaders inordinate power and influence. Related to this is the enormous budget at their command. With so many eyes and ears, the Defense Department has sources of information which the few diplomats on a particular country team cannot possess or assess; and in many cases information is power.

Other advantages the Defense Department enjoys stem from its organization and mission, as compared with those of State. The Defense Department has a substantive and relatively clear-cut purpose, to be strong enough to deter and to be prepared to defend. The State Department diplomats, on the other hand, have no well-defined substantive mission of their own. They are the advocates, the negotiators for other American interests. The diplomats are attorneys; the Defense Department in many instances is their client.

The State Department's style is reactive; the Defense Department's is planned. State focuses on responding to crisis after crisis; Defense, with its five-year budgets, contingency plans, and command and control, moves in more directed paths. The military's direction is toward action; the diplomat's toward inaction. The military is trained to meet a crisis. The diplomat is trained to avoid one.

The factors that military men tend to deal with are in many instances more manageable than those weighed by State Department officials. Generals and admirals deal in quantities of men, tanks, vessels, and aircraft. Diplomats deal in the qualitative and ambiguous elements of foreign policy. This in turn leads to clear-cut advice from the military and to qualified, conditional advice from the State Department.

The knowledge of a military man is technical knowledge; the knowledge of a diplomat tends to be general knowledge. Too often the answer of a technical expert, irrefutable because of his expertise, is accepted as conclusive on a general question of policy, as to which he is really no expert, simply because his information happens to relate to a portion of the problem. His answer may even sound as if it is responsive to the entire question when in fact he knows about only a part of the problem. For instance, on the question whether an American base should be located in a particular country, the expert military officer can probably give "irrefutable" military justifications for placing one there, but he knows little about the more general political and financial reasons for not doing so.

In the last dozen years, although good men have served at the heads of both departments, the particular personalities of the high officials in both departments have had their effects. The tendency of several presidents to concentrate foreign policy decisions more and more in the White House has also played its part in State's decline and, unfortunately, the damaging effect on morale and recruiting at the State Department caused by Senator Joseph McCarthy lingers on.

Another difference in organization that counts for greater effectiveness in the Defense Department is its orientation toward the management of a vast enterprise and the execution of enormous programs; whereas the emphasis of the State Department is on rendering advice to one's superior.

The constant choosing that goes on in the Defense Department among alternative strategies, programs, deployments, and weapons systems sharpens the advocacy of those who have to defend the results selected. The State Department has few vested interests to preserve, the Defense Department many. The planning that goes on at State tends to be rather abstract; whereas that at Defense is much more closely integrated into operations.*

The effective intrusion of the Defense Department into the formulation of foreign policy is seen in various ways. One instance is the admission by the State Department that it has to take on faith what military men tell it concerning strategic requirements. The civilians in Secretary McNamara's Pentagon never gave such deference to military judgment. Another instance is the ease with which American military officers are able to get along with other military men who rule in some of the countries with which this country is allied. One case in point seems to have been in Greece.

In some cases ambassadors have confided that they have felt as if they were no longer the highest ranking American official in the country. In other cases, high embassy officials have intentionally refused to learn about military programs going on in the countries in which they were posted, under what would appear to be a misconception of the division of responsibility.

The disadvantages of turning more and more of our foreign policy over to the military—and it is not so much a problem of intention as of structure—is that military officers, capable though they may be in their own profession, are ill-equipped by training or experience to resolve matters of foreign policy. The military man is guided by the principle of effectiveness, not efficiency. He legitimately wants all that will assist him in defeating a possible enemy. He cannot balance this factor against the competing considerations of political relationships. Yet time and again military men are asked to make judgments about matters on which they are only partially qualified. Take, for instance, the question whether the threat in a particular area justifies the expenditure to support the American forces in that area. A military man will invariably interpret the threat to mean the enemy's capability in terms of armed

* For a further discussion of some of these points, see Adam Yarmolinsky, "Bureaucratic Structures and Political Outcomes," *Journal of International Affairs*, vol. 23, p. 225 (1969).

men, tanks, aircraft, and naval vessels and will give scant attention to the political probability, or improbability, of attack.

COMMITMENTS AND THE MILITARY BUDGET

Some people say that if only we could cut our overseas commitments, we could reduce our military budget substantially. This, unfortunately, is an overstatement. If we could reduce, or reinterpret downward, our treaty and other commitments, this might allow for a minor reduction in the defense budget. But equally important in determining the size of our peacetime defense forces is a perception of American security interests abroad combined with an assessment of the threat against those interests and the degree to which we are willing to risk the unforeseeable. Without reducing these factors, a reduction in commitments by itself will have little effect upon the defense budget.

One reason that a reduction in the scope of what is promised in American commitments will not, standing alone, achieve large-scale savings in the defense budget is that the major items in the budget, whether Army divisions, air wings, or naval task forces, exist to provide a readiness to meet any one of a number of similar contingencies. To give up one commitment and keep another similar one would provide very little savings in our defense budget.

Some reductions in American ground forces in Asia have come about through a combination of: (1) a more moderate view of what the Asian commitments actually require; (2) a more realistic appraisal of American interests there; and (3) a reassessment of the likely threat to allied and friendly countries. In the President's Report on United States Foreign Policy for the 1970s, issued on February 18, 1970, the President announced that peacetime forces would be maintained ready to fight one and one-half major wars (one in Europe or in Asia, plus a minor contingency elsewhere) instead of two and one-half (in both Europe and Asia, plus the minor contingency) as in the past; and, upon that new premise, this country began to reduce the number of active Army divisions toward the level that existed in the 1950s. In the same pronouncement, however, the President also announced that we were going to keep all our treaty commitments.

Substantial savings can in fact be achieved within our military forces without endangering American security. The analysis by which such a conclusion is reached, however, does not rest significantly on a paring down of American commitments abroad, if by that term is meant explicit and implicit promises to defend in the future. The concept is too amorphous, too elastic, and too disconnected from tanks, guns, airplanes, and ships to help much in reducing the budget.

Instead, the analysis followed by Dr. Carl Kaysen, the Director of the Institute for Advanced Study at Princeton and a former Deputy Special Assistant to President Kennedy for National Security Affairs, in his testimony before the Subcommittee on Commitments Abroad is likely to be more productive. Dr. Kaysen testified on the basis of the 1971 budget. Extrapolating from Dr. Kaysen's approach, one could well conclude that the current defense budget could be reduced by more than $6 billion for conventional forces without regard to possible further reductions in existing strategic forces or the war in Vietnam.

The 1972 defense budget of about $75.8 billion was composed of $17.4 billion for strategic (nuclear) forces, $7.1 billion as the incremental costs of the Vietnam war that year, and $51.3 billion for the base line general purpose forces; i.e., the pre-Vietnam Army divisions, Air Force wings, and Navy task forces at 1972 prices.* Out of this $51.3 billion important savings can be made.

Let us consider first the savings that can be achieved among the Army and Marine Corps divisions. The sixteen Army and Marine Corps divisions this country has are roughly allocable as nine to

---

* See Charles L. Schultze, *Setting National Priorities: The 1973 Budget* (Washington: Brookings Institution, 1972), p. 42.

Europe, four to Asia, and three to a strategic reserve. Some of these, though allocable to a contingency beyond our borders, are of course stationed within the United States.

Under the recently announced doctrine that the United States will henceforth stand ready to engage in one and one-half major contingencies, the Nixon Administration reduced the number of active divisions from nineteen and two-thirds to the present sixteen divisions. Units based in the United States under this theory could be made to be available to go to Europe or Asia. Accordingly, it would seem feasible under this concept to reduce the number of active divisions by three more, leaving a total of thirteen. There would still be well above the number needed to meet either a European or an Asian contingency and a minor contingency at the same time. In 1971 only eight land divisions were allocable to Europe. Accordingly one could be reduced for that area of responsibility, and either out of the Pacific area or out of the strategic reserve two further divisions could be demobilized. Based upon calculations made by the Brookings Institution, each division deactivated would represent annual savings of at least $1 billion. Thus three divisions would represent $3 billion in savings.*

In 1971 this country had twenty-three tactical air wings (comprised of fighter/attack aircraft such as the F-4). Although the Administration announced plans to reduce this number by two, the United States ended up instead with twenty-four such wings in 1972. Of these twenty-four wings, eight and one-third are allocable to Europe, five and one-third to the Pacific, and ten and one-third to a strategic reserve. Likewise, under the one and one-half wars theory, a reduction in this enormous force by three air wings would seem appropriate, making an annual savings of $1.2 billion.

The analysis of naval forces must be somewhat different. Naval task forces cannot readily be shifted from one ocean to another.

* See Charles L. Schultze, *Setting National Priorities: The 1971 Budget* (Washington: Brookings Institution, 1972), p. 44; Roland A. Paul, "The $10 Billion Misunderstanding," *New York Times,* February 12, 1971.

Presently we have fifteen fighter/attack wings located on sixteen aircraft carriers. When, in 1971, the Pentagon announced a reduction from the previously existing fifteen carriers to fourteen, the Navy compensated by placing the equivalent of a wing of aircraft onto two former ASW (antisubmarine warfare) carriers (which are simply older and somewhat smaller attack carriers). These sixteen carriers are presently allocated as five to the Mediterranean, seven to the Pacific, two to the strategic reserve, close to the United States, and two in overhaul. With the advent of home-porting of one aircraft carrier in Greece and one in Japan, adequate on-station presence can be achieved with as few as twelve carriers. Even with fifteen carriers in service, which was the number in 1971, the Navy was only maintaining two carriers continually on station in the Mediterranean and three in the Pacific. With home-porting abroad and only four carriers allocated to the Mediterranean, four to the Pacific, two in the strategic reserve and two in overhaul, we could maintain two carriers on station at all times in the Mediterranean and two in the Pacific. The savings from reducing our sixteen carriers to twelve would be at least $2 billion annually. With the use of greater home-porting, which is possible in the future, and more reliance on land-based aircraft (i.e., Air Force aircraft) an even lower number of aircraft carriers would be feasible.

The one notable function served by carriers which is not readily replaceable by land-based aircraft is the pre-crisis signal. Carriers have been used for this purpose in the Six-Day War in 1967, the Jordanian civil war in 1970 and the Indian-Pakistan conflict in 1971. The movement of carriers is well suited for this diplomatic maneuvering. The deployment of large numbers of Air Force aircraft to new bases is not as subtle a stroke. However, the smaller number of carriers recommended above is fully adequate for this purpose as well as actual combat.

Thus the total savings which are achievable from all three services is more than $6 billion. Further savings, perhaps $1 billion or more, could result from a reduction in our tactical nuclear weapons abroad as discussed in Chapter IX.

The suggestion that such reductions are tantamount to a return to the doctrine of massive retaliation is not so. These reductions are feasible because American interests abroad can be adequately protected with a smaller American force, considering the reduced risk of overt aggression against those interests today, both in Europe and in Asia. The flexible response policy would continue, but with greater peacetime efficiency.

ABILITY TO INFLUENCE FRIENDS AND ALLIES

There is an assumption in some quarters that the United States, even though it is a superpower, has a very limited capacity to influence its clients in the direction it wishes them to follow. On the contrary, both superpowers, the United States and the Soviet Union, have many times (although not always) been able to bring their will to bear on the behavior of their friends and allies. The United States prevented Turkey from launching an imminent invasion of Cyprus in 1964 by threatening to remove its defense guarantee should such an attack lead to Soviet intervention. The United States was also able to influence events in Laos by its control of military aid to that country. It was able to induce a reluctant Israel to participate in the 1971 truce with the Arab states. The Soviet Union has had similar success in other instances with North Korea, Iraq, and Syria, and in influencing East Germany to participate in negotiations with West Germany over the normalization of relations between those two countries.

One of the most dramatic instances of this country's ability to influence events occurred in South Vietnam in 1963. American suspension of certain economic assistance, including the $100 million Commercial Import Program, cessation of support for the elite Vietnamese Special Police controlled by Diem's brother, Ngo Dinh Nhu, and other direct criticisms of the Diem regime could not have failed to impress some Vietnamese military leaders with the belief that the United States would be receptive to a change of government in South Vietnam.

In spite of all this, Secretary Rogers announced on December 24, 1969:

. . . we have had a study made of how many times we have been able to influence the policy of another government by withholding military aid, and we find that it has not been successful in any instance.

However, the study referred to by the Secretary of State actually concluded only that

An examination of the cases where a program of military aid has been suddenly modified or curtailed suggests, however, that the results desired by the donor can only be achieved under the rather exceptional circumstances of a total and exclusive dependence by the recipient on the supplier.

In fact, the instances analyzed in the study, some of which have been mentioned above, do not support the implication that American influence upon its friends and allies is insignificant, whether that influence is represented by the supply of military assistance or otherwise.

ELECTRONIC INTELLIGENCE-GATHERING

In various parts of the world, the United States operates land-based, airborne, and, until recently, seaborne electronic intelligence-gathering efforts. The information intercepted by these facilities, some of which is enciphered and some of which is not, is subjected to local analysis and also, in part, reported to central locations for further, more sophisticated analysis.

These operations are run predominantly by military personnel, but some civilians are also involved. No attention, naturally, is drawn to the operations, but in general, members of the host governments are aware of the nature of a given program, and in some places the operation is hardly a secret at all to those who care to know, whether friend or foe.

However, a general aura of secrecy does attend intelligence-gathering operations such as these, and therefore, even the United States Congress paid little attention to the electronic intelligence program until the inquiry by the Subcommittee on Commitments Abroad. This general lack of review and oversight has in some instances led to evident redundancy and inefficiency in the program.

Not only are all three services involved, but several separate members of the intelligence community participate in similar functions. There have been cases where each of the services has operated a separate facility close to one run by another service, although there has been some trend in recent years toward consolidation.

If one compares the product-to-personnel ratio among the various facilities, one is struck by the wide variance among them in the number of people needed to achieve a given result. This suggests that the logistical and administrative support for some facilities is unnecessarily large. Invariably the civilian-operated units require fewer people than do the military-operated units to accomplish the same results. It appears that servicemen, even in this field, need a logistical tail that civilians simply do not need.

Another dimension of this possible inefficiency resulting from the overmilitarization of this program can be seen by comparing the typical pattern followed by service personnel and by civilian personnel in their tours of duty. A serviceman in this program enlists for a four-year tour. The first year is spent in training. If he is not accompanied by dependents, the next twelve to twenty-four months are served in useful work overseas. Then the serviceman is entitled to return to the United States for the remainder, if any, of his enlistment. Although he can do useful work in the United States, it is obvious that, in general, his most productive work is done overseas. Service personnel have a very low reenlistment rate, usually below twenty percent. Some of the reasons for this are that they are among the more intelligent and well-educated servicemen and that during their tours they acquire skills in electronics or language which qualify them for higher paying jobs in the civilian economy.

The civilian operators, on the other hand, have average tours of duty of a significantly longer period, and many are career personnel. One reason for the preponderant number of military personnel in the program is the fact that military commanders have a large voice in determining the nature of the program.

The question whether it is more economical, on a cost-effectiveness basis, to have greater civilian operation or to continue with the same level of military participation would be a suitable question for those trained in systems analysis to study. The lower pay for military personnel must be weighed against the much lower turnover rate among civilians, which of course represents a saving in training costs. Furthermore, the intangible factor of greater competence, experience, and enthusiasm among the civilians must be considered in the balance.

It is true that a certain number of military personnel must be trained to be available for this intelligence-gathering operation in tactical areas under combat conditions. However, even in wartime much of this work is conducted well behind the lines. During World War II much of this type of work was done by civilians.

Another possibility for achieving greater cost-effectiveness may be to encourage our allies to do a greater proportion of this work in the interest of the common defense. Some of the functions involve an inquiry into the substance of a message, but many others relate merely to locating the source from which the message comes. Particularly for these latter functions, it would seem that our allies could help more than they do. High standards of security would not be of prime relevance for such aspects of the program. Furthermore, in some cases, our allies would have language advantages which we lack. It would seem possible to get a greater total output for less money by moving further in this direction.

CONCLUSIONS

The United States does of course have some verbal commitments to other countries. However, the nature of the action called for by these verbal commitments is very elastic. This country probably has a greater degree of commitment in those places where large numbers of its armed forces are present. The consequences of this presence, in terms of the commitment it conveys, are to draw the line, as in South Korea, West Germany and Berlin, South Vietnam and Thailand, beyond which the adversaries of the United States (including those countries and factions perceived to be surrogates or proxies for our major opponents) may not adavnce without requiring this country to engage in large-scale military action. The risk that these forces stationed abroad will involve this country in extensive hostilities against forces other than those of our own adversaries seems remote. And the risk of excessive engagement even against our own opponents may not be great where the American operation is kept to a low profile, as in Laos.

In the interest of American security, the desired standard may be to have manifest, but nonthreatening, American strength in places where such presence can be expected to provide effective deterrence against the relevant threat, such as in Western Europe, Turkey, South Korea, Taiwan, the Mediterranean, and probably Thailand; and, on the other hand, a low profile, but without total withdrawal, in places where a large American military presence does not provide a high degree of deterrence against the relevant threat, such as in Laos, Cambodia and South Vietnam. One country—Japan—presents a unique situation. There, the better term perhaps is "absorption" instead of "deterrence"—the capacity to absorb into the international system Japan's bounding energy, with all its likely tensions. To this end, some American military presence, at least in the area, is probably necessary, although it should be flexible and not overbearing. This varied posture according to the place and the nature of the threat would seem to maximize American security interests abroad, reducing the likelihood of hostilities and preserving American flexibility in areas of likely crisis.

Appendix A

WITNESSES APPEARING BEFORE THE SENATE FOREIGN
RELATIONS SUBCOMMITTEE ON UNITED STATES SECU-
RITY AGREEMENTS AND COMMITMENTS ABROAD

Country	Dates and Principal Witnesses
Spain	March 11, April 14, 1969, and July 17, 1970. Elliot L. Richardson, Under Secretary of State; Earl G. Wheeler, Chairman of the Joint Chiefs of Staff; George Landau, State Department, Country Director for Spain; Walter Pincus, Chief Consultant, and Roland Paul, Counsel of the Subcommittee.
Greece, Italy, Portugal, Spain and Turkey	May 22 and 27, 1969. Walter Pincus and Roland Paul.
Philippines	September 30, October 1, 2 and 3, 1969. James M. Wilson, Jr., Deputy Chief of Mission, U.S. Embassy, Manila; Lt. General Francis C. Gideon, Commander, 13th Air Force; Lt. General Robert H. Warren, Deputy Assistant Secretary of Defense for Military Assistance and Sales; Major General George B. Pickett, Jr., Chief, Joint U.S. Military Advisory Group, Philippines; Rear Admiral Draper L. Kauffman, Commander, U.S. Naval Forces, Philippines; Colonel Ernest W. Pate, Commander, 6th Air Division.

Country	Dates and Principal Witnesses
Laos	October 20, 21, 22 and 28, 1969. William H. Sullivan, Deputy Assistant Secretary of State for East Asian and Pacific Affairs; G. McMurtrie Godley, U.S. Ambassador to Laos; Robert H. Nooter, Deputy Assistant Administrator, Bureau for East Asia, Agency for International Development; Daniel Oleksiw, Assistant Director, East Asia and Pacific Affairs, U.S. Information Agency; Colonel Robert L. F. Tyrrell, Air Attaché, U.S. Embassy, Vientiane; Colonel Peter T. Russell, Deputy Chief Joint U.S. Military Advisory Group/Thailand; Lt. Colonel Edgar W. Duskin, Army Attaché, U.S. Embassy, Vientiane; Major Robert W. Thomas, former Army Attaché, Luang Prabang, Laos; Loring A. Waggoner, Agency for International Development Advisor, North Nam Ngum, Laos.
Thailand	November 10, 11, 12, 13, 14, and 17, 1969. Graham A. Martin, former U.S. Ambassador to Thailand; Leonard Unger, U.S. Ambassador to Thailand; George Tanham, Special Assistant to Ambassador for Counterinsurgency, U.S. Embassy, Bangkok; Lt. General Richard G. Stilwell, former Commander, U.S. Military Assistance Command, Thailand; Major General Louis T. Seith, Commander, U.S. Military Assistance Command, Thailand; Major General Robert L. Petit, Deputy Commander, 7/13th Air Force; Brig. General David E. Ott, Commander, U.S. Army Support Command, Thailand; Lt. Colonel Robert A. Bartelt, former Commander, 46th Special Forces Unit, Thailand.
China (Nationalist)	November 24, 25 and 26, 1969 and May 8, 1970. Walter P. McConaughy, U.S. Ambassador to the Republic of China; Vice Admiral John L. Chew, Commander, U.S. Taiwan Defense Command;

Country	Dates and Principal Witnesses
	Major General Richard G. Ciccolella, former Commander, Military Assistance Advisory Group, Republic of China; Colonel Robert D. Yocom, Assistant Chief of Staff, Military Assistance Advisory Group, Republic of China; Colonel Roy L. Tweedie, Deputy Commander, 327th Air Force Division.
Japan and Okinawa	January 26, 27, 28 and 29, 1970. U. Alexis Johnson, Under Secretary of State for Political Affairs; Lt. General James B. Lampert, High Commissioner of the Ryukyu Islands; Lt. General Thomas K. McGehee, Commander U.S. Forces, Japan; Major General Jerry D. Page, former Commander, 313th Air Division; Rear Admiral Daniel F. Smith, Jr., Commander, U.S. Naval Forces, Japan; Brig. General Frank E. Garretson, former Commander, U.S. Marines, Okinawa; Scott George, Political-Military Affairs Officer, U.S. Embassy, Tokyo; Colonel Charles M. Simpson, First Special Forces Group.
Korea	February 24, 25 and 26, 1970. William J. Porter, U.S. Ambassador to Korea; General John H. Michaelis, Commander in Chief, United Nations Command; Major General Leland G. Cagwin, former Commander, 2d Infantry Division; Major General Livingston N. Taylor, Chief, Joint Military Assistance Advisory Group, Republic of Korea; Brig. General Arthur W. Holderness, Jr., Commander, 314th Air Division.
NATO	May 25 and 26 and June 16 and 24, 1970. Martin J. Hillenbrand, Assistant Secretary of State for European Affairs; Gen. Andrew J. Goodpaster, Supreme Allied Commander, Europe; General David A. Burchinal, Deputy Commander in Chief, European Command; General James H. Polk, Commander in Chief, U.S. Army, Europe.

Country	Dates and Principal Witnesses
Greece and Turkey	June 9 and 11, 1970. Rodger Davies, Deputy Assistant Secretary of State for Near Eastern and South Asian Affairs; Roswell D. McClelland, former Deputy Chief of Mission, U.S. Embassy, Athens; Robert J. Pranger, Deputy Assistant Secretary of Defense, International Security Affairs.
Ethiopia	June 1, 1970. David D. Newsom, Assistant Secretary of State for African Affairs; George W. Bader, Director, Africa Region, International Security Affairs, Department of Defense.
Morocco and Libya	July 20, 1970. David D. Newsom; William E. Lang, Deputy Assistant Secretary of Defense, International Security Affairs.
Broader Aspects of U.S. Commitments	November 24, 1970. Carl Kaysen, former Deputy Special Assistant to President Kennedy for National Security Affairs.

Appendix B

CONGRESSIONAL RESOLUTIONS

The five congressional resolutions in the nature of security commitments abroad read, in relevant part, as follows:

1. Formosa Resolution, H.J. Res. 159, 69 Stat. 5, approved January 29, 1955:

> *Resolved* . . . That the President of the United States be and he hereby is authorized to employ the Armed Forces of the United States as he deems necessary for the specific purpose of securing and protecting Formosa and the Pescadores against armed attack, this authority to include the securing and protection of such related positions and territories of that area now in friendly hands and the taking of such other measures as he judges to be required or appropriate in assuring the defense of Formosa and the Pescadores.

2. Middle East Resolution, as Amended, H.J. Res. 117, 71 Stat. 5, approved March 9, 1957, as amended by the Foreign Assistance Act of 1961, 75 Stat. 424, approved September 4, 1961:

> [T]he United States regards as vital to the national interest and world peace the preservation of the independence and integrity of the nations of the Middle East. To this end, if the President determines the necessity thereof, the United States is prepared to use armed forces to assist any nation or group of such nations requesting assistance against armed aggression from any country controlled by international communism: *Provided,* That such employment shall be consonant with the treaty obligations of the United States and with the Constitution of the United States.

211

3. Cuban Resolution. S.J. Res. 230, 76 Stat. 697, approved October 3, 1962:

Resolved . . . That the United States is determined—

(a) to prevent by whatever means may be necessary, including the use of arms, the Marxist-Leninist regime in Cuba from extending, by force or the threat of force, its aggressive or subversive activities to any part of this hemisphere;

(b) to prevent in Cuba the creation or use of an externally supported military capability endangering the security of the United States; and

(c) to work with the Organization of American States and with freedom-loving Cubans to support the aspirations of the Cuban people for self-determination.

4. Berlin Resolution, H.C. Res. 570, 87th Congress, passed October 10, 1962:

Resolved . . .

(a) that the continued exercise of United States, British, and French rights in Berlin constitutes a fundamental political and moral determination;

(b) that the United States would regard as intolerable any violation by the Soviet Union directly or through others of those rights in Berlin, including the right of ingress and egress;

(c) that the United States is determined to prevent by whatever means may be necessary, including the use of arms, any violation of those rights by the Soviet Union directly or through others, and to fulfill our commitment to the people of Berlin with respect to their resolve for freedom.

5. Vietnam Resolution, H.J. Res. 1145, 78 Stat. 384, approved August 10, 1964 [rescinded January 13, 1971]:

Resolved . . . That the Congress approves and supports the determination of the President, as Commander in Chief, to take all necessary measures to repel any armed attack against the forces of the United States and to prevent further aggression.

Sec. 2. The United States regards as vital to its national interest and to world peace the maintenance of international peace and security in southeast Asia. Consonant with the Constitution of the United States and the Charter of the United Nations and in accordance with its obligations under the Southeast Asia Collective Defense Treaty, the United States is, therefore, prepared, as the President determines, to take all necessary steps, including the use of armed force, to assist any member or protocol state of the Southeast Asia Collective Defense Treaty requesting assistance in defense of its freedom.

Bibliography

GENERAL

Allison, Graham; May, Ernest; and Yarmolinsky, Adam. "Limits to Intervention," *Foreign Affairs,* vol. 48, no. 2 (January, 1970)

American Foreign Service Association. *Toward a Modern Diplomacy* (Washington, 1968)

Ball, George W. *The Discipline of Power* (Boston: Little, Brown & Co., 1968)

Bloomfield, Lincoln P., and Leiss, Amelia C. *Controlling Small Wars: A Strategy for the 1970's* (New York: Alfred A. Knopf, 1969)

Department of Defense. *Military Assistance and Foreign Military Sales Facts* (Washington, 1971)

Department of State. *Diplomacy for the 70's* (Washington, 1970)

Enthoven, Alain C., and Smith, K. Wayne. *How Much Is Enough?* (New York: Harper & Row, 1970)

"Global Defense, U.S. Military Commitments Abroad," *Congressional Quarterly Service* (Washington, 1969)

Hearings Before the Subcommittee on United States Security Agreements and Commitments Abroad of the Senate Committee on Foreign Relations, 91st Cong. (1969-70)

> Part 1—Philippines
> Part 2—Laos
> Part 3—Thailand
> Part 4—China (Nationalist)
> Part 5—Japan and Okinawa
> Part 6—South Korea

Part 7—Greece and Turkey

Part 8—Ethiopia

Part 9—Morocco and Libya

Part 10—Europe

Part 11—Spain

Part 12—Broader Aspects of U.S. Commitments

Hearings on Worldwide Military Commitments before the Preparedness Investigating Subcommittee of the Senate Committee on Armed Services, 89th Cong., 2d sess., and 90th Cong., 1st sess. (1966–67)

Institute for Strategic Studies. *The Military Balance, 1969–70* (London, 1969)

International Monetary Fund. *International Financial Statistics,* vol. 23, no. 7 (Washington, July, 1970)

Johnson, Lyndon B. *The Vantage Point: Perspectives of the Presidency, 1963–1969* (New York: Holt, Rinehart & Winston, 1971)

Kaysen, Carl. "Military Strategy, Military Forces, and Arms Control," *Agenda for the Nation* (Washington: Brookings Institution, 1968)

Kennedy, Robert F. *Thirteen Days, A Memoir of the Cuban Missile Crisis* (New York: W. W. Norton & Co., 1969)

Kristol, Irving. "We Can't Resign as 'Policeman of the World,' " *New York Times Magazine,* May 12, 1968

Paul, Roland A. "The $10-Billion Misunderstanding," *New York Times,* February 12, 1971

———. "Toward a Theory of Intervention," *Orbis,* vol. XVI, no. 1 (Spring, 1972)

Report of Subcommittee on U.S. Security Agreements and Commitments Abroad of the Senate Committee on Foreign Relations, 91st Cong., 2d sess. (1970)

Schultze, Charles L. "Budget Alternatives after Vietnam," *Agenda for the Nation* (Washington: Brookings Institution, 1968)

———. *Setting National Priorities: The 1971 Budget* (Washington: Brookings Institution, 1970)

———. *Setting National Priorities: The 1973 Budget* (Washington: Brookings Institution, 1972)

Senate Executive Report No. 9, "Treaty on the Nonproliferation of Nuclear Weapons," 90th Cong., 2d sess. (1968)

Senate Report No. 91–239, "National Commitments," 91st Cong., 1st sess. (April 16, 1969)

Symington, Stuart. Speech on the nuclear veil and the right of the Senate to know, *Congressional Record,* S1643 (February, 1970)

"United States Foreign Policy for the 1970's: A New Strategy for Peace." Message from the President of the United States, 91st Cong., 2d sess., February 18, 1970 (House Doc. 91–258)

Wallich, Henry C. "Whatever Became of the Balance of Payments?" *Atlantic Community Quarterly,* vol. 8, no. 2 (Summer, 1970)

Warnke, Paul C. "National Security: Are We Asking the Right Questions?" *The Washington Monthly,* October, 1969

Yarmolinsky, Adam. "Bureaucratic Structures and Political Outcomes," *Journal of International Affairs,* vol. 23, no. 2 (1969)

FAR EAST

Amfitheatrof, Erik. "The Forgotten Front at the 38th Parallel," *The Reporter,* April 18, 1968

Axelbank, Albert. "Short Fuse in Japan," *The Nation,* February 3, 1969

Baldwin, Hanson W. "U.S. Military Weaknesses Are Underlined by *Pueblo* Incident," *New York Times,* March 24, 1968, p. 44

Ball, George W. "We Should De-escalate the Importance of Vietnam," *New York Times Magazine,* December 21, 1969

Bundy, William P. "New Tides in Southeast Asia," *Foreign Affairs,* vol. 49, no. 2 (January, 1971)

Campbell, Alex. " 'Come and Establish More Bases Here,' " *The New Republic,* June 7, 1969

Chapin, Emerson. "Success Story in South Korea," *Foreign Affairs,* vol. 47, no. 3 (April, 1969)

Dommen, Arthur. *Conflict in Laos: Politics of Neutralization* (New York: Frederick A. Praeger, 1964)

Emmerson, John K. "Japan: Eye on 1970," *Foreign Affairs,* vol. 47, no. 2 (January, 1969)

Goodwin, Richard N. *Triumph or Tragedy: Reflections on Vietnam* (New York: Random House, 1966)

Goulden, Joseph C. "The Military Saboteurs," *The Nation,* March 2, 1970

Halloran, Richard. "Okinawa: 'New Era' as U.S. Agrees to Return It to Japan," *New York Times,* November 23, 1969, p. E4

Halperin, Morton H. "Act of Statesmanship Ceded Okinawa," *Washington Post,* November 30, 1969, p. B1

Hoopes, Townsend. *The Limits of Intervention* (New York: David McKay Co., 1969)

Kahn, Herman. *The Emerging Japanese Superstate, Challenge and Response* (Englewood Cliffs, New Jersey: Prentice-Hall, 1970)

Kamm, Henry. "C.I.A. Role in Laos: Advising an Army," *New York Times,* March 11, 1972, p. 6

Kim, Shim-Jo. "Mission: To Murder a President," *Reader's Digest,* July, 1968

Mecklin, John M. "The Philippines: An Ailing and Resentful Ally," *Fortune,* July, 1969

Paul, Roland A. "Laos: Anatomy of an American Involvement," *Foreign Affairs,* vol. 49, no. 3 (April, 1971)

Ravenal, Earl C. "The Nixon Doctrine and Our Asian Commitments," *Foreign Affairs,* vol. 49, no. 2 (January, 1971)

Reischauer, Edwin O. *Beyond Vietnam: The United States and Asia* (New York: Alfred A. Knopf, 1967)

———. "Transpacific Relations," *Agenda for the Nation* (Washington: Brookings Institution, 1968)

Shaplen, Robert. *Time out of Hand* (New York: Harper & Row, 1969)

Staff report of Subcommittee on United States Security Agreements and Commitments Abroad of the Senate Committee on Foreign Relations, 92d Cong., 1st sess., *Laos: April 1971* (1971)

———, 2nd sess., *Thailand, Laos, and Cambodia: January 1972* (1972)

Staff Report of the Senate Committee on Foreign Relations, 92d Cong., 2d sess., Vietnam: May 1972 (1972)

"The U.S. Tightrope in Korea," *Newsweek,* February 26, 1968

Wakaizumi, Kei. "Japan beyond 1970," *Foreign Affairs,* vol. 47, no. 3 (April, 1969)

" 'We Take the U.S. at Its Word—a Pacific Power, Here to Stay,' Interview with Park Chung Hee, President of the Republic of Korea," *U.S. News & World Report,* August 25, 1969

EUROPE

"As West Huddles Again to Meet Russian Threats," *U.S. News & World Report,* November 25, 1968

Beecher, William. "The Bomb? or the Bayonet? the Paradox of NATO," *The National Guardsman,* June, 1968

Brzezinski, Zbigniew. "America and Europe," *Foreign Affairs,* vol. 49, no. 1 (October, 1970)

Buchan, Alastair. "NATO and European Security," *Orbis,* vol. 13, no. 1 (Spring, 1969)

————. "The Purpose of NATO and Its Future Development," *NATO's Fifteen Nations* (February-March, 1969)

Burchinal, General David A. "Transportation and the NATO Deterrent," *Transportation Proceedings,* January, 1969

Church, Senator Frank. Speech on S. Res. 469 relating to the Spanish Base Agreement, *Congressional Record,* S16122 (September 22, 1970)

Department of State Press Release No. 18. Address by Under Secretary Elliot L. Richardson before the Chicago Council on Foreign Relations on American policy toward Europe, January 20, 1970

————. No. 123. TV Interview of Secretary William P. Rogers, April 16, 1970

Enthoven, Alain C. "Arms and Men: The Military Balance in Europe," *Interplay,* May, 1969

————, and Smith, K. Wayne. "What Forces for NATO? and from Whom?" *Foreign Affairs,* vol. 48, no. 1 (October, 1969)

Farbstein, Leonard. *Report of Special Study Mission to Europe,* 91st Cong., 2d sess. (March 29, 1970)

Finney, John W. "Dissent over U.S. Accord with Spain," *New York Times,* August 9, 1970, p. E4

Fried, Edward R. "The Cost of Alliance," *Interplay,* June-July, 1969

Friendly, Alfred. "Low U.S. Profile Pays off with Few Turkish Incidents," *Washington Post,* March 14, 1970, p. A17

Goodpaster, General Andrew J. "The Double Spirals," *Atlantic Community Quarterly,* Winter, 1969-1970

Harrison, Stanley L. "Defense of the Atlantic Community," *United States Naval Institute Proceedings,* October, 1969

Healey, Denis. Speech on British policy in NATO, *British Information Services,* March 5, 1970

Hearing on Spanish Base Agreement before the Senate Committee on Foreign Relations, 91st Cong., 2d sess. (1970)

Hearings on the Crisis in NATO before the Subcommittee on Europe of the House Committee on Foreign Affairs, 89th Cong., 2d sess. (1966)

Hearings on S. Res. 49 and 83 before the Combined Senate Subcommittee on United States Troops in Europe, 90th Cong., 1st sess. (1967)

Hearings on United States Policy toward Europe (and Related Matters) before the Senate Committee on Foreign Relations, 89th Cong., 2d sess. (1966)

Hearings on United States Relations with Europe in the Decade of the 1970's before the Subcommittee on Europe of the House Committee on Foreign Affairs, 91st Cong., 2d sess. (1970)

Herald, George W. "New Challenge to NATO," *The New Leader,* vol. 51 (November 4, 1968)

Mansfield, Mike. Speech on reduction of U.S. forces in Europe, *Congressional Record,* S5957 (April 20, 1970)

———. Speech on S. Res. 292 relating to reducing U.S. forces in Europe, *Congressional Record,* S15162 (December 1, 1969)

———. Speech on U.S. force levels in Germany, *Congressional Record,* S5050 (April 3, 1970)

Mendershausen, Horst. "Fetishes of NATO and the Dollar," *Orbis,* vol. 12, no. 2 (Summer, 1968)

NATO Information Service. *NATO Facts and Figures* (Brussels, 1969)

Nino, Pasti. "NATO's Defense Strategy," *Orbis,* vol. 13, no. 1 (Spring, 1969)

Nixon, Richard M. "NATO: Facing the Truth of Our Times," address before the North Atlantic Council, April 10, 1969, reprinted in *Atlantic Community Quarterly,* Summer, 1969

Percy, Senator Charles. Speech on U.S. commitment to NATO, *Congressional Record,* S2058 (February 20, 1970)

Report of the Combined Senate Subcommittee on United States Troops in Europe, 90th Cong., 2d sess. (1968)

Report of the United States Delegation to the 14th Meeting of the North Atlantic Assembly, 91st Cong., 1st sess. (1969)

Reuss, Henry S. Speech on military costs in Europe, *Congressional Record*, H1823 (March 16, 1970)

Schmidt, Helmut. "Germany in the Era of Negotiations," *Foreign Affairs*, vol. 49, no. 1 (October, 1970)

———. "The Consequences of the Brezhnev Doctrine," *Atlantic Community Quarterly*, Summer, 1969

"Secretary Rogers Interviewed on 'Issues and Answers,' " *Department of State Bulletin*, February 9, 1970

"Secretary Rogers Interviewed on 'Today' Program," *Department of State Bulletin*, April 6, 1970

Shulman, Marshall D. "Relations with the Soviet Union," *Agenda for the Nation* (Washington: Brookings Institution, 1968)

Staff report of the Senate Committee on Foreign Relations, 92d Cong., 1st sess., *Greece: February, 1971* (1971)

Stewart, Michael. "Britain, Europe and the Alliance," *Foreign Affairs*, vol. 48, no. 4 (July, 1970)

Index

Adana, Turkey, 171
Advanced Research Projects Agency (ARPA—Thailand), 117
Africa, 175, 182–83, 184, 185–93. *See also specific countries*
Agnew, Spiro T., 167
Agreements of Cooperation of March 5, 1959 (CENTO), 8, 26, 27–28
AID Mission, Vientiane, 56, 61, 64
Air America, 57, 60
air bases: in Europe, 4n, 128, 130, 137, 140–41, 142, 163, 169, 175–83, 184; in Japan, 40–45, 48, 51, 52, 176; in Laos, 58–59; in Morocco, 4n, 192; in the Philippines, 79, 80, 82–85, 90, 91–92, 176; in South Korea, 96, 97; in Taiwan, 32, 35; in Thailand, 91, 107, 108–109, 111, 112, 113, 116, 121, 122, 123–24; in Turkey, 171   ,
aircraft, 11, 12, 195, 200–201; in Ethiopia, 187; in Greece, 167–68; in intelligence gathering, 10, 32, 34, 57, 97, 98, 102, 107, 203; in Japan, 41, 44, 45, 51; in Laos, 56, 57, 58, 59–60, 64–65, 69, 107; for NATO, 131, 132, 141–42, 153, 182, 184; in nuclear warfare, 131, 161, 176; numbers (1960, 1965, 1970), 13; in the Philippines, 83–84; in South Korea, 96, 97–98, 100, 102; in Spain, 175, 176, 180, 181–82; in Taiwan, 31, 32, 34, 35, 36; in Thailand, 107, 109, 110, 111, 116, 118;

treaty terms on, 17–18; U.S. losses in North Vietnam, 67–68. *See also* air bases; bombing; *and see specific types of aircraft,* e.g., helicopters
aircraft carriers, 13, 98, 109, 201
Allende, Salvador, 4
alliances, *see* commitments; treaties; *and see specific allies*
Alps, 131
Amharas, 188
ammunition depots, 40, 43, 45
Anderson Air Base, Guam, 92
Angeles City, Philippines, 87
Ankara, Turkey, 28, 141, 171, 172
anticommunism, *see* Cold War; communism
ANZUS Security Treaty (Australia, New Zealand, United States), 15, 17–18
Arab states, 10, 189, 193, 202. *See also specific countries*
Argentina, 14
Armée clandestine, 55. *See also* Meo tribes; Montagnard tribes
Asia, 3, 198, 200; Japanese role in, 39–40, 46–47, 48, 49–50, 52; Nixon Doctrine on, 81–82, 107; nuclear war and, 24. *See also specific countries*
Asmara, Ethiopia, 185
Athens, Greece, 163, 164
Athens Airport, 163, 164
Atlantic area, 13, 20, 182, 193
Atsugi Naval Station, Japan, 41, 44

Australia, 15, 18, 106; Vietnam War and, 88, 91
Australia, New Zealand, United States Security Treaty (1951), 15, 17–18
Austria, 156
Azores islands, Portugal, 142, 181, 182, 184

B-47 bombers, 176
B-52 bombers, 62, 111; nuclear, 131; in Okinawa, 32, 35, 51, 85, 92; Philippines and, 85, 91–92
Balgat, Turkey, 171
Ball, George, quoted, 19
Bangkok, Thailand, 107, 117, 121, 122; Nixon (1969) in, 106; North Vietnamese negotiations (1965) in, 110; roads, 108, 112
Bataillons guerriers (BGs), 55. See also Meo tribes; Montagnard tribes
Belgium, 15, 168
Berlin, 134–35, 150; Congressional resolution (1962) on, 25, 212; occupation forces in, 3, 18, 128, 130, 136, 137, 157, 206
Black Sea, 174
Blessing, Karl, quoted, 144–45
Bohlen, Charles E., 80, 82, 85
Bolivia, 14
bombing: Cuban missile crisis and, 4, 9, 10n, 161; F-4 capability in, 98n; in Laos, 57, 59–60, 62, 63, 68, 73, 75, 77, 91, 107, 111, 120, 125; missile deployment and, 32, 35, 95–96, 131, 139, 142, 163, 168; mission-launching regulation of, 45, 82, 85; NATO capability in, 131, 132; in North Vietnam, 59–60, 67–68, 107, 109, 110, 111; ranges, 40, 42, 96, 175, 182; in South Vietnam, 107, 111; submarines for, 131, 175, 176, 181. See also nuclear weapons
Borneo, 17
Brazil, 14

Brookings Institution, 130, 148, 199n, 200
Brown, Winthrop, 103
Buell, Edgar "Pop," quoted, 64
Bundy, McGeorge, quoted, 19, 151
Bundy, William P., 66
Burchinal, General David A., 178
"Bureaucratic Structures and Political Outcomes" (Yarmolinsky), 197n
Burma, 125

C-5A aircraft, 153
C-47 aircraft, 116
C-130 aircraft, 83, 84, 142, 184
C-141 aircraft, 184
Cambodia, 7, 21, 54, 73, 74, 206; invasion (1970) of, 63, 125; Vietnam War entry of, 91
Camp Page, South Korea, 96
Cam Ranh Bay, South Vietnam, 84
Canada, 15, 37, 168
Caribbean Sea, 13
Caribou Trail, 87
casualties: in Ethiopian insurgency, 189, 190; in Korean DMZ, 101, 102; in Laos, 59, 63–64, 72; in Nigerian civil war, 192; in nuclear warfare, 159–60; in Philippine insurgency, 86; South Korean, in Korean War, 99; South Korean, in Vietnam War, 103; in South Vietnam, 67, 88; in Thailand, 116
Cebu, Philippines, 84
Central Luzon Plain, Philippines, 86
Central Treaty Organization (CENTO), 8, 26, 27–28, 155
Ceuta, 183
Cheju island, South Korea, 97
Chiang Kai-shek, 37, 70
Chile, 4, 14
China, People's Republic of, 49; American détente and, 4, 5, 37–38, 45, 47, 104, 126, 127; Laos and, 54, 56, 71, 72, 125; North Korea and, 100; nu-

clear policy and, 26, 82; Philippines and, 82, 86; South Korea and, 93; Soviet disputes with, 133, 154; Taiwan China and, 30–31, 32–34, 37, 91; Thailand and, 125–27

China, People's Republic of. Air Force, 33

China, People's Republic of. Army, 33

China, People's Republic of. Navy, 33, 36

China, Republic of. (Taiwan Nationalists), 15, 30–38, 40, 45, 70, 91, 206, 208–209

China, Republic of. Army, 33, 37

China, Republic of. National Assembly, 37

China, Republic of. National Salvation Force, 34

China (Republic of)–United States Mutual Defense Treaty (1954), 15, 30–31

Ching Chuan Kiang Air Base, 32

Chou En-lai, 38

Church, Frank, 180

Cigli, Turkey, 171

Clark Air Base, Philippines, 82, 83, 84, 85, 92; Huk forces and, 86, 87–88

Clark, Clifford, 114

Cold War, _détente_ efforts, 135, 150, 154–55. _See also_ communism

Colombia, 14

Commander-in-Chief, United States Forces in Europe (CINCEUR), 179

commitments, 194, 198–202; defined, 3–8, 18–19; response flexibility, 19–25, 28–29, 31, 70–71, 106–107, 127, 128–29, 158, 187, 202, 205–206; types of, 8–12, 25, 66–67, 70, 81, 121–22, 123–24, 126, 176–77, 178, 179–80, 190

communism: in Europe, 131–32, 134, 135, 150–51; Laos and, 53–54, 55, 57–58, 63, 66, 70–76, 119, 125; the Middle East and, 169–70; the Philippines and, 86, 90; policy of "containment" of, 3–4, 7, 17, 69, 124; South Vietnam and, 19, 69, 124; Taiwan and, 37; Thailand and, 72, 106, 114–16, 121–22, 155; Turkey and, 171

Congo, 186, 192

Constantine II, king of Greece, 164

containment doctrine, 3–4, 7, 17, 69, 124

Continental Air Services, 57, 60

Costa Rica, 14

costs (defense), 12, 194, 195, 197–202, 204–205; in Africa, 180, 186, 190–91, 193; in Guam, 85, 111; in Japan, 40, 42, 49, 51; in Laos, 61, 70, 72, 73; in NATO Europe, 130–31, 133, 137, 138–39, 140–49, 157, 158, 159, 160–61; 164, 167–68, 171, 174, 180, 184; in the Philippines, 82–83, 87–88, 89, 91–92; in South Korea, 95, 96, 98, 102, 103, 104; in Spain, 175, 177, 178, 180, 181, 182; in Taiwan, 32, 33, 35–36; in Thailand, 107, 108, 110, 111–12, 113, 114, 117, 127; U.S. balance of payments and, 5, 137, 140, 141, 142–45, 164, 171, 184, 186

counterinsurgency, _see_ insurgency

Crested Cap program, 137, 142

Crete, 163

crime rates, in the Philippines, 86, 87–88

Cuba, 25, 185; missile crisis and (1962), 4, 9, 10_n_, 161, 212

Cyprus, 22, 163, 170, 172–73, 183, 202

Czechoslovakia, 132, 134, 136, 154–55; Greece and, 167; Morocco and, 193

Defense Appropriations Act, amendments, 62, 65

defense budgets, _see_ costs (defense)

demilitarized zone (Korean DMZ), 95–96, 100–102

Demirel, Suleyman, 172

democracy, 5, 129; Greece and, 165–67, 169, 170; Laos and, 73; the Philippines and, 85–86; South Korea and, 100; Spain and, 176; Taiwan and, 34, 36–37; Turkey and, 170–71

Denmark, 15

deterrence doctrine, 4–5, 206; NATO and, 129, 131, 134, 149–50, 151, 155–56, 157, 158–62

Deutsche Bundesbank, 144–45
Diem, Ngo Dinh, 11, 69, 202–203
Dien Bien Phu, North Vietnam, 56
"Diplomacy for the 70's" (U.S. State Department), 194–95
Discipline of Power, The (Ball), 19
Dominican Republic, 3, 12, 14
"domino theory," 124
Don Muong Air Base, Thailand, 107
"dual-basing," 137, 141–42
Dulles, John Foster, 31, 80; quoted, 16–17

EC-121 aircraft, 42; shoot-down of (1969), 10, 32, 97, 98, 102
Eastern Europe, 129, 131–33; Cold War détente and, 154; Western European fears of, 133–36, 142, 145, 149–56, 157, 168, 169–70. See also specific countries
East Germany, 133, 134, 138, 150; West German relations with, 151, 152, 156, 202
economic assistance, 3, 24, 49–50; to Ethiopia, 188, 192; to Morocco, 193; to the Philippines, 90–91; to South Korea, 103–104; to Taiwan, 37; to Thailand, 106, 110, 112, 116, 124; to Turkey, 174; to Western Europe, 135, 179
Economic Stabilization Program (U.S.), 145
Ecuador, 14
Eisenhower, Dwight D., 30, 80, 105, 136, 192
elections: in France, 135; in Greece, 164, 165, 166, 170; in Japan, 47–48; in Laos, 63, 74; in Thailand, 113; in Turkey, 170, 171
El Salvador, 14
employment: in the Philippines, 86; in West Germany, 139, 140
Enthoven, Alain, cited, 143, 147
Eritrea Province, Ethiopia, 189, 192

Eritrean Liberation Front, 189
espionage, see intelligence
Ethiopia, 4n, 180, 185–92, 210
Ethiopia. Army, 187, 188–89
Europe, 3, 12, 13, 127, 128–62, 198, 200. See also Eastern Europe; Western Europe; and see specific countries
European Common Market, 154
executive commitments, 8, 25–27, 196; in Laos, 66–67; in the Philippines, 80–81; in South Korea, 93–94; in Thailand, 105–106, 120
Export-Import Bank, 180
Express Transport Organization (ETO), Thailand, 113

F-4 aircraft, 200; in Europe, 137, 175, 180, 181–82; in Japan, 41, 42, 44; in Laos, 58; in the Philippines, 83; in South Korea, 97, 98, 100; in Taiwan, 36; in Thailand, 110
F-5 aircraft, 58, 83, 98n, 100, 187
F-100 aircraft, 36, 109
F-102 aircraft, 83, 100, 167
F-104 aircraft, 36
F-105 aircraft, 109, 110
F-106 aircraft, 100
Far East, see Asia
Felt, Harry, quoted, 66
Focus Retina exercise, 96
Fond Memory exercise, 35
Foreign Affairs (periodical), 3, 19, 32, 147
foreign aid, see economic assistance; military assistance
Foreign Assistance Act (1961), 211
Formosa island, 25, 31, 34. See also China, Republic of. (Taiwan Nationalists)
Formosa Resolution (January 29, 1955), 31, 211
Forward Thrust exercise, 34–35
Four Power Agreements on Berlin, 128
Fourth U.S. Missile Command, 96

France, 15, 22, 124, 129, 182; defense capabilities of, 131, 133; defense expenditures of, 147; Greece and, 168, 170; Indochina War (1954) and, 70; Morocco and, 192, 193; NATO withdrawal, 137, 154, 156; strike of 1968 in, 135; West German troops of, 155
Franco, Francisco, 183
Friendship Highway, 108
Fukuoka, Japan, 42
Fulbright, J. William, 36, 60

Garcia, Carlos P., 80
Gaullist party (France), 135
Geneva Accords (1962), on Laos, 21, 53–54, 56, 61, 63, 65, 69, 72, 74, 75, 76–77, 78, 108
German Central Bank, 144–45
Germany, 128, 129, 151, 152. See also East Germany; West Germany
Ghana, 186
Gibraltar Straits, 182, 183
gold, 144–45
Goodwin, Richard, quoted, 19
Greece, 15, 150, 155, 163–70, 180, 207, 210; Cyprus dispute of, 22, 163, 170, 173, 183, 202; U.S. bases in, 142, 145, 163–64, 167, 169, 197, 201
Greece, February, 1971 (Senate Committee on Foreign Relations), 167n
Greece. Foreign Office, 164–65
ground combat, 11; in Laos, 55–56, 57, 58, 59, 60, 62, 63, 64–65, 67, 68, 69, 70–71, 78, 119; NATO and, 132, 146; nuclear weapons and, 160; in South Vietnam, 83, 111, 119, 154, 198; in Thailand, 120–21; training for, 35
Guam, 24, 65, 81, 106; B-52 bombers in, 85, 92, 111
Guatemala, 14
guerrillas, see insurgency
Gulf of Tonkin, 10, 25, 67, 109

Haile Selassie, emperor of Ethiopia, 187, 188

Haiti, 14
Halperin, Morton, quoted, 126
HAWK air defense units, 95–96, 114, 139
Heidelberg, West Germany, 141
helicopters, 36, 57, 87, 97, 168; in Thailand, 107, 109, 110, 116, 118, 120
Herald, George W., cited, 159n
Ho Chi Minh Trail, 55, 59, 71; bombing of, 57, 68, 73, 75, 91; cease-fire proposals and, 74
Holy Loch, Scotland, 181
Honduras, 14
Honshu, Japan, 41
Howze, Hamilton H., quoted, 95
Huks, 86–87
Humphrey, Hubert, quoted, 93–94
Hungary, 134

Iceland, 15
Incerlik, Turkey, 171
Inchon/Ascon, South Korea, 96
India, 17, 201
Indian Ocean, 186
Indochina War (French), 70
Indonesia, 17, 33, 90, 126
infiltration: in South Korea, 97, 100–102, 103; in Thailand, 72. See also insurgency
Inonu, Ismet, 173
Institute for Strategic Studies, cited, 131
insurgency: in China, People's Republic of, 33–34; in China, Republic (Taiwan) of, 36, 37; in Eastern Europe, 132, 133, 134, 154–55; in Ethiopia, 189–90, 192; in the Philippines, 86–87, 90, 119; in South Vietnam, 69, 119; in Spain, 183; in Thailand, 72, 106, 110, 114–16, 117–20, 123, 124, 125, 126–27; treaty obligations and, 17, 19, 21–22; in Western Europe, 135
intelligence, 194; aircraft in, 10, 32, 34, 57, 97, 98, 102, 107, 203; civilian

operation of, 204–205; Japanese aid in, 50; ships in, 10, 45, 97, 102, 203
Inter-American Treaty of Reciprocal Assistance (Rio Treaty), 14, 16, 17
interests, see national interests
international law: Taiwan status in, 31; treaties and, 18
Iraklion, Crete, 163
Iran, 27–28, 155
Iraq, 27, 189, 202
Israel, 11, 155, 202; CENTO and, 27; Ethiopia and, 189; Johnson and, 10
Istanbul, Turkey, 172, 173
Italy, 15, 130, 147, 207; communism and, 134, 135, 151; Ethiopia and, 187, 189; Greece and, 164, 168; U.S. bases in, 141, 142, 175, 181
Itazuke Air Base, Japan, 41, 42, 44
Iwakuni Air Base, Japan, 41
Izmir, Turkey, 171, 172

Japan, 7, 15, 19, 39–52, 97, 179, 206, 209; Philippines and, 18; Taiwan and, 31, 33, 38, 40, 45, 70; U.S. military bases in, 40–45, 48–49, 51, 52, 145, 176, 201
Japan. Air Force, 49, 51, 139
Japan. Defense Ministry, 48, 49
Japan. Diet, 40
Japan. Navy, 49
Japan. Self-Defense Forces, 49
Japan Atomic Fuel Corporation, 42
Japan–United States Joint Communiqué of November 21, 1969, 39–40, 45, 46, 47–48, 50–52
Japan–United States Security Treaty (1952), 39, 50
Japan–United States Treaty of Mutual Cooperation and Security (1960), 15, 19, 39, 40, 47, 50; on troop deployment, 45
Japan–United States Treaty of Peace (1952), 39, 50, 51–52
Javits, Jacob, 136, 180; quoted, 46
John Hay Base, Philippines, 88

Johnson, Lyndon B.: quoted, 10, 66, 105; Philippines and, 80, 89; South Korea and, 93, 94, 102; Turkey and, 173
Johnson, U. Alexis, quoted, 8, 19, 47, 177
Joint Resolution to Promote Peace and Stability in the Middle East, 28. See also Central Treaty Organization (CENTO)
Jordan, 10n, 201
Journal of International Affairs, 197n

Kabinburi, Thailand, 110
Kadena Air Base, Okinawa, 44, 51, 85, 92
Kaemphaeng Saen, Thailand, 113
Kagnew Station, Ethiopia, 185–92
Kamiseya Naval Facility, Japan, 41, 45
Kanto Plain, Japan, 43
Karamanlis, Constantine, 166
Karamursel, Turkey, 171
Kavalla, Greece, 164
Kaysen, Carl, cited, 199
Kenitra, Morocco, 186, 192–93
Kennan, George, 3
Kennedy, John F., 136, 199; quoted, 9, 66; Thailand and, 105, 121n
Kennedy, Robert F., cited, 9n
Ketsana, Colonel, 54
Kiesinger, Kurt G., 144, 145
Kimpo Air Base, South Korea, 96
Kissinger, Henry, 38
Korat Air Base, Thailand, 107, 109, 110, 113
Korea, see North Korea; South Korea
Korean War, 3, 25, 30, 89; consequences of, 7, 11, 93–94, 99–100, 103, 176; demilitarized zone and, 95–96, 100–102
Kunsan Air Base, South Korea, 96
Kuomintang party, 37
Kwang-ju Air Base, South Korea, 96

Labor party, Turkey, 171
Laird, Melvin, quoted, 138

Lajes Air Base, Azores, 142, 181, 182, 184
Lambert, James B., quoted, 52
land reform movements: Philippines, 85–86; Taiwan, 37
LANDSOUTHEAST (NATO headquarters), Turkey, 171
Laos, 21, 53–78, 109, 119, 122, 124, 202, 206, 208; Thailand roads of, 56, 108, 112, 115, 125; U.S. bombing of, 57, 59–60, 62, 63, 68, 73, 75, 77, 91, 107, 111, 120, 125
Laos. Air Force, 58, 60–61, 67
Laos. Army, 55, 58, 61, 67, 73
Lebanon, 3
Liberal Democratic party (Japan), 40
Liberia, 186
Libya, 175, 186, 190, 193, 210
London, England, 140–41
London and Zurich Accords (1959), 173
Long Tieng, Laos, 60, 62, 63, 72
Lon Nol, 65, 125
Lopburi, Thailand, 117
Luang Prabang, Laos, 58, 71
Luxembourg, 15, 168
Luzon island, Philippines, 81, 82

Macapagal, Diosdado, 80
McCarthy, Joseph, 196
McConaughy, Walter P., 36n
McNamara, Robert, 159, 197; on NATO troop reductions, 137, 154
Mactan Air Base, Philippines, 83, 84, 85, 88, 92
Madrid, Spain, 175
Malaya, 119
Malaysia, 17, 18, 91, 115, 126
maneuver areas, in Japan, 40, 42–43, 45
Manila, Philippines, 82
Manila Conference (1966), 90
Manila Evening News (newspaper), 85
Mansfield, Mike, 136
Marcos, Ferdinand E., 80, 81, 89, 90
Marshall Plan, 3
Martin, Graham A., 114; quoted, 123

Martin, William McChesney, 144
Matsu island, 31, 34
Mediterranean, 10, 13, 131, 193, 201, 206; Greece and, 163, 164–65; Spain and, 176, 181, 182; Turkey and, 174
Mekong River Valley, 54, 71, 74, 76
Melilla, 183
Meo tribes, 55, 59, 60, 64; in Thailand, 115
Mexico, 14
Middle East, 9–10, 25, 202; Greece and, 164, 169–70. See also specific countries
Middle East Resolution (March 9, 1957), 211
MIG aircraft, 33, 100, 132
military advisors: in Africa, 187, 188; in Laos, 57, 60–61, 63, 67, 75; in the Philippines, 87; in South Korea, 96, 98, 103; in Taiwan, 31–32, 33, 34–35; in Thailand, 107, 117–18, 123; U.S. State and Defense Departments expertise and, 194–98, 205
military assistance, 3, 49–53, 202–203; to Ethiopia, 185–92; to Laos, 56–57, 59–61, 63, 75–76, 202; to Morocco, 193; Nixon Guam Doctrine on, 24, 106–107; to the Philippines, 79, 86–87, 88, 89, 90, 91; to South Korea, 95–102, 103–104; to Thailand, 106–107, 108–109, 110–14, 116, 117–25, 126–27; to Turkey, 172, 173, 174; to Western Europe, 128–36, 167–68, 169, 170, 175–80, 184; as virtual commitment, 6, 11, 21, 22, 70–71. See also specific forms of aid, e.g., troops
Military Assistance Advisory Group (MAAG), in Ethiopia, 188, 190
Military Assistance Command, Thailand (MACTHAI), 117, 124; command of, 107, 108, 109, 110, 111, 123; construction program and, 122–23
Military Assistance Command, Vietnam (MACV), 123
Military Balance, The (Institute for Strategic Studies), 131n

military bases, *see* air bases; naval bases

military personnel, *see* troops

Minneapolis, Minnesota, 66

Min River raid (1969), 34

Minuteman missiles, 131

Misawa Air Base, Japan, 41, 42, 44, 97

missiles, 33, 131, 139, 142, 163; in Cuba, 4, 9, 10*n*, 161; in Greece, 168; in South Korea, 95–96; submarine-launched, 131, 175, 176, 181; in Taiwan, 32, 35

Mito Bombing Range, Japan, 42, 44

Mohammed V, king of Morocco, 192

Montagnard tribes, 55, 60, 68

Montreux Convention, 174

Morocco, 4*n*, 180, 182–83, 185, 192–93, 210

Morón Air Base, Spain, 175

Moslems, 189

Mount Fujiyama, 42–43, 45

Mu Gia Pass, 55

Muong Phalane, Laos, 58–59, 68

Muong Soui, Laos, 57, 58

Naha Air Base, Okinawa, 51

Nakhon Phanom Air Base, Thailand, 107, 108, 112

Namfi, Crete, 163

Nam Phong, Thailand, 113

Naples, Italy, 141

National Commitments Resolution, S. Res. 85, 6

national interests, 4–5, 194–98, 202–203; in Europe, 128–29, 147–49, 151, 153, 156, 163, 169–70, 176; in Laos, 65, 66–67, 68–69, 72, 73, 74, 75; in Thailand, 105, 124–25, 126–27; treaties and, 7, 11, 18–19, 20–21, 128

nationalism: in East Europe, 134; in Japan, 46–48; in Laos, 72, 73; in the Philippines, 79, 81, 82; in the Somali Republic, 187; in Thailand, 115; troop commitment and, 102, 120

Nationalist China, *see* China, Republic of (Taiwan Nationalists)

National Press Club, 40

NATO, *see* North Atlantic Treaty Organization

naval bases, 4*n;* Ethiopia and, 185–92; in Europe, 141, 145, 163, 169, 175–83, 192, 193, 201; in Japan, 40–45, 48–49, 145, 201; in Morocco, 186, 192–93; in the Philippines, 79, 80, 82, 83, 90, 91; in Thailand, 122, 123

naval vessels, 195; aircraft carriers, 13, 98, 109, 201; attacks upon, 17–18, 67; intelligence-gathering duties, 10, 45, 97, 102, 203; Japanese home-porting of, 43, 201; numbers (1960, 1965, 1970), 13; submarine, 36, 83, 131, 175, 176, 181; Taiwan Strait deployment of, 30–31; treaty terms on, 17–18. *See also* naval bases; *and see specific ships*

Nea Makri, Greece, 163, 169

negotiations, 202; arms limitation, 25–27, 46, 150, 154, 161; on Cyprus, 163; on European troop reductions, 138, 150, 153–54, 157; on Korean unification, 104; on Laos, 53, 63, 65, 68, 72, 74, 75–76, 78; military conduct of, in Greece, 164–65, 167; on refugee problems, 110, 116; secrecy in, 38, 110; for Spanish bases, 176–81

Netherlands, 15, 130

"New Challenge to NATO" (Herald), 159*n*

New Leader (periodical), 159*n*

Newsom, David D., quoted, 191

New Yorker (periodical), 64

New York Times (newspaper), 32, 47*n*, 166, 200*n*

New Zealand, 15, 106

Ngo Dinh Nhu, 202

Nicaragua, 14

Nigeria, 186, 192

NIKE Hercules, 35, 95–96, 139

Nixon, Richard M.: China *détente* and, 4, 38, 45, 104, 126; Economic Stabilization Program of, 145; on Laos, 69–

70, 78; NATO and, 138, 144, 150, 154; Okinawa and, 50; South Korea and, 94; on South Vietnam troop withdrawals, 111; on treaty obligations, 24–25, 64, 65, 81–82, 106–107, 198–99, 200; and Vietnam War cease-fire proposals, 63, 74, 75

Nixon (Guam) Doctrine, 24–25, 64, 81–82; Thailand and, 106–107

North Atlantic Treaty Organization (NATO), 4n, 7, 128–62, 209; Greece and, 15, 163–64, 168, 169, 170, 173; Portugal and, 15, 184; Spain and, 179, 182, 183; terms of, 16, 17–18, 20–21, 22, 79; Turkey and, 15, 22, 141, 142, 155–56, 163, 171, 172, 173, 174

North Korea, 7, 32, 202; South Korean relations with, 95, 96, 97, 99, 100–102, 104, 127. See also Korean War

North Korea. Air Force, 100

North Korea. Army, 100

North Vietnam: Cambodia and, 63; harbor mining of, 10n; Laos and, 21, 53, 54, 55, 56, 57–58, 59–60, 62, 63, 71, 72, 110; Southern offensive (1972), of, 111, 113; U.S. bombing of, 59–60, 67–68, 107, 109, 110, 111. See also Vietnam War

Norway, 15, 150

Nuclear Non-Proliferation Treaty, 25–27, 46, 154

nuclear weapons, 4, 5, 11, 97, 134, 149; costs, 131, 148, 160–61, 199, 202; Japanese nationalism and, 46–47, 48–49; Nixon (Guam) Doctrine on, 24, 106–107; Philippines and, 82, 85; Soviet, 155; storage of, 32, 33, 45, 51, 52; submarine, 131, 175, 176, 181; tactical, 131, 158–62, 202; United Nations Declaration (1968) on, 25–27; West European capabilities in, 151, 152, 154

O'Donald Base, Philippines, 88

Ogaden Province, Ethiopia, 187

Okinawa, 12, 43, 44, 97, 209; B-52 bombers and, 32, 35, 51, 85, 92; reversion to Japan, 39, 45, 46, 47–48, 49, 50–52

Organization of American States. Charter, 14

Osan Air Base, South Korea, 96

P-3 aircraft, 83–84

Pacific area, 13, 20–21, 22–23, 28, 39, 148, 200, 201. See also specific countries

Packard, David, 182; quoted, 181

Pakistan, 15, 17, 27, 28, 201

Palomares incident, 161

Panama, 14

Papadopoulos, George, 164, 166

Papandreau, George, 166

Paraguay, 14

Park, Chung Hee, 94, 99, 102; assassination attempt, 97, 100–101

Pathet Lao, 53, 54, 55, 72, 78, 91

Pathfinder Express exercise, 183

Paul, Roland A., 200n; quoted, 8

Pearl Harbor, Hawaii, 67

Pentagon, see United States. Department of Defense

Persian Gulf, 186

Peru, 14

Pescadores Islands, 31

Philippines, Republic of, 15, 17–18, 33, 79–92, 106, 126, 176, 207; insurgency in, 86–87, 90, 119

Philippines, Republic of. Air Force, 84

Philippines, Republic of. Civic Action Group, Vietnam (PHILCAGV), 88–90

Philippines, Republic of. Congress, 90

Philippines–United States Memorandum of Agreement (1959), 80, 82, 85

Philippines–United States Military Assistance Agreement (1947), 79

Philippines–United States Military Bases Agreement (1947), 79

Philippines–United States Mutual Defense Treaty (1951), 15, 17–18, 79–81

Phoumi Nosavan, 53, 56
Phou Pha Thi, Laos, 59, 68
Phu Phan Mountains, 117
Piraeus, Greece, 164
Plaine des Jarres, Laos, 57, 62, 71–72
planning, bilateral, 109, 110, 121–22, 124
Pleiku, South Vietnam, 67, 109
Pohang, South Korea, 96
Poland, 134, 154, 155, 156
Polaris submarines, 131, 175, 176, 181
political parties: in Europe, 135, 170; in Japan, 40, 47–48; in the Philippines, 85; in Taiwan, 37; in Turkey, 171, 172
population: of Ethiopia, 188, 189; of Europe, 133; of North Korea, 100; of the Somali Republic, 187; of South Korea, 100; of Taiwan, 33, 36–37
Poro Point, Philippines, 83
Portugal, 15, 180, 183, 207; U.S. air base in, 142, 181, 182, 184
post-exchange (PX) and commissary privileges, 140
President's Report on United States Foreign Policy for the 1970s (Nixon), 24, 198–99, 200
press, the: on Cambodia, 7; on Greece, 166, 170; on Laos, 62, 63, 66, 70, 76, 78; on Spanish bases, 178–79; on Turkey, 170. See also specific journals
Princeton Institute for Advanced Study, 199
prisoners, in Greece, 165–66, 170
protest demonstrations: on Cambodian invasion, 63; in Japan, 40, 42; in the Philippines, 85; in Turkey, 173–74
Pueblo (vessel), 10, 45, 67, 97–98, 102
Pusan, South Korea, 96
Pyonyang, North Korea, 101

Quemoy island, 30, 31, 32
Quinim Pholsema, 54

radar facilities, 83, 139
Ramos, Narciso, 80

Ramstein, West Germany, 140, 141
REDCOSTE program, 137
Reforger program, 137, 157
refugees: in Laos, 64, 107; in South Korea, 99; in Thailand, 110, 116
Reischauer, Edwin, 47
Rhodes, 164
Rio Treaty (Inter-American Treaty of Reciprocal Assistance), 14, 16, 17
Rogers, William P., 186; quoted, 203
Romulo, Carlos P., 81
"Roosa bonds," 145
Rota Naval Communications Station, Spain, 175, 182, 192, 193
Route 19, Laos-North Vietnam, 56
Route 223, Thailand, 112
Rusk, Dean, 80, 137, 154; Thailand and, 105–106, 108, 120, 124
Ryukyu Islands, 50, 51

Sabah, Borneo, 17
Saigon, South Vietnam, 108, 110, 123
Sakon Nakhom, Thailand, 112
Salazar, Antonio de Oliveira, 183
SALT (Strategic Arms Limitation Treaty) talks, 150
Sam Neua, Laos, 58
Sam Thong, Laos, 60, 62
Sangley Air Station, Philippines, 83–84, 88
San Miguel Naval Communications Station, Philippines, 82, 83, 84, 88
Sardinia, 182
Sasebo Naval Base, Japan, 41, 44
Sato, Eisaku, 45, 46, 50; quoted, 40, 47
Sattahip, Thailand, 110, 112, 122, 123
Schultze, Charles L., cited, 199n, 200n
Sea of Japan, 10, 45, 97
Sea of Marmara, 171
SEATO, see Southeast Asia Treaty Organization
secrecy: equipment sales and, 36; intelligence-gathering and, 203–204, 205; Laos operations and, 61–62, 69–70, 76–78; in negotiations, 38, 110; nu-

clear weapons and, 162; political motives and, 124–25; war costs and, 61, 89
Seoul, South Korea, 95, 96, 101
Serrano, Felixberto M., 80, 82, 85
Setting National Priorities: The 1973 Budget (Schultze), 199n, 200n
Shinjuku Station, Japan, 41
Shulinkuo Air Base, Taiwan, 32
Siberia, 133
Sicily, 182
Singapore, 122, 123, 136
Six-Day War (1967), 10n, 201
Sixth Allied Tactical Air Force, 171
Sliz, Stanley, 59n
Smith, K. Wayne, cited, 147
Somaliland, 187
Somali Republic, 187, 189, 190, 191
Somali Republic. Army, 187, 189
Souda Bay, Crete, 163
Souphanouvang, prince of Laos, 54
Southeast Asia Collective Defense Treaty (SEATO), 14, 15, 213; Laos and, 21, 54, 65, 72; Philippines and, 79–81, 85, 88; terms of, 16–17, 19–20, 79; Thailand and, 105–106, 107, 108–109, 120, 122, 124
South Korea, 15, 18, 33, 42, 155, 209; Japan and, 7, 40, 45, 47, 49; North Korean relations with, 95, 96, 97, 99, 100–102, 104, 127; U.S. troop commitments in, 9, 12, 44, 48, 93–99, 102, 127, 206; Vietnam War involvement of, 88, 91, 94, 95, 97, 98, 101, 102–104, 113. *See also* Korean War
South Korea. Air Force, 98, 100
South Korea. Army (ROK), 96, 98, 100, 102, 103; costs, 104
South Korea. Defense Ministry, 98, 99
South Korea-United States Mutual Defense Treaty (1954), 8, 11, 15, 93, 94
South Ruislip, England, 141
South Vietnam, 18, 49, 84, 109, 115, 206; Cambodia and, 63, 125; Diem fall and, 11, 202–203; foreign troops

in, 12, 21, 25, 83, 89–91, 97, 102–104, 111, 113–14, 119, 129, 141, 198; Laos and, 54–55, 56, 57, 58, 66–67, 68–69, 71, 73, 75, 125; Okinawa and, 51; SEATO and, 14, 15, 19–20, 124; U.S. bombing of, 107, 111. *See also* Vietnam War
South Yemen, 189
Souvanna Phouma, prince of Laos, 53–54, 56, 58n, 125; Ho Chi Minh Trail and, 57, 68, 73; Johnson and, 66; U.S. secrecy and, 76, 77, 78
Soviet Union, 3, 5, 127, 135; Africa and, 187, 190, 191, 193; Cuba and, 9, 10n; Cyprus and, 22, 173, 202; Czechoslovakia and, 132, 134, 136, 154–55, 167; Laos and, 53, 54, 58, 71, 76–77; Middle East and, 9–10, 202; NATO and, 129, 131–33, 138, 148, 149–50, 154–56, 158, 161, 162; North Korea and, 100, 202; nuclear policy and, 26, 27, 47, 155, 158, 160, 161, 162; Philippines and, 86
Soviet Union. Navy, 174, 181
Spain, 8, 79, 207; U.S. bases in, 4n, 9, 128, 130, 141, 142, 175–83, 185, 192, 193
Spain. Army, 180
Spain–United States Base-Rights Agreement (1953), 176
Spain–United States Five-Year Agreement (1970), 179–81
Spain–United States Joint Declaration (1963), 176–77, 179
Spanish-American War, 79
Spanish Sahara, 183
Special Logistics Action for Thailand (SLAT), 108–109
Stillwell, Richard, 109; quoted, 123
Straits of Gibraltar, 182, 183
Strategic Air Command (SAC) bases, 84, 92, 192
Strategic Arms Limitation Treaty (SALT) talks, 150
strategic weapons, *see* nuclear weapons

Stuttgart, West Germany, 141
Subic Bay Naval Station, Philippines, 82, 83, 84, 88
submarines, 36, 83; nuclear, 131, 175, 176, 181
Sudan, 189
Sullivan, William, quoted, 64, 68
Supreme Allied Commander, Europe (SACEUR), 158, 161
Suwon Air Base, South Korea, 96
Sweden, 156
Symington, Stuart, 8n, 136
Symington Subcommittee, see United States. Senate. Foreign Relations Committee, Subcommittee on United States Security Agreements and Commitments Abroad (Symington)
Syria, 189, 202

Tachens islands, 30
Tachikawa Air Base, Japan, 42, 45
Taegu Air Base, South Korea, 96
Taipei, Taiwan, 35, 36n, 66
Taiwan, see China, Republic of (Taiwan Nationalists)
Taiwan Defense Command (U.S.), 32, 34, 35
Taiwan Strait, 30–31, 32
Takhli Air Base, Thailand, 107, 109
Tama Ammunition Depot, Japan, 43, 45
tanks, 195; NATO, 131, 132
tariffs, Philippines and, 90–91
Taylor, Maxwell, 114
"$10 Billion Misunderstanding, The" (Paul), 200n
Tet offensive (1968), 58
Thailand, 3, 10, 15, 84, 85, 88, 91, 92, 105–27, 206, 208; communism and, 72, 106, 114–16, 121–22, 155; Laos and, 54, 56, 57, 58, 60, 61–62, 64, 68, 71, 72–73, 78, 125
Thailand. Accelerated Rural Development Program, 116
Thailand. Air Force, 110, 112–13
Thailand. Army, 113–14

Thailand. Defense Ministry, 109
Thailand Mobile Development Unit, 116
Thailand–United States Joint Communiqué (1962), 105–106, 108, 120, 124
Thanat Khoman, 105–106, 108, 120, 124
Thanom Kittikachorn, 109; quoted, 121–22
That Phanom, Thailand, 112
Thessalonika, Greece, 164
Thirteen Days, A Memoir of the Cuban Missile Crisis (Kennedy), 9n
Thrace, Greece, 150
Tigres, 188
Tito (Josip Broz), 134
Tobago, 14
Tokorozawa Logistics Depot, Japan, 43, 45
Tokyo, Japan; U.S. troops in, 40, 41, 42, 43, 44, 48, 49
Tong Won Lee, 103
Torrejón Air Base, Spain, 141, 175, 181
treaties, 4, 14–29, 65, 128, 185, 198–99; informal commitments and, 6, 7, 8–9, 11, 18–19, 23, 25, 105, 180; and renunciation consequences, 23–24. See also specific treaties
Trinidad, 14
Triumph or Tragedy: Reflections on Vietnam (Goodwin), 19
troops, 12, 197–98, 199–200; commitment obligations and, 6, 9, 11, 67, 68, 80–81, 102, 105, 119–20, 206; deterrence doctrine and, 4, 160; in Ethiopia, 185, 188; intelligence-gathering and, 204–205; in Japan, 40–41, 42–43, 44–45, 47, 48, 49, 61; in Laos, 53, 54, 55, 56, 58, 60, 61, 62, 64–65, 67, 68, 70–71, 75–76, 119, 120; in Morocco, 192–93; for NATO, 129–31, 136–58, 163–64, 171–72; in the Philippines, 79, 80–81, 83–84; in Portugal, 184; in South Korea, 9, 12, 44, 48, 93–99, 101–102, 103; in South Vietnam, 12, 21, 83, 88–91, 97, 102–104, 111, 113–14, 116, 119, 141, 198; in Spain, 175;

in Taiwan, 31–32; in Thailand, 105, 107, 108, 109–10, 111, 112, 113, 116, 117, 121*n*, 127; treaty obligations and, 17–18, 24, 31; Warsaw Pact and, 131–33, 155

Truman, Harry S., 3, 30

Truman Doctrine, 3, 163, 171

Tumpane Company, 172

Tunisia, 186

Turkey, 15, 27, 28, 150, 170–74, 206, 207, 210; Cyprus dispute, 22, 163, 172–73, 183, 202; U.S. bases in, 141, 142, 155–56, 171–72, 175, 181, 182

Ubon Air Base, Thailand, 107, 116

Udorn Air Base, Thailand, 60, 107, 116

Unger, Leonard, quoted, 122

United Kingdom, 15, 22, 27, 106, 187; Common Market entry, 154; defense expenditures of, 147; Greece and, 168; nuclear policy and, 26; Spain and, 183; U.S. air bases in, 130, 140–41, 142

United Nations, 38, 187, 189; nuclear warfare casualty estimates, 159*n*

United Nations Charter, 26

United Nations Command, 93, 95, 99, 101

United Nations Security Council, 93

United Nations Security Council Declaration of June 19, 1968, 25–27

United States: balance of payments, 5, 137, 140, 141, 142–45, 164, 171, 184, 186; defense budget, 146–47, 198–202 (*See also* costs); foreign policy of, 3–13, 145, 146, 194–99, 202–203, 206; secrecy and, 36, 38, 61–62, 69–70, 76–78, 89, 124–25, 162, 203–204, 205; treaty obligations of, 8, 14–29, 39–40, 79–82, 93–94, 128–29, 146. *See also* national interests; *and see specific government departments and agencies*

United States. Air Force, 13, 199, 200, 201; in Europe, 130–31, 137, 140–42,

146, 153, 175; Greek junta diplomacy and, 164–65, 167, 197; intelligence-gathering and, 203, 204; in Laos, 58–59, 60–61; in the Philippines, 83; in South Korea, 96, 102; in Thailand, 107, 109, 110, 111, 123; in Turkey, 172

United States. Air Force. Fifth Tactical Control Group, 83

United States Air Force. First Mobile Communications Unit, 83

United States Air Force. Thirteenth Air Force, 83, 107

United States Air Force. Seventeenth Air Force, 137, 141

United States Air Force. Sixteenth Air Force, 141

United States Air Force. 606th Air Commando Squadron, 110

United States Army, 12, 60, 95, 102, 146, 199–200; Ethiopia and, 188; European Command, 140; intelligence-gathering and, 203–204; Thailand and, 107, 109, 110–111, 123

United States Army. Ninth Logistics Command, 109

United States Army. Second Division, 95

United States Army. Seventh Army, 130, 137, 140, 141

United States Army. Seventh Division, 95

United States Army. Special Forces Command, 188; in Thailand, 111, 117, 123, 124

United States Army. Support Command, Thailand, 107, 111

United States Army. 24th Infantry Division, 137

United States Bureau of the Budget, 144

United States Central Intelligence Agency, in Laos, 55, 57, 60, 61, 78, 120

United States Congress: Ethiopia and, 187; intelligence-gathering and, 204; Laos and, 62, 65, 66; military allocations and, 6–7, 36, 62, 65, 124–25,

138; resolution of, on security commitments, 8, 23, 25, 211–13; Taiwan and, 31; war powers of, 16, 23. *See also* United States Senate
United States Congress. Berlin Resolution (1962), 212
United States Congress. Combined Subcommittee on U.S. Forces in Europe in 1967, 137
United States Congress. Joint Resolution of January 29, 1955, 31, 211
United States Congress. Joint Resolution of March 9, 1957, amended September 4, 1961, 211
United States Congress. Vietnam Resolution (1964), 212–13
United States Constitution, 16, 22–23, 28
United States Declaration of July 28, 1958, 25–26, 27–29
United States Department of Defense, 194–98, 201; Ethiopia and, 191; Greece and, 164; Japan and, 48; NATO and, 130, 137, 138, 143, 157; South Korea and, 98, 99; Spain and, 181, 182; Taiwan and, 36; Thailand and, 113, 123, 124–25
United States Department of State, 194–98, 203; "commitment" definition by, 6, 20–21; Ethiopia and, 191; Japan and, 48; Laos and, 65, 76–78; NATO and, 138, 145; the Philippines and, 80, 89; Spain and, 4n, 177, 178, 180; Taiwan and, 31, 36; Thailand and, 105
United States Embassy in China (Taiwan), 35, 36n
United States Embassy in Ethiopia, 191
United States Embassy in Greece, 165
United States Embassy in Laos, 65
United States Embassy in the Philippines, 82
United States Federal Reserve System, 144
United States General Accounting Office, 89, 113

United States Information Service (USIS), 116
United States Joint Chiefs of Staff, 137
United States Joint Security Consultative Committee, 47, 48
United States Logistics Group (Turkey), 171
United States Marine Corps, 12, 146, 199–200; in Europe, 131; in Japan, 42–43, 51; in Thailand, 108
United States Naval Institute Proceedings, October, 1969, 159n
United States Navy, 13, 141, 182, 199, 200–201; Greek junta diplomacy and, 165, 167, 197; intelligence-gathering and, 203, 204; Japan and, 43, 44–45, 145; the Philippines and, 83, 84
United States Navy. Seventh Fleet, 30, 44, 49, 83
United States Navy. Sixth Fleet, 163, 164, 173, 182; NATO and, 130, 141, 148, 151
United States Presidency, 196; Laos and, 62, 64, 65, 66, 78; the Philippines and, 80; South Korea and, 93–94; war powers and, 23, 25, 26–27
United States Selective Service (draft), 156
United States Senate, 6, 28–29, 52, 180; Cuban Resolution (1962), 212; NATO reduction proposals in, 136, 138; nuclear policy and, 25, 26–27
United States Senate. Foreign Relations Committee, 16–17, 26–27, 31, 167n; on the North Atlantic Treaty Organization, 7, 21–22, 151; Spain and, 177, 180, 181, 182
United States Senate. Foreign Relations Committee, Subcommittee on United States Security Agreements and Commitments Abroad (Symington), 6, 8, 29, 194, 195; defense budget (1971) testimony in, 199; Ethiopia and, 191, 210; Greece and, 166, 207, 210; on intelligence-gathering, 204; Japan and,

19, 46–47, 52, 209; Laos and, 59*n*, 62, 76–78, 208; the Philippines and, 18, 85, 87, 89, 90, 207; South Korea and, 97, 99, 209; Spain and, 181, 182, 183, 207; Taiwan and, 36, 208; Thailand and, 114, 122, 124–25, 208; on treaty terminology, 20–21

Uruguay, 14

U Tapao Air Base, Thailand, 84, 85, 92, 107, 111

Vang Pao, 55, 60, 63, 68; Plaine des Jarres seizure (1969), 62, 71–72; recruits for, 64

Vantage Point, Perspectives of the Presidency, 1963–1969, The (Johnson), 10*n*

Venezuela, 14

Vienna, Austria, 53

Vientiane, Laos, 56, 58*n*, 60, 65, 67; communist threats to, 71, 72

Vietnam, *see* North Vietnam; South Vietnam

Vietnam Resolution (1964), 212–13

Vietnam War, 3, 4, 11, 147; costs (1971), 144, 199; Japan and, 40, 46, 51; Laos and, 54–55, 57, 58, 65, 66–67, 68-72, 73, 74, 75, 125; the Philippines and, 81, 83, 84–85, 88–92; South Korea and, 88, 91, 94, 95, 97, 98, 101, 102–104, 113; Taiwan and, 31–32, 34, 35, 91; Thailand and, 10, 88, 91, 105, 107, 108, 110, 111, 112, 113–14, 115–16, 119, 121, 122, 123, 124–25; treaty obligations and, 19–20; troop/command ratios, 141; U.S. ground troop withdrawals, 12, 154, 198

Voice of America, 164

Voice of the United Nations Command, 96

Wallace Air Station, Philippines, 83, 88

Warsaw Pact, 131–33, 134, 158; troop reduction proposals and, 138, 150, 152, 153, 155

Washington, D.C., 46, 48

weapons, 20, 35–36, 160. *See also* aircraft; bombing; missiles; naval vessels; nuclear weapons; submarines; tanks

Western Europe, 16, 128–62, 206. *See also* North Atlantic Treaty Organization; *and see specific countries*

Western European Union Assembly, 159*n*

Western Hemisphere defense doctrine, 4, 16, 128

West Germany: defense capability and expenditures of, 147, 148–49, 152, 153, 156; East German relations of, 151, 152, 156, 202; Greece and, 168; *Ostpolitik* of, 150, 154, 156; postwar recovery of, 129; treaty obligations to, 9, 15, 22; U.S. balance of payments and, 139, 140, 143–45; U.S. troops in, 48, 130, 137, 139–40, 141, 142, 143, 151, 155, 156, 206

Wheeler, Earle, quoted, 9, 177–78

Wheelus Air Base, Libya, 175, 190, 193

Wiesbaden, West Germany, 140–41

World War II, 3, 159, 205; Berlin and, 128; Ethiopia and, 185, 189; France and, 129; Japan and, 31, 39, 48, 50; Philippines and, 79, 81; Taiwan and, 31, 36

Yakosuka Naval Base, Japan, 41, 44

Yankee Station, Philippines, 84

Yarmolinsky, Adam, cited, 197*n*

Yeh, George K. C., 31

Yokohama, Japan, 45

Yokota Air Force Base, Japan, 41, 42, 44, 45

Yosuhiro Nakasone, 48

Yugoslavia, 134

Zaragoza Air Base, Spain, 175